BÁRBARA WAGNER
BENJAMIN DE BURCA

BÁRBARA WAGNER
BENJAMIN DE BURCA
Five Times Brazil

Edited by Margot Norton and Bernardo Mosqueira

NEW MUSEUM

Contents

Foreword

—

Lisa Phillips

Working together for a decade, Bárbara Wagner (b. 1980, Brasília, Brazil) and Benjamin de Burca (b. 1975, Munich, Germany) produce films and video installations that feature protagonists engaged in cultural production. The duo typically collaborates with nonactors who participate in the making of their films—from writing scripts to staging performances on camera. The resulting works are marked by the economic conditions and social tensions present in the contexts in which they are filmed, giving urgency to new forms of self-representation through voice, movement, and drama.

Occupying the New Museum's third-floor galleries, "Five Times Brazil" focuses on projects developed by the artists over a period of particular sociopolitical turmoil in Brazil. *Faz Que Vai* [Set to Go] (2015) focuses on four dancers whose practices complicate the relationship between traditional and contemporary *frevo* dance in northeast Brazil; *Estás Vendo Coisas* [You Are Seeing Things] (2016) delves into the landscape of *brega* music in Recife; *Terremoto Santo* [Holy Tremor] (2017) investigates the accelerated growth of evangelical religions; and *Swinguerra* (2019), commissioned for the Brazilian Pavilion in the 58th Venice Biennale, looks into popular dance competitions in Pernambuco. Their new piece, *Fala da Terra* [Voice of the Land] (2022), features the practice of Colectivo Banzeiros, a theater group composed of members in the Movimento dos Trabalhadores Rurais Sem Terra (Landless Workers Movement)—an organization that fights for land reform and against social inequities affecting rural workers in Brazil. Together, the works in the exhibition highlight the strength and complexity of artistic expression, demonstrating how culture can offer rich and enduring sources of resistance and community during particularly turbulent times.

This catalogue serves to elucidate critical ideas explored in "Five Times Brazil" and Wagner and de Burca's practice to date. Within these pages, Bernardo Mosqueira's essay traces the diverse dynamics of collaboration in each of the films in the exhibition. Vivian A. Crockett's piece focuses on questions of representation, interpretation, and articulation in Wagner and de Burca's work over the past decade. Artist Wendelien van Oldenborgh's text centers on her experiences working with and knowing the artists over many years. The catalogue also features a conversation between Wagner and de Burca and Margot Norton. We are grateful to all of the authors as well as to Sarah Stephenson for her attentiveness in editing this publication. The catalogues in this series have been elegantly designed by Nicholas Weltyk.

I would like to thank the curators of the exhibition, Margot Norton, Allen and Lola Goldring Curator, and Bernardo Mosqueira, ISLAA Curatorial Fellow, who worked collaboratively with Wagner and de Burca to realize this show and accompanying catalogue. This exhibition is the result of the combined efforts of the entire New Museum staff. I would like to thank David Hollely, Director of Exhibitions Management, and his entire team for their work in realizing such an ambitious installation—in particular, Abby Lepold, Senior Registrar; Carlos Yepes, Registrar; Patrick Foran, Chief Preparator; Arkadiy Ryabin, Audio Visual Preparator; and Olivia Biggs, Production Preparator. We are grateful to Massimiliano Gioni, *Edlis Neeson Artistic Director*; Isolde Brielmaier, Deputy Director; Dennis Szakacs, Chief Operating Officer; Diane Vivona, Vice President, Advancement; Mariah Mazur, Director of Development; and their teams for their support in making this exhibition possible.

The New Museum gratefully acknowledges our Board of Trustees and generous sponsors for their support of "Five Times Brazil." Major support for this exhibition is provided by the International Leadership Council of the New Museum. Support for this exhibition is provided by the Toby Devan Lewis Emerging Artists Exhibitions Fund. Artist commissions are generously supported by the Neeson/Edlis Artist Commissions Fund. Additional support provided by Marcelo Martins, Frances Reynolds/Instituto Inclusartiz, and Brenda Valansi. Education and community programs are supported, in part, by the American Chai Trust. Thanks to Camila Yunes Guarita. Support for the publication has been provided by the J. McSweeney and G. Mills Publications Fund at the New Museum. This exhibition is made possible, in part, by in-kind support from Kvadrat.

The exhibition would not have been possible without the support and collaboration of Wagner and de Burca's studio and gallery. In particular, I would like to thank Camila Goulart, Studio Coordinator; Marcus Vinicius Santos, Exhibition Designer; and Aline Arroyo, Exhibition Design Assistant; they all provided critical assistance with the planning and coordination of the exhibition. At the artists' gallery, Fortes D'Aloia & Gabriel, São Paulo/Rio de Janeiro, I would like to thank Alexandre Gabriel, Ana Varella, and Ligia Carvalhosa for their expertise throughout this project. We would also like to thank João Sánchez at Estudio Baren, Marina Neder at 321 Studio, and Samuel Murray at Hilt Projects for their collaboration.

Finally, and most importantly, I would like to thank Bárbara Wagner and Benjamin de Burca for their courageous, inspiring films that continue to shed light on important issues affecting society today and for their hard work and generous collaboration in producing this exhibition.

Lisa Phillips
Toby Devan Lewis Director, New Museum

Staying with the Tension

—

Bárbara Wagner and Benjamin de Burca in Conversation with Margot Norton

Margot Norton: I know that you both had independent practices before you came to collaborate—Bárbara in photojournalism, and Benjamin, as a studio-based artist. How did you meet and decide to work together?

Bárbara Wagner: I was in Berlin in 2010 and visiting an exhibition by the artist Phil Collins, who was my professor in the MFA program at the Dutch Art Institute in the Netherlands. Benji was working for the institution at that time and assisting Phil on the show—though they already knew each other from Belfast and Glasgow.

When I arranged to meet Phil, he didn't show up, and neither of us had mobile phones at that time. Benji appeared in the reception area, and I suddenly knew I had to spend more time around that person.

Benjamin de Burca: Mystical. I also had a feeling, like, "There she is."

After a couple of years, we moved to Brazil. At that time, we hadn't yet worked together. Our initial work together was more us supporting one another.

When we moved to Brazil, Bárbara was so pumped to make new work there, particularly against the backdrop of what was happening in the country since she'd left for the MFA program.

BW: In that span of four to five years, something really particular was happening in Brazil. It was the second term of President Dilma, and we were experiencing an understanding of how the economy was connected to dignity.

For example, the labor party's policies of ending hunger in Brazil at the beginning of the 2000s were gaining results. The majority of the population finally didn't have to worry about whether they could get three meals a day. In terms of the domestic economy, people were starting to have a life.

What we saw at this time, in 2012–13, has been the focus of what we have been looking at from our first film in Brazil until now. It has a lot to do with forms of production and knowledge that constitute popular culture, and how, up to that point in Brazilian history, they were not considered relevant, economically speaking. That's when we started looking at forms like *brega* and gospel.

BdB: Our first works were instigated by helping each other but also provoking each other. Our first collaboration was a series of photographs called *Edifício Recife* [2013].

BW: There's something really anarchic about *Edifício Recife*. It documents public sculptures in front of residential buildings that were erected following a municipal law that, since the 1960s, has mandated that three-dimensional artworks be placed at the entrances of edifices over a certain size. The work includes testimonials from guards about these art objects.

BdB: Though it may have begun as some form of utopian idea for art in Recife's residential spaces, over the decades, it degraded into something more emblematic of class divide, with electric fencing behind which the sculptures are interred. Residences over a thousand square meters already represent the interests of the upper classes, and the art object becomes a symbol of status. But the porters, who sit in security cabins right beside those sculptures, open up a discourse more about taste and class and reveal something of the imaginary of the majority of the city, of those who don't live in these buildings.

MN: As you are talking, I keep thinking about this tension between being an insider and an outsider and approaching situations when bringing your experiences from somewhere else. I feel that all of your works operate from within this tension and stay inside it in order to better explore it—rather than trying to come up with some simple answer as to what it means. This is so rooted in your collaborations and the fact you experience things from very different perspectives.

After *Edifício Recife*, which was a photo-based project, how did you begin working in video, which neither of you had a background in previously?

BW: The idea of translating the world in two dimensions is common in our practices. Video came naturally when we realized that the phenomenon we were investigating really had to "move." In a big city like Recife, those who hold traditions in music and dance have to constantly fight against exclusion. When we met cinematographer Pedro Sotero, our main collaborator, we understood the value of the moving image as a medium for what we were trying to convey as artists, thinkers, and practitioners.

BdB: It was a nice coincidence to meet Pedro. At the time, Bárbara and I were documenting photographically, and I remember we had a conversation that led to us making *Faz Que Vai* [Set to Go; 2015]. We were living close to an artisanal shop where young *frevo* dancers from the area would perform for tourists intermittently, and we could always hear bars with frevo music playing. I said to Bárbara, "You know, it's really nice to hear the music and know what's happening but not see it and leave it to the imagination." Then Bárbara came back suggesting we should make a work about frevo.

BW: Yes, we began working with Pedro on *Faz Que Vai*, but we had been previously researching frevo, brega, and *swingueira*.

MN: So you were looking at frevo, brega, and swingueira simultaneously, even though the works on brega and swingueira came later?

BW: Yes. Connecting *Edifício Recife* to the interest we developed in dance and music, we were looking at how vernacular knowledge and culture reach a level of being recognized.

BdB: It becomes crystalized somehow into a form of the past. For example, in 2012, frevo was inscribed on the UNESCO Representative List of Intangible Cultural Heritage of Humanity.

This kind of labeling moves a cultural form from an area of resistance directly to one of celebration without having a moment to reflect upon it, as it exists in the present as something constantly refashioned by the people living and practicing it every day.

BW: We had just finished *Edifício Recife* and were planning to turn it into a publication. Lisette Lagnado, who curated the 2006 São Paulo Biennial, was the first to say that we were an artist duo. We were researching *Edifício Recife* and starting to look at the brega music scene in nightclubs, and when she visited our studio, she said, "Wow, you are an artist duo. I didn't know your work."

BdB: We didn't either!

BW: She invited us to exhibit in the 33rd edition of the Panorama of Brazilian Art at the Museu de Arte Moderna de São Paulo and encouraged us to apply for a residency where we would make our first video work together, called *Cinema Casino* [2013]. We were already looking at brega as a form of music and dance and how it is practiced by people connected to frevo and other traditional forms. We wanted to understand how the same bodies could perform the past and the future, so we went to the island of La Réunion on this residency, focusing on two main musical forms: *séga* and *maloya*, a dance connected to the people from Africa brought to La Réunion. The island had no population before it was colonized by the French.

BdB: It was utilized as a slave-trade byway.

BW: Exactly. And maloya became a form of resistance.

BdB: Maloya was banned as well. Later, it became celebrated as a currency of tourism and inscribed on the UNESCO list, some years before frevo. Like frevo, it never went through a process of reflection, as I mentioned—it went from resistance and banishment to celebration and cultural currency. We went to maloya schools during our residency to understand how it was taught and found it similar to frevo in Brazil. The maloya dancers we got to know in the schools were performing it in hotels for tourists, but for themselves, they were recording dancehall music videos for YouTube. It was a similar relationship to what we saw in Recife between frevo and brega. *Cinema Casino* inaugurated what would become our methodology and would continue with *Faz Que Vai*.

MN: It's interesting that right as maloya and frevo were stamped on UNESCO's heritage list, you were looking into them as living forms of resistance—almost as if you were refusing to allow them to become solidified. You're looking at what the dancers bring to these traditional art forms, which seep out in their movements from under the surface.

Going back to *Faz Que Vai* and knowing these dancers from your neighborhood, how did you actually go about approaching them to collaborate? How does that conversation develop?

BW: At the same time that we were seeing the frevo dancers performing in the neighborhood, we were going to nightclubs and would see the same performers dancing brega onstage. We were also looking at how they were producing these brega YouTube music videos while also performing frevo during carnival. Edson, one of the dancers in *Faz Que Vai*, for example, was part of a group called Guerreiros do Passo that was rehearsing every week in a public square, and Benji and I would go there.

BdB: The schools that taught frevo would teach a very specific set of dance steps that had to be followed. It was much more rigid than frevo performed on the street, which allowed movements to be more improvised and mixed.

BW: We were interested in everything—the most schematic methods of frevo alongside those that were more experimental.

BdB: The organic nature of how we got to meet the dancers was fundamental. It wasn't as if we were going out to find the best dancer, or the most representative. Edson also happened to be teaching voguing in a rented dance studio. When it came to working with him, we would challenge exactly that intersection between frevo and the other forms of dance they would perform and would make exercises in workshops together.

So, for example, if Madonna's songs play at 120 BPM, there are also frevo pieces that are 120 BPM, and we would make a mix of different music to see how these two dance forms would interact in the same body. We would also take out the music altogether, put on a metronome, and call out the different dance forms to see where these styles intersect, among other exercises.

MN: So there's this whole experimentation and rehearsal phase that doesn't get shown before you finalize the scenes?

BdB: Yes, because of the intensity of our meetings beforehand, when it comes to the days of filming, everybody knows pretty much how it's going to be.

BW: I don't think we really knew how to work in cinema at first. We never studied theater, scriptwriting, or acting. We undergo this intuitive and participatory method in every project. We wanted to look at how these traditions were once banned and then celebrated and the coexistence of opposing motivations, such as resistance and tourism.

Historically, frevo was an aggressive kind of dance that came from capoeira, which is connected to the history of slavery in Brazil. Then, over fifty years later, it became more commercial, and they started dancing with a little umbrella with the colors of the Pernambuco state flag. How did this happen? We don't aim to come up with answers, but we wanted to understand how the dancers embody those contradictions. This is the question we pose to the people interested in collaborating with us.

BdB: They are not just interested in being on the screen. It's also a professional undertaking; they want to learn through the process.

MN: I feel like this collaborative aspect, which is part of everything you do, also contributes to how you approach documentary filmmaking from a completely different place. There is a loss of control in the process of creating these works. It's not about coming in and dictating exactly what is going to be shown—instead, you have no idea what the outcomes are going to be!

It is also significant that you approach these works as cinema, in terms of the equipment and technology you use—the look and feel of these works as cinema. You mentioned before that a lot of the artists you collaborate with make videos for YouTube and Instagram and how technology has been such a crucial tool for getting their work out into the world. What does it mean to take this work, typically shot on a smartphone, and give it the production value of cinema?

BW: It's fundamental to understanding their distribution—who consumes what they are making, and where can it be seen? Framing their work through filmmaking in the way we do allows it to be carried into film festivals, galleries, and museums. We now have a team of professionals that work closely with us, including our cinematographer Pedro Sotero, our sound designer Nicolau Domingues, and editor Eduardo Serrano. We have learned a lot from them.

The language of cinema makes our works more accessible to audiences, as well. There's something conventional about this language—the way we follow a body in a certain space, or the pace through music.

The experimental part of what we are making is our process—the process of collaborating with those we film, developing a script, storyboarding, and how we translate this process to the screen. We don't know what the films will be until just before we shoot, which makes the cinema crew we work with completely crazy; it's almost the opposite of what they typically do. But the language of cinema has the capacity to connect to people of different ages and backgrounds.

This was the case with *Swinguerra* [2019], which we developed for the Brazilian Pavilion at the Venice Biennale. In Venice, it was interesting to see how people who couldn't speak Portuguese would engage with the rhythm and power of the movements on-screen even though they didn't understand the words. These levels of understanding are present in the film. A lot of it has to do with the technical approach to the work and the quality of image and sound, which I consider to be quite conventional. It is a way to engage with different audiences and cultural contexts.

MN: In the works, there are often moments of rehearsal and people getting ready that are part of the narratives, and they get the same treatment as the final performances. It complicates the whole idea of performance—where the fantasy begins or ends and what parts are documentary and what aren't.

BdB: Each of our films is inextricable from the moment it's made. There are aspects that are like portraits—of people, of artists at a given time, and against the political backdrop of that moment. It's like the metaphor of stepping into a stream—it's never the same river and never the same experience. Each work captures a specific local context and group of people. They are snapshots of a particular place, person, time, and setting.

BW: We choose to include the whole process of getting into the performance and getting out of it. All the films have a moment after the dance number ends, and the performers stare back at the viewer for a long time. In *Estás Vendo Coisas* [You Are Seeing Things; 2016], the narrative in the nightclub is broken up by two music video productions. In both, we see what happens when the recording stops and how the performers get out of the characters they are playing. For us, it is important to make it clear that we are talking about labor—people are working as artists to survive. It is their profession and a crucial part of our economy.

This is an important part of the conversation about the recognition and value that this vernacular form of knowledge carries. As a Brazilian in the northeast, I wanted to work in image-making to observe and convey this information. The media industry in Brazil is problematic for what it omits, what is not being discussed. We want this information, this labor, to stay in the work. The complexity and tension are there, and we want to stay with it, rather than narrow it down. This is why it is important for us to film the rehearsal and everything behind the curtain; it is important for us to go there.

MN: It needs to be there. This brings me to talking about the new film you are making with MST—Movimento dos Trabalhadores Sem Terra [Landless Workers Movement]. In all of these past works we're speaking about, you are looking at cultural production, which becomes a powerful lens to view the complex social and political issues that surround it—they bubble up to the surface in the pieces. In *Fala da Terra* [Voice of the Land; 2022], the culture—the theater they produce—is directly tied to a political and social movement, and it is within this framework the culture emerges. What led you to looking at MST, and how does this work extend from the different forms of culture you were looking at previously?

BdB: MST, as an organization, is decidedly striving to exist outside the structures of capitalism in order to survive and have dignity. If rural farmers are forced into situations where they're producing food to sell and don't have enough money to feed themselves, we recognize there's a problem with capitalism. MST comes from a Marxist doctrine, and it is deeply important for the social movement to address these problems. With the pandemic, we've seen how globalization and the networks in place pose a problem to survival, and we don't know how to undo them in order to do the most basic things. MST represents a return to forms of living where we might better understand nature, work with it, and survive.

In MST, theater is an active form for bringing these oppressive systems to light, and they use techniques developed by Augusto Boal in his Theater of the Oppressed in their daily life and political struggles.

BW: The body of films we built in Brazil up to *Swinguerra* was a reaction to what we saw happening here. At the same time, the current president, Jair Bolsonaro, has completely mismanaged the country during the pandemic. MST, which has been an important force in Brazil for the last forty years, got to an emblematic place with their fight for land reform.

From what we are seeing now, MST has reached a point where its mission is more important than ever. The movement is also being criminalized by the government, and members have been called terrorists—they are criminalizing those fighting for the right to remain on their land.

BdB: They occupy land that has been destroyed by large-scale farming production and is not in use anymore. They agro-ecologically return it to a place full of insect life with variation of vegetation—not just one crop sprayed with hundreds of chemicals, leaving the land barren and lifeless.

BW: We are interested in looking at the movement now and how theater is one of their most important pedagogical tools to inform new generations.

This new work can be seen as a continuation of what *Swinguerra* did in showing these dancers as warriors, moving with order and synchronicity. MST members are warriors of our time.

MN: It's interesting you bring up this aspect of fighting. When rewatching your works, I was thinking about how many of the performers are fighting, resisting, or asserting their identities through acts of creativity and joy, and how these things that are thought to be oppositional are actually very much connected. Seeing the images of you both when you visited MST last month, I was struck by how much joy is a part of that, too. How they resist and fight through collaboration to produce something beautiful and joyful.

BdB: Recently, MST has taken an interesting direction and created their first project in urban spaces to feed people experiencing hunger and desperation. They did this in direct opposition to Bolsonaro's denialist approach to the pandemic and distributed seven thousand tons of organically grown vegetables and fruit and millions of lunchboxes across Brazil's urban centers; it is a mammoth task. MST is countering the direction we're moving on this planet and returning dignity to everyone, not just representing the interests of the wealthy.

BW: For us, it's not difficult to understand why looking at MST is important, or how we can observe traditions that have been exploited, but this idea of joy is interesting. Where does it come from? What compels people to do what they're doing in an artistic way?

MN: And where does the art end and the activism begin?

BW: Totally. These sentiments are something you don't often see in the art world. We are not afraid of them for this very reason. With the people we have been working with, their emotions are connected to their fight for survival. It's a fight for change and against exclusion—the right to participate as a form of liberation. I'm constantly learning from the artists we work with. It's because of them that we keep going.

MN: Our exhibition "Five Times Brazil" focuses on five films you have made in Brazil since 2015. The title comes from the 1962 Cinema Novo film *Cinco Vezes Favela* [Five Times Favela], in which five directors direct different segments about the experiences of people living in the favelas of Rio de Janeiro. None of the directors of that film were from the favelas, but in 2010, another film came out titled *5 x Favela, Agora por nós Mesmos* [5 x Favela, Now by Ourselves], which was directed by filmmakers from the favelas about their own experiences. It complicated the traditional binary opposition between those filming and those being filmed.

Our title also reflects on ideas of what it means to represent a country or place multiple times. What does it mean to you to bring these five works together, and how might they generate something between them that they might not by themselves?

BdB: With cachaça, for example, we can drink it here in Brazil, but if you bring a bottle to Europe, somehow it doesn't taste the same. This is true with films as well. When I see our films in other cultural contexts, I see them differently. While we are only showing the five films we made in Brazil, and the title is "Five Times Brazil," it suggests the number could be infinite in terms of perspectives on the country. It also recognizes the "outsider" and "insider" viewpoints in terms of our contribution in their making.

BW: There are ambivalences in all of our works. *Terremoto Santo* [Holy Tremor; 2017] is a good piece to look at regarding this. It has been read as either propaganda for the Evangelical church or an ironic or satirical portrait of the Evangelical singers. For us, it was neither: it was an opportunity to come closer to understanding the recent accelerated growth of gospel singers—noticeable on the radio and television and being consumed by the majority of the population in Recife. Some thought the work was celebrating the gospel singers, while others argued we were ridiculing them. There was very little understanding of the film at the time or how it would be possible for us to have a conversation with those that think differently.

MN: Right, or how you might choose to stay in that tension or deal with an uncomfortable situation. It's a very brave thing to do. People might want the work to have a clean viewpoint or thesis, but it refuses a neat summation, which makes it so interesting—these contradictions are a part of life. A key part of collaboration is not only having one voice in the work.

BW: Exactly, multiple values are present, and it's not as simple as having one or even two viewpoints. That's part of the open-endedness in making these works, seeing what happens in the process of making them, and allowing these multiple viewpoints to exist.

Most of the people we work with know how to be collaborative in this way. It's not an issue, which is progressive in many ways. We actually hope that having these five works coexist in the same space can make this aspect of our work more evident. Even if they talk about specific circumstances, communities, or cultural practices, the methodology for making them is similar, and perhaps seeing them together will highlight this aspect of our collaborations.

BdB: Each work is a different encounter. Our task now is to arrange these pieces in a way that you would arrange dinner courses. It's a new experience for us to gather together five very separate, individual works; it's exciting.

BW: I think of the exhibition as another work itself. Again, it's something completely unknown, and we're curious to see what happens.

5 × Brazil =

—

Bernardo Mosqueira

Bárbara Wagner + Benjamin de Burca + Collaborators =

Working together for over a decade, Bárbara Wagner and Benjamin de Burca have developed their works as speculative studies on diverse cultural movements. Collaborating with different artists and groups, the duo has been making films, video installations, and photographic series that combine documentary and fiction. Their projects have focused on *frevo* dance culture in Recife, the *brega* music scene in Pernambuco, the *Schlager* music of Münster, the spoken-word scene in Toronto, Evangelical gospel singers from Zona da Mata, and *swingueira* dance competitions, among others.

Proposing different dynamics of intimacy and collaboration, Wagner and de Burca established a methodology that entangles the process of representation by shuffling the roles of subjects and objects. Every participant in their films contributes to all project phases—discussing the theme, composing the script, staging the sets, and directing their performances in front of the camera. However, in this practice of "collective imagination," rather than forming a single, coherent voice, the duo intertwines multiple perspectives without trying to appease the differences. These polyphonic compositions are marked by tension, conflict, contradiction, and ambivalence and reflect intricate social relations, often touching on issues related to class, gender, race, and sexuality. With a specific interest in the production systems of different cultural movements, their works portray culture, economy, and politics as intricate knots, inseparable and fascinating in their complexities.

Denying strategies of representation of the other and self-determination, Wagner and de Burca's pieces aspire to radical self-indetermination in refusing to adhere to traditional categorization systems. The portrayed contradictions are signs of resistance in a struggle for the right to live together without being defined, explained, or ordered by others. Their collaborators dedicate themselves daily to the creation of language as a constituent element of common life. In their works, people and the images they create coexist in the same universe—forming, informing, and transforming one another. Ultimately, at the heart of their practice, they investigate what moves people to produce art and culture together, looking deep into the desires, exchanges, and challenges that generate diverse textures of collaborative relationships.

5 × Brazil =

The exhibition "Five Times Brazil" focuses on five video installations developed by Wagner and de Burca in Brazil: *Faz Que Vai* [Set to Go] (2015), *Estás Vendo Coisas* [You Are Seeing Things] (2016), *Terremoto Santo* [Holy Tremor] (2017), *Swinguerra* (2019), and a new work developed for the exhibition, *Fala da Terra* [Voice of the Land] (2022). Each piece was created following the experiences of the previous one, and showing them side-by-side allows viewers to find meaningful resonances between them.

Rather than "explaining" Brazil, this exhibition points to the fallacy of a singular national identity. The title of the show can be read as an equation, highlighting the abstract dimension of the term "Brazil"—which, in its concrete form, suffers from extraction and appropriation directly from bodies and land. As an equation, it is about value—cultural, economic, political—but breaking with the numerical system, it does not intend determination (of a single result) but rather imagination (of multiple passages). Analogous to Wagner and de Burca's portrayal of complex social landscapes, this exhibition highlights the contradictions that coexist in order to be experienced rather than explained.

The title, "Five Times Brazil," also directly references two important Brazilian films: *Five Times Favela* (1962) and *5 x Favela, Now by Ourselves* (2010). The first is composed of five separate narratives, directed by five middle-class university students who would become some of the greatest directors in the history of Brazilian cinema (Marcos Farias, Miguel Borges, Joaquim Pedro de Andrade, Cacá

Diegues, and Leon Hirszman). None were raised in favelas, and one of the most common criticisms of the film is that it romanticizes or exoticizes the favelado in a stereotypical way.

The process for *5 x Favela, Now by Ourselves* began in 2007 when Cacá Diegues and Renata Almeida Magalhães produced cinema workshops in partnership with important NGOs in Rio de Janeiro. More than six hundred young favela residents signed up for the process, with over two hundred participating in professional training workshops and more than eighty selected to join the film's crew.[1] Of these, seven were collectively chosen to be directors of the five chapters: Cacau Amaral, Cadu Barcellos, Luciana Bezerra, Luciano Vidigal, Manaíra Carneiro, Rodrigo Felha, and Wagner Novais. The entire crew was formed of favela residents, and the entire process (choice of themes, scripts, costumes, photography, direction, and production) was collectively discussed.

Wagner and de Burca's methodology is situated at a crossroads between these two films: neither representation of the other nor the self, but the collective imagination. In a way, they refuse the ethnographic gaze that prioritizes definition, classification, and hierarchy in favor of a practice that approaches the ungraspable, indefinable, unclassifiable, contradictory, and transmutable.

(5 × Brazil) / 2022 =

In 2022, Brazil is celebrating its two-hundredth anniversary of independence. Conventional historical narratives state that on September 7, 1822, the voice of Emperor Dom Pedro I cut the silence on the banks of the Ipiranga Brook, in what is now São Paulo, crying "Independence or death!" This myth, forged to portray Dom Pedro I's heroism, continues to be repeated in schools. But in 2022, as Brazil still suffers from economic, political, cultural, epistemic, and symbolic dependence built by more than 520 years of colonization and coloniality, we need to ask: Which cries today are capable of carrying out movements of emancipation and empowerment? If the notion of national identity is constructed by shared fictions, which images and discourses do we need to create and share to transform the mythical dimension of Brazil? And furthermore, how can we go beyond historical narratives to create new forms of storytelling, address social issues, and build communities?

Wagner and de Burca's films are created with people whose voices and experiences have been systematically ignored by Brazilian hegemonic narratives. The duo's practice explodes persisting, arbitrary borders between high and low culture, compelling viewers to hear cries for freedom and empowerment through movements, songs, and theater. They highlight how artists use their bodies as territory for political disputes, but not necessarily creating gestures as a means to future political goals. What's emphasized here is the fact that, while they create their forms of art, they invent their forms of living. This is autopoiesis as political action.

Collaborating with artists whose social contexts are far from the typical urban, economically privileged category of "contemporary art," Wagner and de Burca make evident how "culture" is far broader and more complex than the reach of the institutional-academic bubble. What happens when the subjectivity characteristic of art institutions is confronted with a complexity and richness that they frequently ignore? The duo's collaborations offer us new myths and perspectives that help us establish more nuanced, liberating notions of Brazilian culture and identity.

"Five Times Brazil" also coincides with a crucial election year, when the Brazilian population will have the chance to democratically choose whether or not they want to reelect the current far-right government under Jair Bolsonaro. In this context, the exhibition will contribute to the important debates surrounding the country's identity, shared values, and desires for the future.

Faz Que Vai + Estás Vendo Coisas + Terremoto Santo + Swinguerra + Fala da Terra =

In 2013, Wagner and de Burca moved to Olinda, a historic city just outside Recife. From the apartment where they lived during that period, they could often hear frevo music through the window but were unable to see the dancers performing. Inspired by this experience, the duo began to think about ways of imagining frevo and studying the social dynamics underlying this practice. Frevo had also just been recognized by UNESCO as an Intangible Cultural Heritage of Humanity and was being used by the Pernambuco tourism industry as a "traditional" cultural attraction of the region. After spending time researching in spaces where frevo was investigated, taught, and performed, the duo noticed certain contradictions between the definition of it as an "intangible heritage" to be preserved and their experience of it as a living art form in constant transformation.

After many meetings and workshops, Wagner and de Burca selected four dancers to collaborate with in the production of *Faz Que Vai* (2015). The title comes from the expression "*Faz que vai mas não vai*" [Do as if you would, but don't], which the duo found in a frevo score written by composer Nelson Ferreira in the early 1900s. The phrase refers to a fundamental frevo step where the dancer interrupts a movement that seems to throw the body forward with an unexpected stop and a jump in the opposite direction. This instant *between* one direction and another, a kind of physical point zero from which any movement could emerge, served as a strong image of a space between tradition and modernity or between genders or identities.

The video consists of four chapters—each focusing on one of the four collaborators: Ryan Neves, Edson Vogue, Bhrunno Henryque, and Eduarda Lemos—and is inspired, in part, by Wagner's earlier photography series, *Brasília Teimosa* (2005–07). The duo and cinematographer Pedro Sotero (who has collaborated with Wagner and de Burca on all of their films since then) chose to orchestrate the scenes as *tableau vivant*, a style that has become a staple in their practice.

Each dancer was invited to choose their own music and imagine a frevo dance to accompany it. The music ranged widely: the sound of a metronome, a house remix of Madonna, a swingueira track, and a sexy carioca funk parodying the song "Heigh-Ho" from Walt Disney's *Snow White and the Seven Dwarfs*. The duo then edited out the original music and collaborated with four percussionists from the Orquestra Popular da Bomba do Hemetério to produce a new soundtrack for the work.

This friction between the visual and auditory dimensions echoes the duo's experience at their Olinda apartment, when they could hear but not see the dance. Portraying the space *between* traditional frevo and other forms of contemporary popular dance, *Faz Que Vai* questions the legitimacy of the category "intangible cultural heritage."

Another crucial aspect of the work is how it makes us look at these artists who have enormous mastery over their bodies' abilities to produce images—transmuting, improvising, hypnotizing, and manipulating. Though none of the dancers express themselves verbally during the film, they actively, powerfully communicate through their movements. At the end of each of the four chapters, they freeze in position and stare at the camera, creating a charged silence and acknowledgment of the viewer's gaze, almost as though they are waiting for us to respond with our own movements.

While making *Faz Que Vai*, the duo began developing their next film, *Estás Vendo Coisas*, which investigates the cultural industry of brega music and similar tensions between tradition, with the classic *brega romântico*, and innovation, with the more recent *brega funk*. In *Faz Que Vai*, the protagonists communicated through movement, while in *Estás Vendo Coisas*, lyrics play an important role in the construction of narrative. Made in collaboration with a large number of brega artists in Pernambuco, the film focuses on two people in particular: the hairdresser and singer MC Porck and the firefighter and singer Dayana Paixão.

The film is composed of three "fictional" moments, in which brega artists imagine and stage important phases of their own creative processes at the nightclub Planeta Show, interlaced with two "documentary" scenes of brega music groups recording their own music videos around Recife. The film starts with MC Porck and Paixão staring closely at one another on Planeta Show's dance floor. When they exit the frame in opposite directions, the empty stage signals that the film's subject is this tense space between the collaborators.

Wearing her firefighter uniform, Paixão sings a brega romântico: "*Ah! É tudo ilusão do seu coração, alucinações, estás vendo coisas!*" [Ah! It's all an illusion of your heart, hallucinations, you're seeing things!]. She is followed by MC Porck with his brega funk: "*De cordão de ouro eu tiro onda onde eu chego! Elas ficam loucas quando sentem o meu cheiro! Cheio de tatuagem, eu chego pra incomodar!*" [With my gold chain, I shake up the scene! The girls go crazy when they smell my scent! Covered in tattoos, I'm here to make trouble!]. The two songs contrast both in terms of their rhythms and lyrical content. Later, we see Paixão fantasizing about being onstage in front of an LED screen showing a pixelated image of a waterfall, with silver metallic confetti falling around her.[2] After a second documentary scene showing the production of an independent music video, we find MC Porck and Paixão side-by-side again on the Planeta Show stage.

In the research process, Paixão expressed that she takes her brega music career seriously but is primarily a firefighter in the service of helping people. In the last scene of *Estás Vendo Coisas*, Paixão leaves MC Porck onstage, heads directly out onto the street, jumps on the back of a fire truck, and flashes a big smile. After the Planeta Show lights are turned off, we hear Paixão singing a song by Banda

Só Brega: "*Vou mudar! Um dia você mesmo vai dizer quem era, quem tu sois, é uma miragem, podes crer! Vou mudar! Um dia você mesmo vai se ver diante do espelho do poder!*" [I will change! One day you too will say who you were, who you are, it's a mirage, believe me! I will change! One day you too will see yourself in front of the mirror of power!].

Intertwining brega romântico and brega funk, *Estás Vendo Coisas* is a rich experience of collective imagination centered on the brega cultural scene of Pernambuco—illustrating tensions related to social class, labor, identity, and especially gender. The emphasis on women's empowerment is particularly meaningful considering that the work was produced in 2016, when Brazil's first woman president, Dilma Rousseff, suffered misogynistic political persecution that ended in a coup d'etat.

Lyrics are also important in *Terremoto Santo* (2017), a work that Wagner and de Burca developed in collaboration with Pentecostal Evangelical singers from the Assembleia de Deus Church, preachers, and music producers in the rural Pernambuco region of Zona da Mata. The duo began their research for this film intrigued by how the accelerated growth of evangelical religions had impacted both the political and cultural spheres of Brazil. The narratives and aesthetic choices in *Terremoto Santo* are directly informed by the visions and values of these singers.

In addition to representing working-class artists and their aspirations for economic success, *Estás Vendo Coisas* and *Terremoto Santo* have relatively similar filmic structures. The latter intersperses excerpts resembling music video clips (in natural environments such as rivers, waterfalls, and quarries) and scenes shot in recording studios and religious temples. In one of the most powerful moments, Tacy Silva sings from behind a simple wooden pulpit in front of a huge waterfall. Initially, she sings about the power of music itself: "*Quando o louvor ungido sai da boca de um fiél, as correntes e grilhões são arremessadas ao chão. . . . Quando Deus recebe o louvor, imediatamente ele age, derrama sua unção e seu poder*."

[When blessed praise falls from the mouth of a believer. The chains and shackles shall be thrown to the ground. . . . When God hears your worship, immediately He acts, pouring forth out His blessing and His power.]

After singing such praise, she announces the "holy tremor" of God's reaction: "*Olha o terremoto! Sinta o impacto, seja abençoado com a glória de deus! É avivamento, é o Pentecostes, é o sobrenatural, é coisa do céu, é o inexplicável, é puro milagre, seja renovado e receba a unção! Entre no mistério, se envolva nesse manto, terremoto santo: poder e unção!*" [Behold the earthquake! Feel the impact! Feel blessed by the glory of God! It's the Revival, it's Pentecost, it's the supernatural, it's a thing of heaven, it's the inexplicable, it's pure miracle, be renewed and anointed! Enter the mystery, wrap yourself in its robes! Holy tremor: the power and the blessing!]

The camera, operated by Sotero, then begins to shake like they are experiencing an earthquake. Although the scene triggers different interpretations, the singer's faith in music (and faith is "courage to believe") resembles the way many understand art's transformative power and capacity to instigate change and renewal.

If Wagner and de Burca's works investigate the production of art and culture in relation to politics and economics, how could they ignore the divine importance given to music by a group that forms almost a quarter of the Brazilian population? This crucial aspect within the country's contemporary culture has been largely ignored (if not condemned) by leftist academic thinkers. And again, rather than imposing a single interpretation, the piece touches on a complex issue and has become the artists' most polemical work.

In the last scene, a space previously seen under construction is revealed to be a new Evangelical church being built in a natural landscape. At this moment, a potential ambivalence opens up: Is nature seen as the material dimension of God? Or is it a potential site to be occupied by the growth of churches? Those who consider the expansion of Evangelical churches as the fulfillment of their God's plan might see this scene as a happy ending. Others might see it as tragic, coloniality, deforestation, epistemicide, and machismo. Those open to embracing ambivalence and contradictions will be able to experience the work (and arguably life itself) in all its complexity.

Created for the Brazilian Pavilion at the 58th Venice Biennale, *Swinguerra* (2019) takes these ideas of ambivalence and contradiction further—into the work's own installation. Composed of two separate video channels, not viewable simultaneously, the piece offers two perspectives on the same narrative. Research for *Swinguerra* began in 2015, when Wagner and de Burca came into contact with the popular swingueira dance competition scene in Recife.

In this work, the weaving of different perspectives and imaginations is particularly evident. The film begins with a slow-motion take, in which Eduarda Lemos walks toward the camera. The dancer, who previously collaborated with Wagner and de Burca in *Faz Que Vai*, triumphantly enters a sports arena where dancers are stretching before rehearsal. While Lemos leads the group in the center of the space, another dancer, Clara Santos, watches from the stands with a look of both admiration and rivalry. In the following scene, Santos imagines a group of men and women confronting one another in a dance battle, appearing both as courtship and competition.

Swinguerra, with its combination of narrative, choreography, and lyrics, questions the social categories of gender and sexuality, presenting them as unstructured, nonbinary, indefinable, and in constant transformation. In a moment of rest, Lemos imagines other scenes of collective dance interrupted by a voice shouting: "*Chega de anarquia! Formação de grupo!*" [No more anarchy! Group formation!]. A voiceover announces: "*Brasil! Um país maravilhoso. Realmente devemos honrar o que está escrito na bandeira: Ordem e Progresso*" [Brazil! A wonderful country. We really must honor what is written on the flag: order and progress.] The dancers are then presented in a heroic V-formation while saluting, with a flag depicting two large, open wings behind them.

This complex image depicts a group of predominately Black and trans people reciting a nationalist-like oath during a time of growing conservatism and militarism. Their praise of “order and progress”—the positivist motto in the center of the Brazilian flag—might initially feel out of place. However, what appear as contradictions are, in fact, subversive gestures: for the scene to happen, this diverse group had to enter Brazilian army headquarters in Jaboatão dos Guararapes[3] to perform a provocative choreography expressing their own vision of Brazil. In this setting, the competition is no longer only between swingueira groups but also between progressive values in Brazil and the death machine of Bolsonaro’s militaristic regime.

Which Brazil does this group salute? Who is to say what the “order” is? What “progress” are they talking about? In this performance, the group adopts nationalist discourse and militaristic gestures to enter this territory, both geographic and symbolic, in order to, from there, reimagine a Brazil that is their own. Rather than wearing the colors of the Brazilian flag, they wear black and red and salute their own flag. In their choreography, they devour militarist language and regurgitate the gesture of the salute contorted in the most beautiful and diverse ways. As part of their dance, we hear several phrases as battle cries: “*Prazer! Estou de Volta!*” [Pleasure! I am back again!] and “*Alegria, Alegria, Alegria!*” [Joy, Joy, Joy!]. Shortly before the dance is over, we hear “*A dança das mulheres! A dança das mulheres! A luta das mulheres! A luta das mulheres!*” [The women’s dance! The women’s dance! The women’s struggle! The women’s struggle!]

In the concluding scene, Lemos is separated from the group and begins to move away from the camera, in the opposite direction she entered originally. She is interrupted by Kinha dos Tamboretes, an older woman who passes by singing and announcing the sale of taborets—a small, traditional stool symbolizing a form of labor and culture now disappearing from the region. A final ambivalence opens up at this point: while we might see Kinha dos Tamboretes in contrast to Lemos (as tradition versus progress), we also see their relationship as a continuum—both performing their art as a way of life, having in common "*A luta das mulheres!*"

The last work in this exhibition, *Fala da Terra* (under development while I write), is a collaboration between Wagner and de Burca and the members of Coletivo Banzeiros, a theater group part of the Movimento dos Trabalhadores Sem Terra (MST) [Landless Workers Movement]—an organization fighting for land reform and against social inequities in Brazil for forty years. Wagner and de Burca have been interested in how Coletivo Banzeiros uses techniques developed by Augusto Boal in his Theater of the Oppressed in their daily life and political struggle in settlements and camps located between Marabá and Parauapebas, two cities in the Brazilian Amazon. In the political trenches against the planetary impact of deforestation and mining, MST has become an organization in danger, being constantly persecuted for its activism by different groups in the region.

Fala da Terra looks into the relationship between activism, life, and art and is directly informed by this group's fight for land rights and the preservation of forests. It addresses the urgency, strength, and beauty of this movement in one of the most dangerous regions for activists in the world. A radically important step in Wagner and de Burca's investigations about why and how different groups develop their art, *Fala da Terra* also contradicts stereotypical ideas of Brazil as a land of hedonism and harmony.

× =

"Five Times Brazil" closes on October 9, 2022—exactly one week after the presidential elections in Brazil. Consequently, the "×" in "5 × Brazil" might be read as a graphic representation of the major crossroads of this moment. With the multiplicity of Brazilian culture presented here, we can only wish that, at the other side of this exhibition/equation/crossroads, we find hope.

1 For more details, see “5 x Favela - Agora por nós mesmos,” Adoro Cinema, accessed February 10, 2022, https://www.adorocinema.com/filmes/filme-180470/curiosidades/.

2 Fantastical moments like this have become a staple in all of Wagner and de Burca’s works—a similar waterfall scene is included in *Terremoto Santo*.

3 Jaboatão dos Guararapes is also the site of the Battle of Guararapes, in which Portuguese forces ended the region’s Dutch colonial project in 1649. Among the Dutch expelled was a group of twenty-three Jewish settlers who tried to return to the Netherlands, but, due to a storm, ended up settling on a sparsely inhabited island in the North Atlantic called New Amsterdam. These twenty-three settlers are the Jewish Pilgrim Fathers who participated in the founding of New York City. See Daniela Levy, *De Recife para Manhattan: os judeus na formação de Nova York* [From Recife to Manhattan: Jews in the Formation of New York] (São Paulo: Planeta, 2018); and Arnold Wiznitzer, “The Exodus from Brazil and Arrival in New Amsterdam of the Jewish Pilgrim Fathers, 1654,” *Publications of the American Jewish Historical Society* 44, no. 2 (December 1954): 80–97.

The Mirror, Five Times

—

Vivian A. Crockett

In the final seconds of Bárbara Wagner and Benjamin de Burca's *Estás Vendo Coisas* [You Are Seeing Things] (2017), Dayana Paixão, one of the film's protagonists, sings the lines of a popular *brega* song: "One day you will see yourself / In front of the mirror of power."[1] Seeing ourselves in the mirror of power is one of the central aims of the filmmakers' body of work. Their projects focus on subcultures and the evolution of historical traditions in the northeastern Pernambuco region of Brazil, as well as those centered in Germany, Ireland, and the RISE spoken-word scene in Toronto.

Perhaps unexpectedly, the effect of watching their films, for me, most closely resembles that of encountering Diego Velázquez's *Las Meninas* (1656), for the ways both embrace representational slippages and indecipherability. Understood by some as a portrait of its central figure, the Infanta Margarita, and her entourage, Velázquez's painting arguably focuses on the viewer as we attempt to decipher the visual riddle before us. Just beyond the head of the Infanta, the hazy visages of her parents, Philip IV and Mariana of Austria, are visible, but rather than being rendered within a portrait alongside the other artworks on the wall, as we might assume, they appear reflected in a framed mirror. Presumably, the queen and king are placed in the same position as us—the painting's viewer-subject—where they/we are the visual focus of the Infanta, two of her *meninas*, the chamberlain at the doorway, and the painter himself. We are both omitted from and implicated in the scene. Quintessentially a representation of representation itself, *Las Meninas* taunts viewers with its lack of narrative fixity, its ever-shifting subject positions, and in the many ways it unsettles our sense of self.[2] So, too, do Wagner and de Burca's films.

Through a range of tactics, Wagner and de Burca's projects highlight structures of representation to distort and displace their authoritative power. Like Velázquez staring at us from his easel (as we stare back at him, his painting, and the painting before us), they self-reflexively invoke the act of filmmaking itself. *Bye Bye Deutschland! Eine Lebensmelodie* (2017), their examination of contemporary *Schlager*, concludes with the singer-protagonists performing a duet in front of two TV cameras. The transmission from one of the cameras plays directly behind them, so their slightly skewed image extends infinitely into a blur. At once a canonical visual trope and a metanarrative tool, this *mise en abyme* conveys Wagner and de Burca's emphasis on how images are variously constructed, distorted, and dispersed and how they function within larger cultural, political, and economic systems.

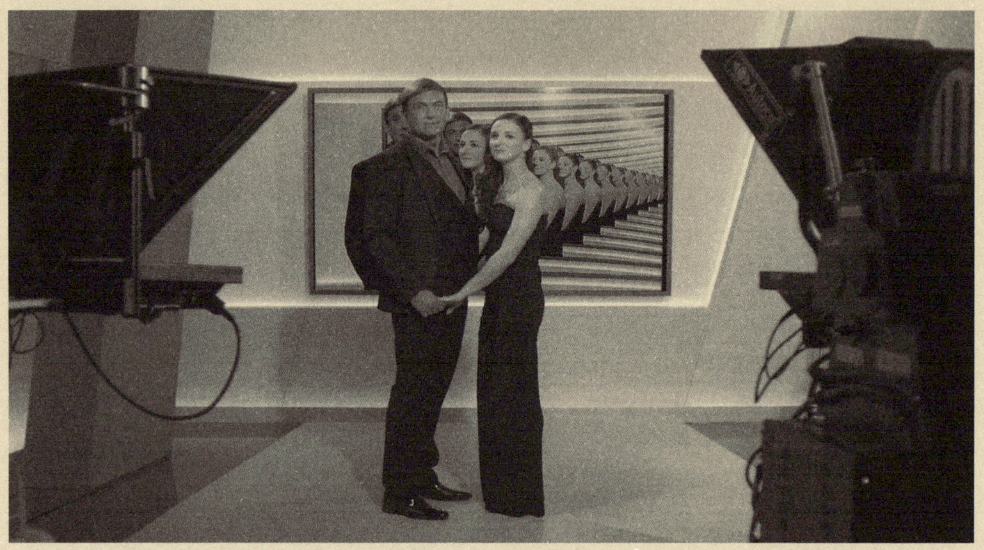

Bye Bye Deutschland! Eine Lebensmelodie [Goodbye, Germany! A Life Melody], 2017 (still). 2K HD video, color, 5.1 sound; 21 min

The camera's perspective often takes a secondary position, as if an omniscient presence within the scene. This is a common thread in most of their films, though made most explicit in *Estás Vendo Coisas*. As they film the music video for "Patrão é patrão" [Boss is Boss], the dancers and singers are seen in profile, directing their efforts toward the live audience and *other* cameras—not the one through which we experience the action [see p. 100]. The people before us, seemingly unaware of this other gaze, break in and out of performance according to the cues of their own recording session, performing for and within their own systems of exchange and representation. We witness the development of other video clips as well, both out in the world and within the insular microcosm of the LEDs and laser beams of Planeta recording studio. Through these glimpses—some staged explicitly for Wagner and de Burca, some not—we come to (partially) understand the economic structures and modes of circulation through which brega music has proliferated.

Evangelical gospel and brega, while seemingly disparate creative forms—one filled with devotional, proselytizing messages; the other with saccharine lyrics about love, lust, and betrayal—both represent popular artistic production growing on the margins of the mainstream market. Wagner and de Burca claim it was brega that led them to gospel, having been drawn to the success of both genres in attracting a young, creative consumer base amidst the growth of a Brazilian middle class during Lula's and Dilma Rousseff's presidencies.[3] Both *Estás Vendo Coisas* and *Terremoto Santo* (2017) emphasize the role of radio and independent record labels in disseminating the work of popular performers.

The latter film chronicles the live transmissions of Mata Sul, a gospel record company based out of Palmares, once the site of a *quilombo*—an autonomous community of formerly enslaved people—and now a creative hub for evangelical music. As the "On Air" neon shines, the radio hosts and amateur performers look away from the camera and perform for their "real" audience: the radio listeners [see pp. 138–39]. Sounds from these transmissions bleed into scenes of Assembleia de Deus [Assembly of God] members from the nearby Zona da Mata region as they enact pseudo-music videos for their original songs. The film's dramatic climax centers around its titular performance, written and performed by Tacy Silva, while the camera trembles to evoke the "holy tremor" of God's power.

As with other projects, *Terremoto Santo* centers the subjects' self-fashioning and self-representation. From their earliest collaboration, *Faz Que Vai* [Set to Go] (2015), to the new project on the Movimento dos Trabalhadores Rurais Sem Terra [Landless Workers Movement], these case studies unfolded during a period of radical political and economic shifts in Brazil. If the earlier films reflect growing creative industries amidst a newly emerging middle class, *Swinguerra* and *Fala da Terra* [Voice of the Land] (2022) portray modes of resistance by historically targeted communities, whose conditions have intensified under Jair Bolsonaro's regime—marked by economic decline, inflation, and political repression.[4] *Terremoto Santo*, the duo's third film and chronological midpoint of the five "views" of Brazil on display in this exhibition, straddles the threshold of this fraught political turning point.

On the one hand, the film provides a platform for members of the broader Evangelical and Pentecostal denominations, a growing religious community whose political influence is largely credited with the 2016 impeachment of Rousseff. On the other, it subtly presents the enduring neo-imperialist structures that account for the proliferation of evangelism within working-class and bourgeoning middle-class communities. More specifically, as Hermano Callou notes, the work portrays a community of mixed race and Indigenous- and African-descendant worshippers in a region where labor is predominantly centered around the sugarcane industry and other forms of manual labor.[5] In the film's final scene, manual and creative labor converge as a construction worker cleans his hands, removes his hardhat, and sings on the pulpit-stage of the still-unfinished site of a church he is ostensibly building himself. As Wagner and de Burca have repeatedly claimed, *Terremoto Santo* is a film about class, not religion.

Wagner and de Burca's process involves spending time with their protagonists to "storyboard" their reality, incorporating larger themes and minute details into the film's final narrative—what Hélio Menezes describes as the "expansion" of factual content.[6] Some of my favorite sequences embrace this blatant fictionalization of reality and nod to the structures of cinematographic storytelling. In *Estás Vendo Coisas*, for example, the dressing room becomes the designated space where Dayanna and other performers break from their public personas, their backs often turned to us. In this off-stage moment, these protagonists step into the "character" versions of their more private selves (to borrow Menezes's phrasing again). Here, we are most aware that our view is always mediated and partial. We see Dayanna clearly from the mirror in which she sees herself—her blurry, dislocated reflection appearing in the other mirror directly in front of her. But rather than look forward at herself—and by extension us—her gaze focuses on her duet partner, who has just exited the frame. There's a feeling of being given exclusive access to this staged "private" moment.

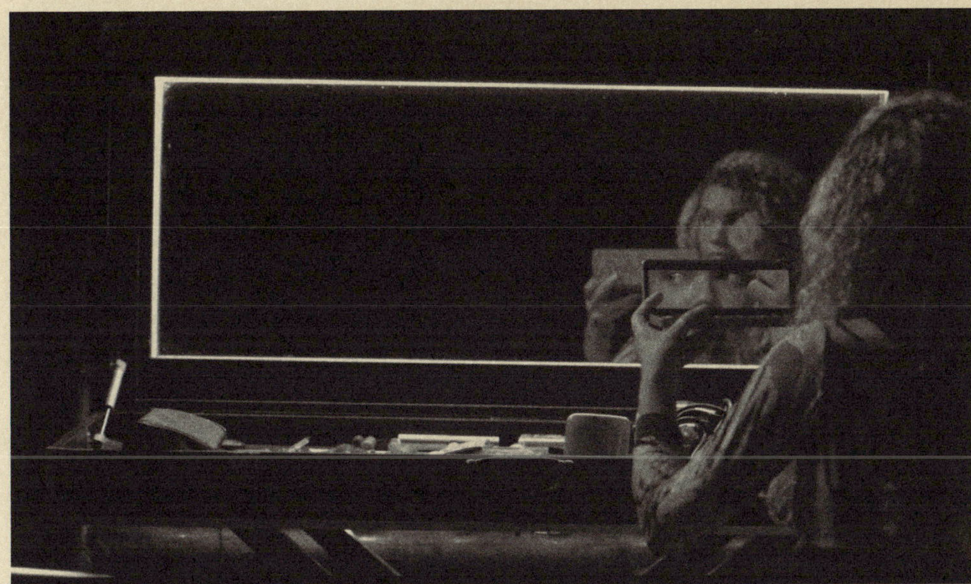

Estás Vendo Coisas [You Are Seeing Things], 2016 (still). 4K HD video, color, 5.1 sound; 16 min.

Another mirror: this time in a scene from *Terremoto Santo*, where a young man, Joalysson Anderson, enacts the story of Joseph in the Old Testament as his mirrored double dons Joseph's tunic. While doubling is a common device in many of Wagner and de Burca's films, its use here takes on an undeniably campy quality, despite the earnestness of Anderson's performance. The dramatic effects used in *Terremoto Santo* have been the cause of much debate, leading some to question whether the protagonists were aware of how their dramatized enactments might be read by a broader public. The critic Bárbara Bergamaschi recounts how, during a now-infamous screening at the 2017 Janela International Film Festival in Recife, an anonymous voice could be heard proclaiming over the audience's laughter: "My maid would love this film."[7]

According to the artists, one of the goals was to provide a different perspective of evangelism, "without judgment," to convey how a hostile force on the macropolitical level might simultaneously represent a more liberal framework of empowerment for a historically disenfranchised community.[8] *Terremoto Santo* followed the same collaborative methodology as Wagner and de Burca's other films; yet, it is the duo's most contentious work to date—not only for its subject matter but also how its methods of creative exchange and development vis-à-vis its subjects appear imperceptible to the majority of its audiences. The film seems to disturb the view of evangelicals as naïve receptacles of indoctrination, rather than as agents capable of creating and disseminating their own ideas.

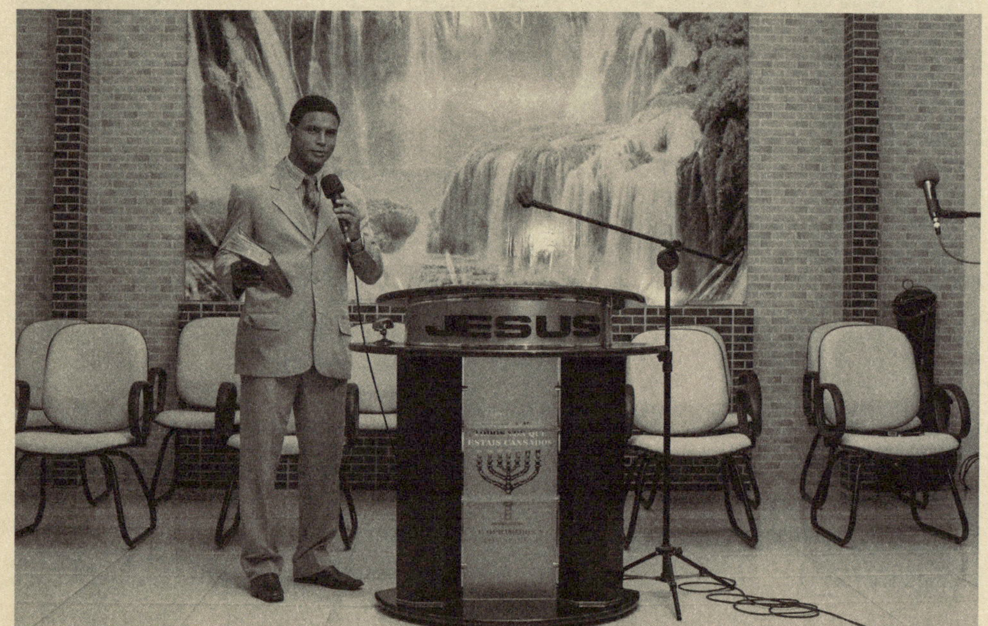

Bárbara Wagner, *Assembleia de Deus* [Assembly of God] from the series "Crentes e Pregadores" [Believers and Truthsayers], 2014. Inkjet on cotton paper, 19 ¾ × 29 ½ in. (50 × 75 cm)

It's helpful to contrast *Terremoto Santo* to the overall effects of Wagner's 2014 photography series, *Crentes e Pregadores* [Believers and Truthsayers], shot on the streets of Recife and in small churches in the city's rural vicinity. The latter images depict subjects of varying ages in stiff poses at the pulpit, alternately holding microphones or bibles, as if in the midst of delivering a sermon. In one, taken at a presumably middle-class church, a young man in a suit stands beside a sleek black-and-gold podium with the word "Jesus" emblazoned across it. It's a striking visual precursor to *Terremoto Santo*, even down to the idyllic waterfall in the background. The later film, when considered alongside this image, explicitly translates this paradisal trope into a symbolic reality, bringing elements of the church directly into a nature so vividly captured it appears almost artificial.

Much has already been written about the bright lighting effects, sharp resolution, and saturated colors of Wagner's photographs, which extend to the cinematographic qualities of her and de Burca's collaborative work with the cinematographer Pedro Sotero. These tactics, nodding to lexicons of advertising and high-gloss editorials, help to emphasize the constructed nature of photojournalistic and documentary traditions while luring viewers in with an irresistible tension between artifice and reality. It is arguably easier to identify the attempts to expose, displace, and denaturalize the ethnographic gaze within the static gloss of Wagner's still photographs, perhaps because we, as viewers, are more accustomed to measuring our own judgments against this style of images. By contrast, there is an unshakeable ambivalence to *Terremoto Santo*'s representational maneuvers. Many (myself included, at times) struggle to dissociate so-called "kitsch" from satire, though the two are not inherently linked. Wagner and de Burca present us with potent, multilayered images with no resolute narrative, and the onus of judgment is displaced from the filmmakers onto the viewers.

Back in 2017, following the Janela festival screening and release of a handful of critical articles, Wagner decided to prompt a debate on her Facebook page. The ensuing thread included comments from fellow artists, cultural workers in the museum and film spheres, and, ultimately, some of the protagonists themselves (who affirmed feeling respected and happy with their involvement in the film). Many comments spoke of the stigmatization of evangelism by the right and left and its ties to blatant and veiled forms of racism and classism. One particularly poignant comment from Julio de Paula addressed the stakes of Wagner and de Burca's open-ended approach: "To me, the laughter was more like bewilderment, the bewilderment of looking into a mirror."[9]

Even as I write on these themes, it is hard to fully convey the stakes of this subject matter to a non-Brazilian reader. If Wagner and de Burca's work engages the limits of representation, interpretation, and articulation, it also points to the inherent limits of translating concepts across regions, countries, classes, and various forms of difference and lived experience. One of the questions in the questionnaire for the series *Como se fosse verdade* [As If It Were True] (2015) asks: "If you could talk to a foreigner about Brazil, how would you describe it?"[10] Within these five views of Brazil, we are confronted with a regionally specific portrait of the country: four are set in the state of Pernambuco and the latest in Pará. These localized contexts—purportedly detached from the realities of the Brazilian art elite of Rio de Janeiro and São Paulo—become placeholders for all of Brazil abroad. With this superimposition, the tensions in the work, on the national level, shift into new modes of tension transnationally.[11] And in each new context, new reflections surface, and with these, new questions. Where do we find ourselves located? In front of the mirror of power? It's a matter of perspective.

1 "Um dia você mesmo vai se ver / diante do espelho do poder." Lyrics from João Gomes's "Espelho do Poder." The song is originally released by Conde Só Brega, an elder in the Recife music scene.

2 Michel Foucault centers the introductory section of *The Order of Things* on an elaborate description and dissection of *Las Meninas* to emphasize the crisis of representation and its authoritative fiction. This interpretation is partially inspired by his reading. See Michel Foucault, *The Order of Things: An Archaeology of the Human Sciences* (New York: Vintage Books, 1994), 3–16.

3 See Bárbara Wagner, quoted in Diogo Rodrigues de Barros, "Os evangélicos na produção visual brasileira contemporâneaa: análise da polêmica em torno do filme *Terremoto Santo*," *Revista de Ciências Sociais, Fortaleza* 50, no. 2 (July–October 2019): 63. Originally in Nelson Gobbi, "Do brega ao gospel, Bárbara Wagner investiga as relações entre cultura popular e os corpos," *O Globo*, May 7, 2018.

4 The Movimento Sem Terra has faced criminalization for many decades—earlier, during the dictatorship, and now under the presidency of Bolsonaro, who has repeatedly referred to the group as a "terrorist organization." Meanwhile, Brazil has the highest global murder rate of trans, *travesti*, and gender-nonconforming people, a reality preceding Bolsonaro's presidency but further bolstered by the current president's openly homophobic and transphobic rhetoric and policies. The *passinho dos maloca* dancers featured in *Swinguerra* humorously and critically respond to the mass criminalization and police brutality experienced by Black youth in Brazil in their work.

5 See Hermano Calou, "Espelhos do poder," *Revista Cinética*, April 13, 2018, http://revistacinetica.com.br/nova/espelhos-do-poder/.

6 Hélio Menezes, "Notes on the Process of *Swinguerra* and on Other Duels at the Margins of the Brazilian Venice," in *The Films of Bárbara Wagner & Benjamin de Burca*, trans. Heitor Augusto (Toronto: Art Gallery of York University, 2019), 19–29.

7 Bárbara Bergamaschi, "Um dia da caça, outro do caçador" [A Day for the Hunted, One for the Hunter], *Janela Crítica – X Janela Internacional de Cinema de Recife*, 2017.

8 Bárbara Wagner, quoted in Guilherme Barbosa Ferreira, "Micropolítica nos trópicos: criação e expressão do comum nas imagens artísticas de Bárbara Wagner" (Master's diss., Universidade Federal do Rio Grande do Sul, Porto Alegre, 2019), 73.

9 "Pra mim, o risível se deu como espanto. Espanto de olhar como que num espelho." Julio de Paula in Bárbara Wagner, November 8, 2017, Facebook comments on *Terremoto Santo*, https://www.facebook.com/barbara.wagner.142/posts/10214378469839582.

10 The original question reads: "Se você pudesse falar sobre o Brasil para um estrangeiro, como descreveria?"

11 See, for example, the presentation of *Terremoto Santo* at the 2018 Berlinale. A discussion of this event can be found in de Barros, "Os evangélicos na produção visual brasileira contemporânea," 51–71.

Cinema as Metaphor

or

Speaking in a Foreign Tongue

or

Entangled Desires

or

If We Work Together,
Does It Mean We Bridge an
Existing Distance?

or

(wh)Y Love Music

—

Wendelien
van Oldenborgh

On the opening page of *The Hour of the Star* [*A Hora da Estrela*], Clarice Lispector lists fifteen possible book titles. I particularly liked *.As for the Future.* [*.Quanto ao Futuro*.], with a period before and after the phrase. Also, *A Culpa é Minha* [It's my Fault]. The latter sounded so familiar and easily spoken by women. But Lispector, or the publishing house, chose *A Hora da Estrela* as the main title. Fair enough. But by showing us the full list on that opening page, she lets us feel the decision.

"How do I know everything that is about to come and that I myself still don't know, since I never lived it?" she writes on the next pages, as a prelude to the story of a girl who remains invisible in society.[1] "Because on a street in Rio de Janeiro," she continues, "I glimpsed in the air the feeling of perdition on the face of a northeastern girl. Not to mention that I as a boy grew up in the northeast. I also know about things because I'm alive." She writes as a boy? Yes, a few paragraphs later, she states that the story could only be written by a male writer: "A woman would make it all weepy and maudlin." I often wonder: How *do* we know about things if we haven't lived them? And how do we create with that which is *not* known to us?

In 2008, I decided to go to Recife, a city not yet known to me, to produce a kind of sequel to a film installation work I made two years earlier, *Maurits Script*.[2] In Recife, I was excited by the idea of encountering a music scene that had caught my attention from afar. For some time, I had been listening to the drum-and-bass-like *manguebeat* movement, originating from Recife with bands like Chico Science & Nação Zumbi and based on the traditional rhythms of *Maracatú*. I also loved DJ Dolores, who, with Orchestra Santa Massa (a band who played more local sounds), produced catchy electronic dance tunes with live voices and instruments.

However, I made *Maurits Script* to come to terms with my surprise in learning that the Netherlands had colonized even more overseas territories than I had realized. Part of northern Brazil was once invaded and governed by the Dutch—a detail barely known in the Netherlands at the time, and in my education, it was never mentioned. I learned that many books dealing with this short-lived Dutch colonization were still being read and used in education in Brazil. But only one of the various studies by Brazilian sociologists and historians, written mainly in the twentieth century, had been translated into Dutch, in 2001.[3] And only after Brazil became part of the BRIC group (Brazil, Russia, India, and China)—four countries suddenly admired as newcomers on the world stage of economic power in the early 2000s—did talks commence around drawing on our "former relations with Brazil." Mostly to do business, obviously. This sudden feeling of brotherliness quickly dissipated when certain Brazilian assets—especially the promised off-shore oil extraction—turned out to be unreliable after all. However, even without the public sentiment of kinship, the Netherlands is still noted as the largest foreign investor in Brazil.[4]

One of the most informative documents from the Dutch exploitation of Brazil was a book compiled in 1647 by Caspar Barlaeus, a humanist now considered one of the first historians (at the time, the specialization didn't exist). The book was a commission from Johan Maurits van Nassau-Siegen, governor of "Dutch Brazil," who fulfilled his role in service of the Dutch West India Company.[5] This text has not yet been translated into contemporary Dutch, and the most recent version is a huge leather-bound volume with beautiful original prints and illustrative maps from 1928, held in Leiden University Library. I was only allowed to handle it with gloves and could copy parts of the text in pencil. Nassau-Siegen is quoted frequently, and among many other stories and analyses, Barlaeus also published reports from informers spending time with the Indigenous peoples—though Barlaeus himself had never been to Brazil. In 2006, a Portuguese translation of the original Latin text was still being printed and distributed in Brazil as a cheap pocketbook. Perhaps it was still being used in education there.

In one of the scenes in *Maurits Film*, the work I made while in Recife,[6] a young Bárbara Wagner is seen from the back, sitting on the edge of the water. She is reading from another seventeenth-century document: *O Valeroso Lucideno, e Triumpho da Liberdade* by the

Luso-Brazilian priest Frei Manuel Calado. The clergyman writes in a gossipy manner, paying special attention to clothing and style during Dutch rule, and calls Nassau-Siegen, whom he befriended, "the Prince of Orange" (the governor was not royalty at all). Interestingly, the tone of the book is wholly against the Dutch invaders.

Another scene sees Wagner flicking through her own publication *Brasília Teimosa*, and over her shoulder, the actual Brasília Teimosa beach is visible. She reads some lines from the essay by DJ Dolores, which prefaces her wonderful series of photographs capturing the pleasure, style, and agency of this resistant community's inhabitants. Dolores writes:

> There is an actual struggle for that part of the beach . . . lately it was desired by real estate speculators. Directly under the sun, in a neighborhood called Pina, a housing complex sprawls. A piece of chaotic urbanism, built by the pressing hands of need. With no money and robbed by the economic reality, our suburban hedonists know that their bodies are their most valuable possessions.[77]

Wagner took her photographs with curiosity, respect, and love for what she saw as an under- or even unrepresented section of Brazilian society. This struggling group somehow created widespread popular urban culture and broke the rules of normative family structure. But there were no images of them in the media, which solely concentrates on the rich and beautiful, or reports on the poorest with stereotypical prejudices.

Benjamin de Burca is an artist educated in Glasgow and Belfast in the early 2000s, where he started to see art as ultimately socially embedded and collectively driven. Connected as he was to artist-led structures with horizontal organization, the politics of working together and finding reasons for art in larger sociopolitical contexts became the norm. Music, as a cultural, collective form, played a role in this. At a young age, in a pre-internet epoch, de Burca would sneak into a local club to hear music not heard anywhere else at the time. Clubs in Galway, where he grew up, mostly pandered to a local audience with predictable playlists, but one place stood out, offering a broad worldview via music and dance.

Galway, a medium-sized city in Ireland, is on one of the very western points of Europe. Across the Atlantic and across the equator, Recife is situated on the eastern point of the South American continent. And across time, in 2012, when de Burca teamed up with Wagner, Recife became a destination and, soon enough, a home. Nothing connected de Burca to the city and its culture other than these experiences in his hometown, which activated his senses: the way poverty showed in people's physiques, and plastic bags and other litter floated in the streets—these were familiar connecting points. The music scene in Recife—self-organized, rough, and lively—also felt familiar, but a distance was felt in many other cultural phenomena and, of course, the language. Even now, after years of speaking Portuguese competently, a gap is still felt. However, the advantage of speaking a language not fully mastered is that it brings a vulnerability and openness with which one can work with the not-yet-known.

While making my work in Recife in 2008, I also had to grasp the language to work with my small, local crew. My Portuguese was primitive, and I learned about the city from a myopic position—an outsider's insight into the social dynamics and variety of inhabitants, some of whom I invited into the film. Among those protagonists was a Dutchman working for the Agencia Comercial Holandesa, housed in the only modernist high-rise in the old center of Recife. A large sign on their entrance read: "Holland! Pioneers in International Business"—an embarrassing level of familiarity. In their own way, each protagonist related their position in the city to the historical facts and myths around the Dutch colonization.

The Fluxus artist Paulo Bruscky is seen showing his impressive archive as he talks about his interventions in 1973 on the Ponte Maurício de Nassau bridge. The community leader Edson Fly, who set up the resistance group Caranguejo-Uçá with the Ilha de Deus community, describes their strategies and how they relate to the power of a governor like Nassau-Siegen. And then, of course, there was Wagner, who could map the social positioning of particular cultural expressions, like music and style, and relate them to observations from four centuries ago. I fell in love with her—with her intelligence and sensitivity toward what is visible in society but not seen by the dominant culture. She guided my understanding of the music genres I already liked, and I introduced her to parts of the art field I was already working in. From that year onward, we shared many thoughts and perhaps became each other's teachers.

There are many good reasons to suspend all presumptions of understanding and get in touch with things that feel different and beyond habit. I always wondered how writers, scriptwriters, and filmmakers invented a character and knew what this character would bring to the story or screen. Lispector has a clear answer: she can't know until she has written the story. But even then, she obscures her clarity by denying herself the "I" as Clarice Lispector by claiming to write as a man called Rodrigo. Is it a second layer of fiction or an acknowledgment that we can speak from all genders anyway? In any case, she admits a certain distance from the girl in the story and removes the possible assumption of being anything like her. Thus, her knowledge about that character comes from elsewhere—not from imagining she *knows* the girl's life, but from another "listening" she has taught herself to do.

Wagner and de Burca don't invent characters from observation but dive into situations they want to learn more about. They work in exchange with real-life characters, creating "cinema" together—cinema as a notion that creates a horizon, not just one image or story. Cinema as a reason to meet, to think together, and, somehow, to use each other's art to open up a space for sociopolitical positions that show themselves in all their complexity. But they also work with the not-yet-known: the distance between them and their protagonists. There's the idea that artists should find their own voices to make work with, but I am always interested in those who can truly listen to the voices of others and make work with that.

The protagonists Wagner and de Burca engage with are performing artists with their own voices: musicians, dancers, poets. Their desire to join in a film project is informed by the knowledge of what exposure to a camera means, and that knowledge forms the grounds for the exchange. Some points may connect to form the basis of a certain recognition, but the situations the artist duo chooses are often outside their own familiar ground. A language has to be found in which the entangled voices can be expressed: the desires of the performers, who might know what they want from a film in which they star, and those of Wagner and de Burca, who come with an idea of why this film has to be made. This language is worked out together, between the artists, a small crew, and the protagonists.

"Prazer!" the dancers shout to the camera toward the end of Wagner and de Burca's *Swinguerra* (2019), "Estou de volta!" The subtitles translate: "Pleasure! I'm coming back!" Even if this statement is ambiguous when it appears after a military salute to the mentioned—but not shown—Brazilian flag, it alludes to an attitude that marks the duo's collaborative works: pleasure! Let's claim it back in how we approach critical issues. Those proud but vulnerable bodies are struggling, at-risk to state violence, yet they honor the flag, representing what the motto "Ordem e Progresso" could stand for. Pleasure! Let the effect of music and dance be the basis for exploring uncertain ground. The basis for questions that do not produce a single narrative or image but show a complex entanglement of desires, creating ambiguous pictures that expose the uncomfortable contradictions we have to deal with in this world.

1 All citations are from the English translation: Clarice Lispector, *The Hour of the Star*, trans. Benjamin Moser (New York: New Direction Books, 2020), 26, 29.

2 Wendelien van Oldenborgh, *Maurits Script* (2006). Two-channel film installation with booklet in an architectural setting. For more details, see https://wendelienvanoldenborgh.info/Maurits-Script.

3 José Antônio Gonsalves de Mello, *Nederlanders, in Brazilië (1624–1654) De invloed van de Hollandse bezetting op het leven en de cultuur in Noord Brazilië*, trans. G. N. Visser (Zutphen, the Netherlands: Walburg Pers, 2001).

4 See "Brazil: Foreign Investment," Santander Trade, last modified March 2022, https://santandertrade.com/en/portal/establish-overseas/brazil/foreign-investment. The high percentage is mainly due to the fact that investments in Brazil by multinationals go through the tax haven of the Netherlands. This structure is also known as the "Dutch sandwich." See Maarten Hietland, "How Tax Havens Like the Netherlands Are Draining Developing Countries of Precious Public Funds," Open Democracy, August 19, 2020, https://www.opendemocracy.net/en/oureconomy/how-tax-havens-netherlands-are-draining-developing-countries-precious-public-funds/.

5 Nassau-Siegen was ultimately made to leave Recife (the city he founded) because, according to the Dutch West India Company directors, he didn't spend the company's funds wisely.

6 Wendelien van Oldenborgh, *Maurits Film* (2008). Digital video, 45 min. For more details, see https://wendelienvanoldenborgh.info/Maurits-Film.

7 Helder Aragão, aka DJ Dolores, "Exatamente Debaixo do Sol," in *Brasília Teimosa: Fotografias* (Recife, Brazil: Bárbara Wagner, 2007), 1 (translation from the subtitles of Maurits Film).

Faz Que Vai
[Set to Go], 2015

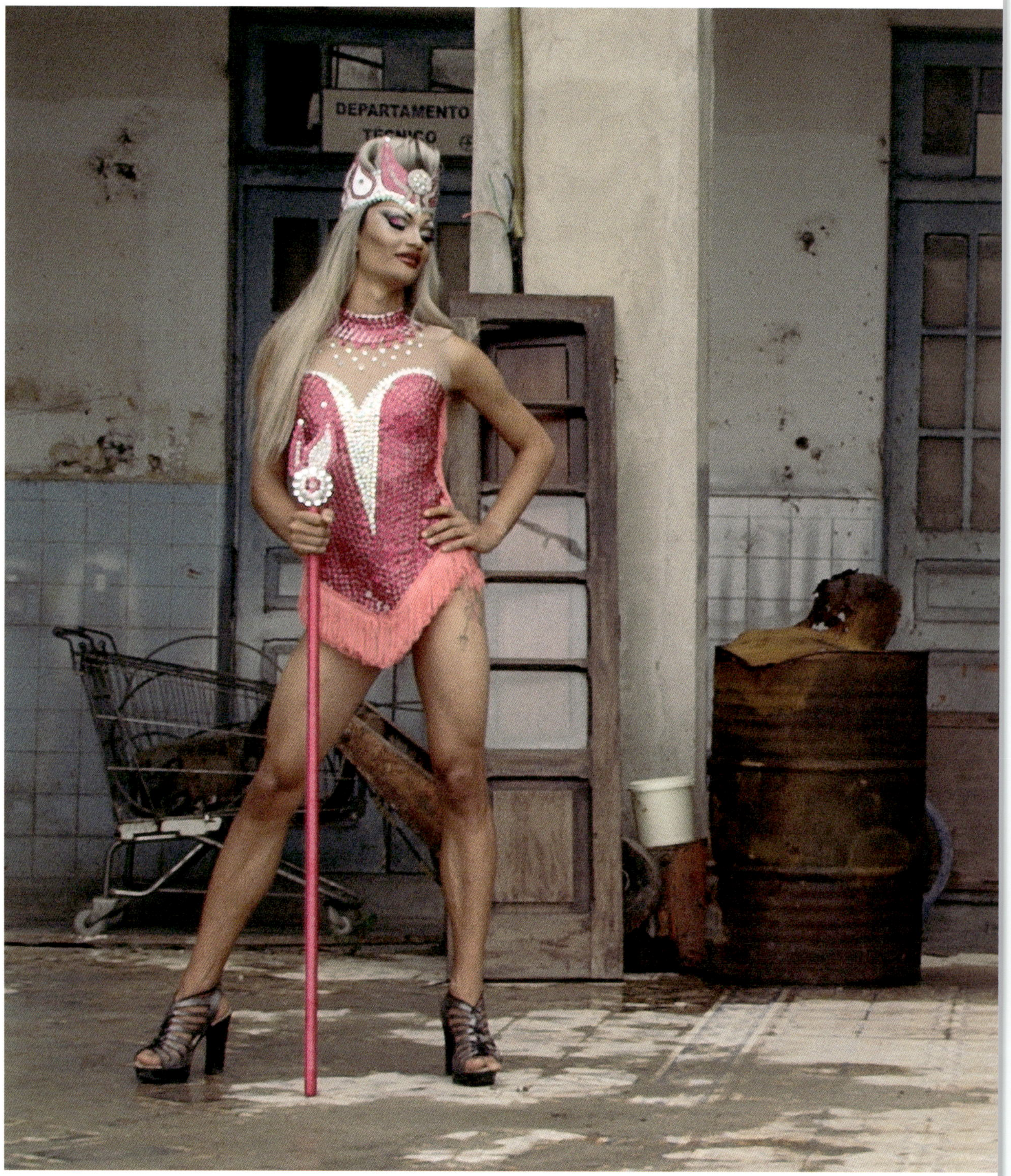
DEPARTAMENTO

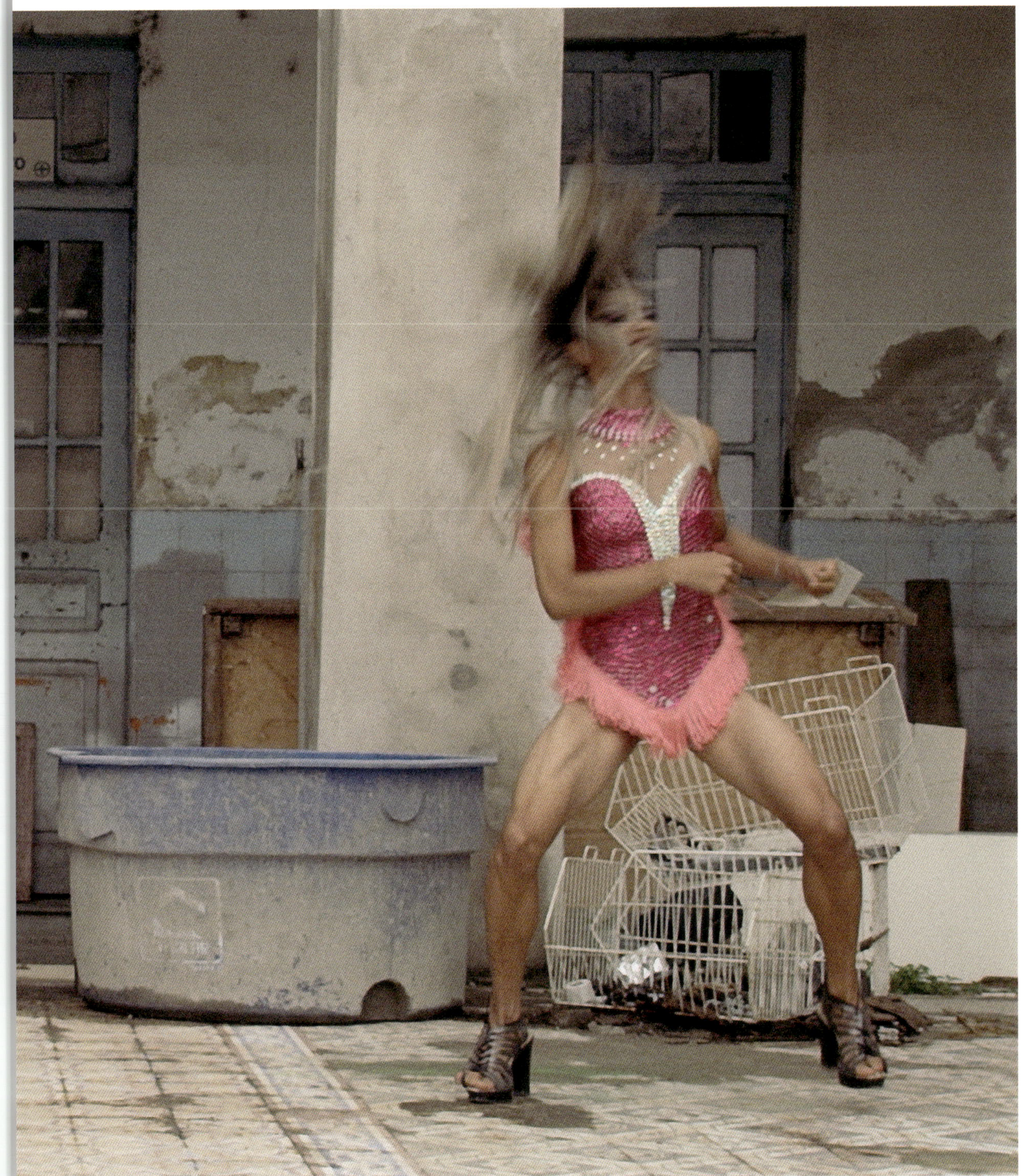

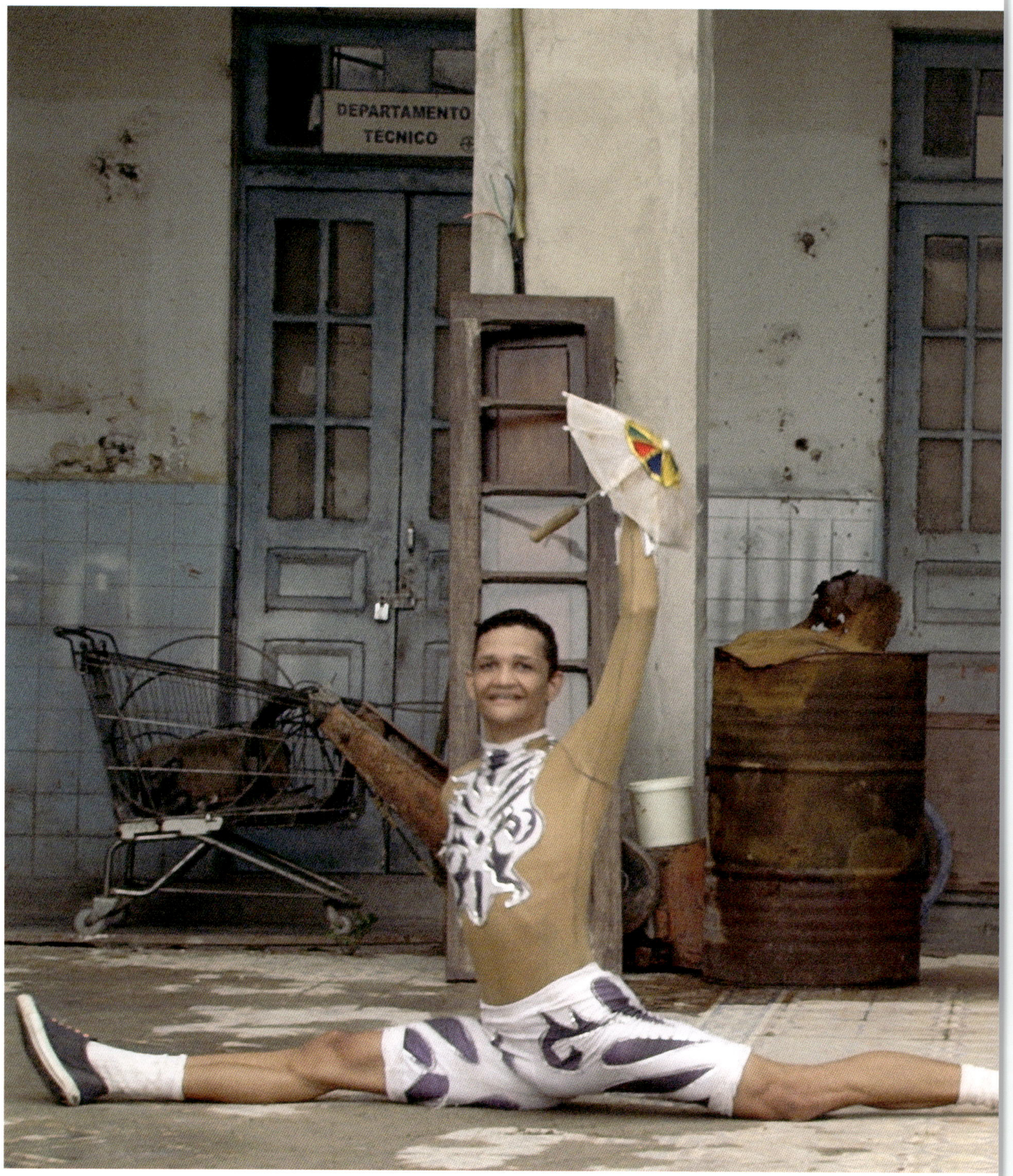
DEPARTAMENTO
TECNICO

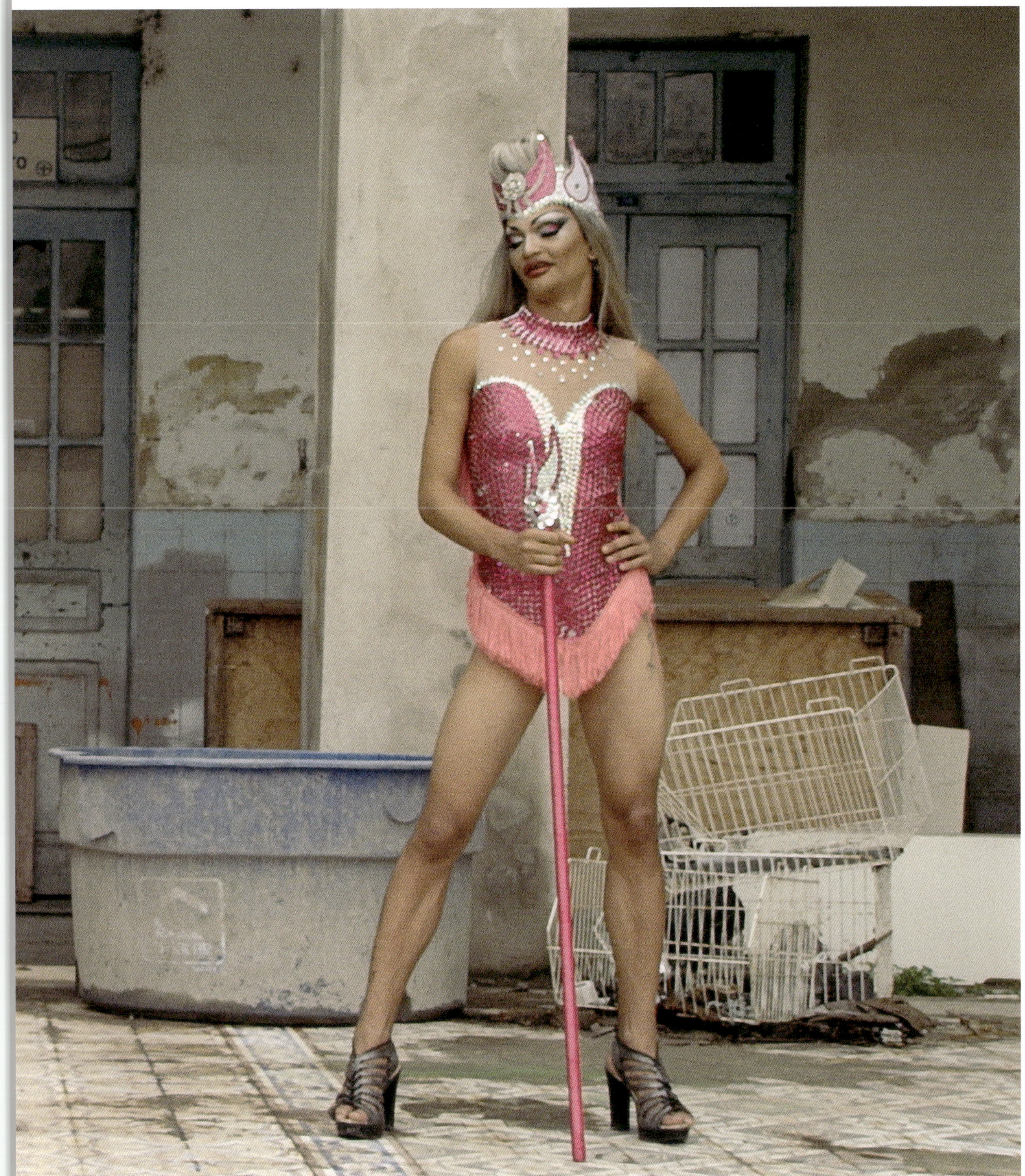

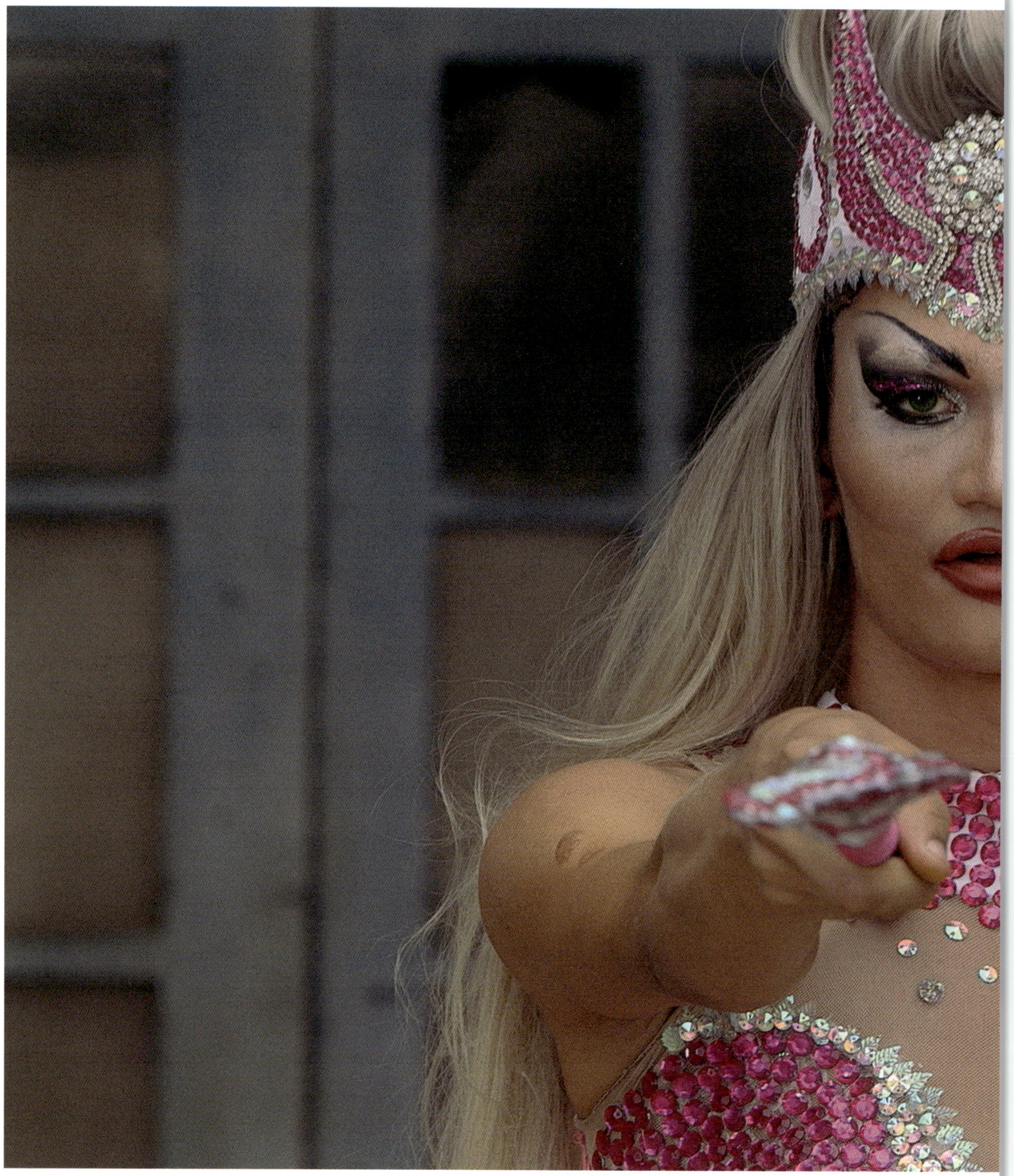

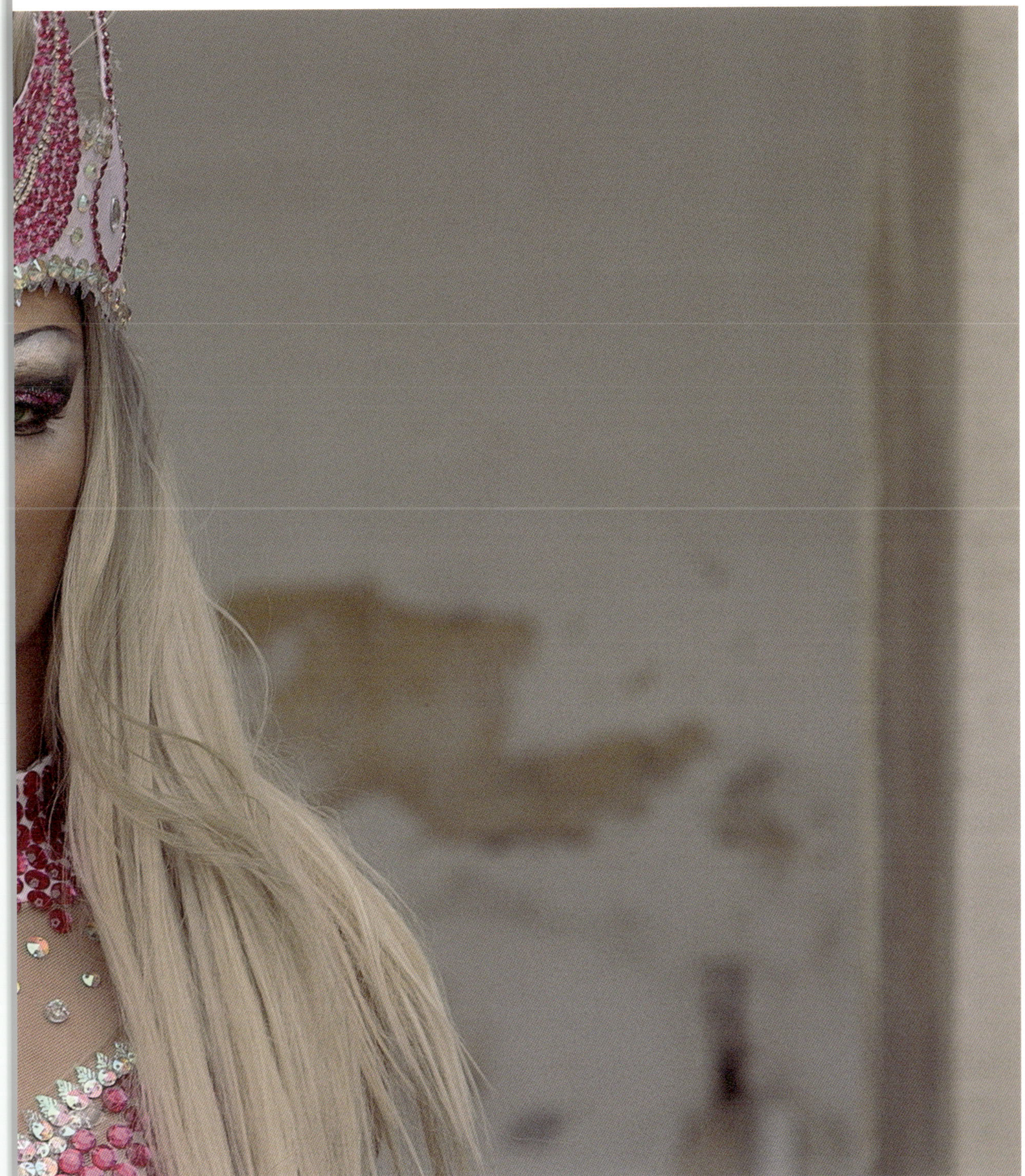

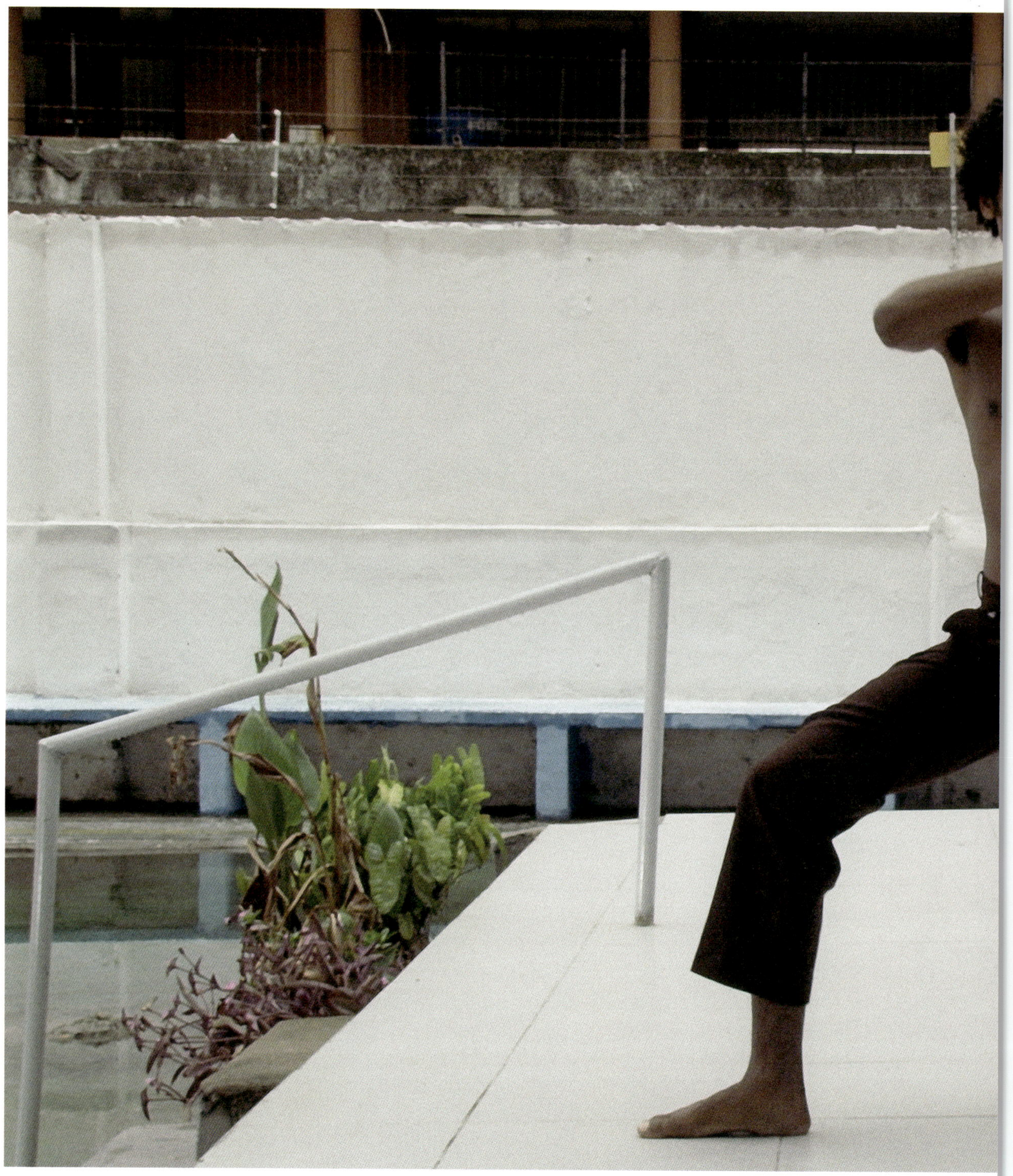

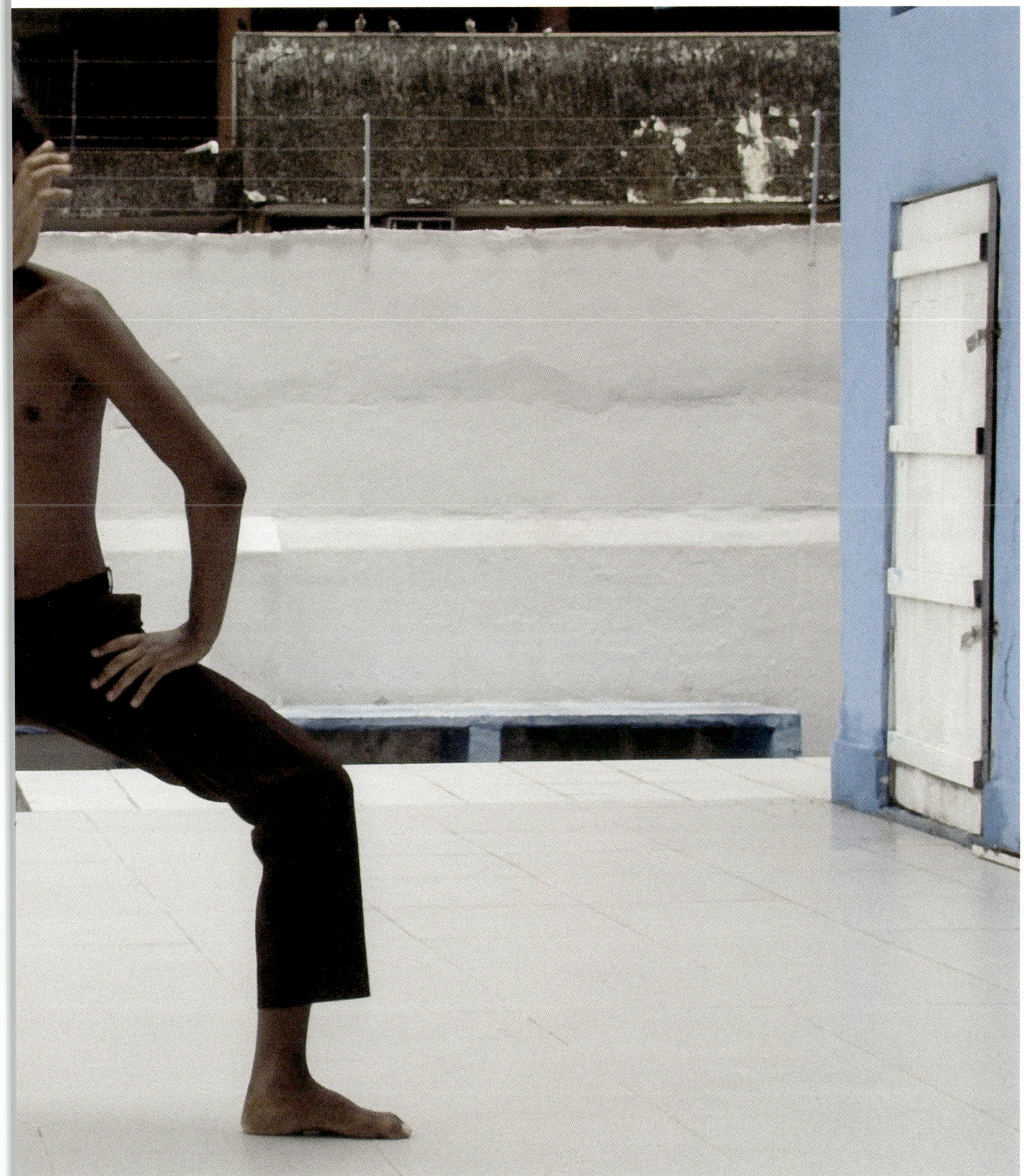

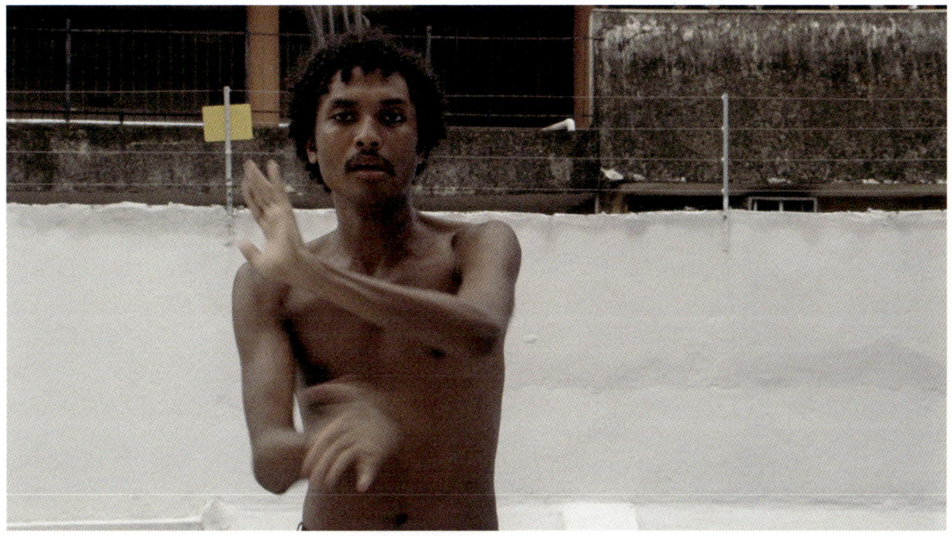

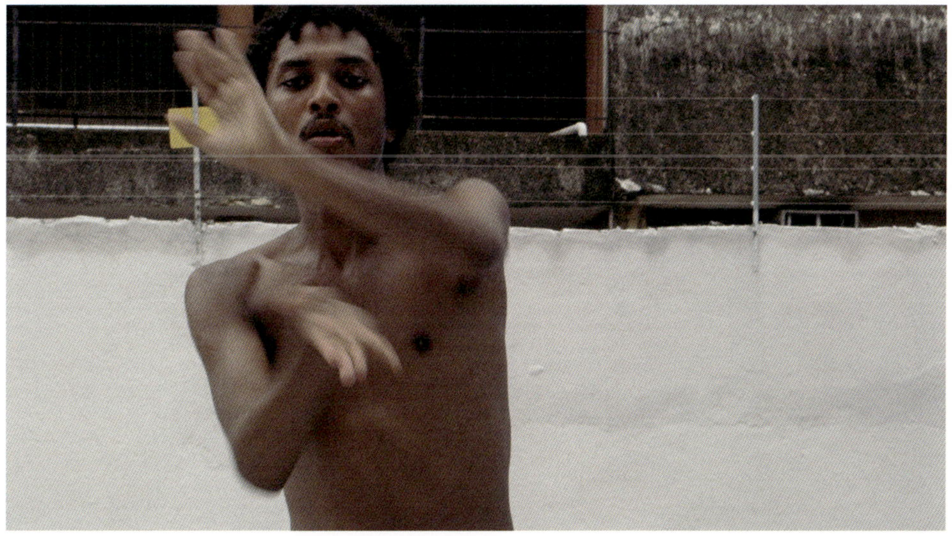

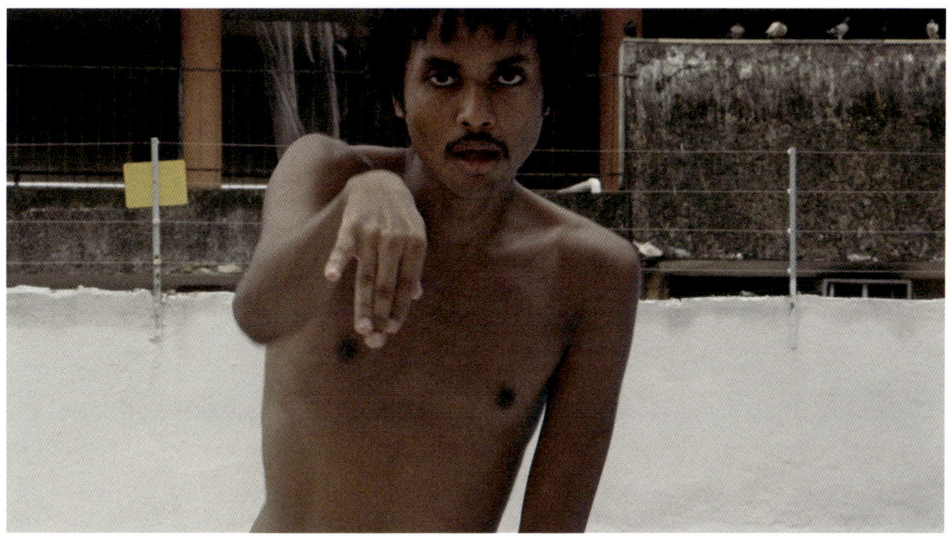

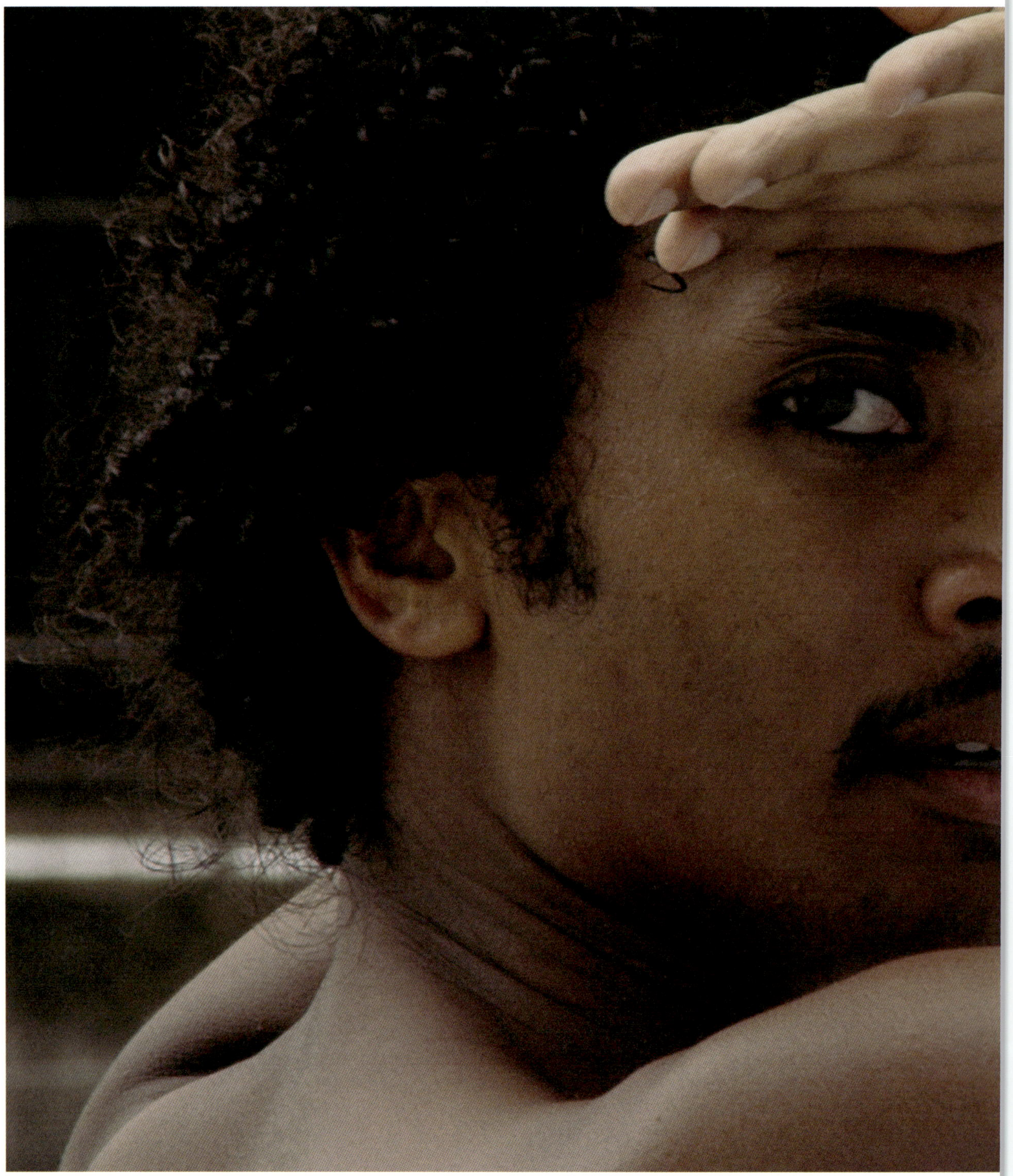

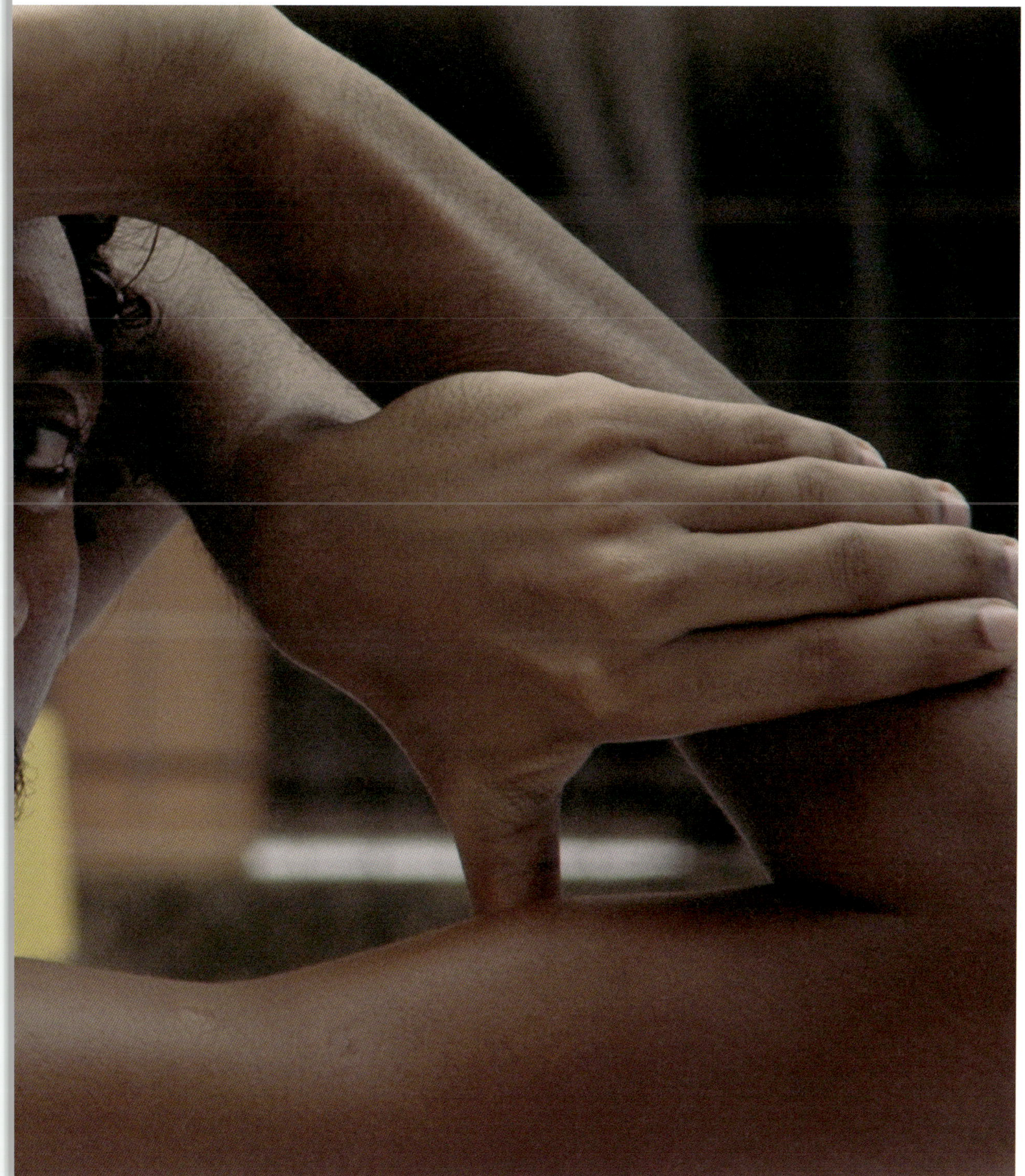

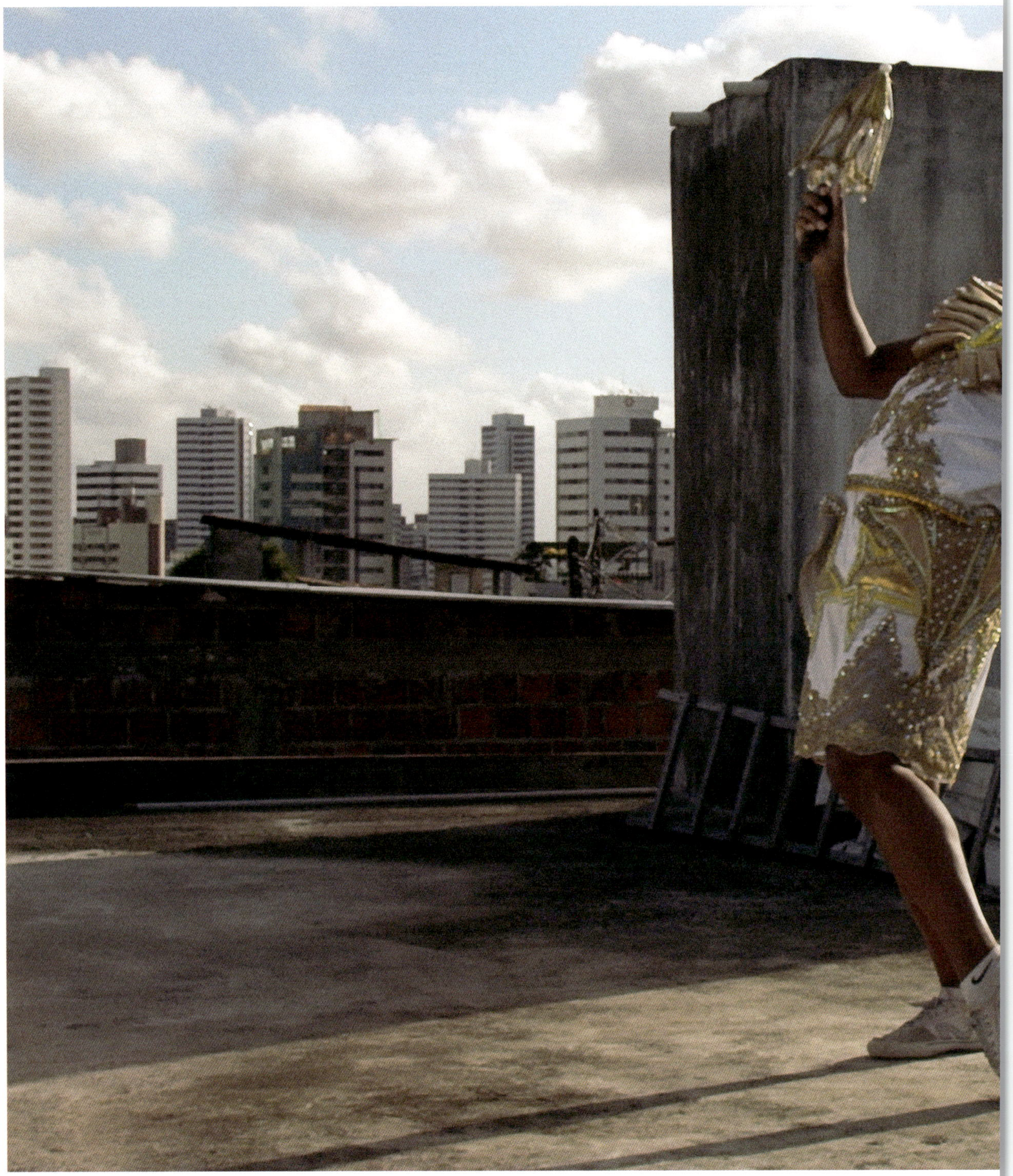

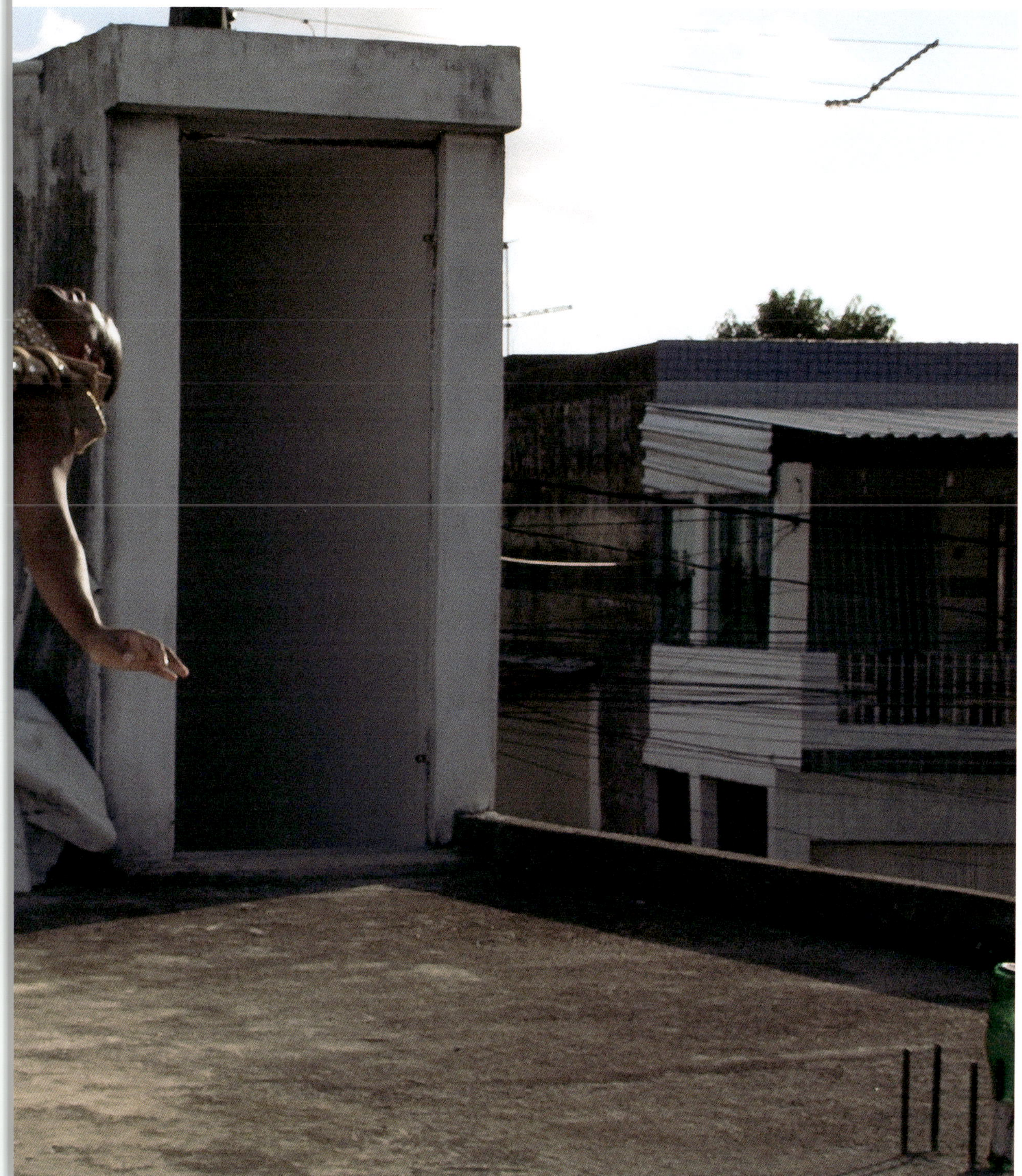

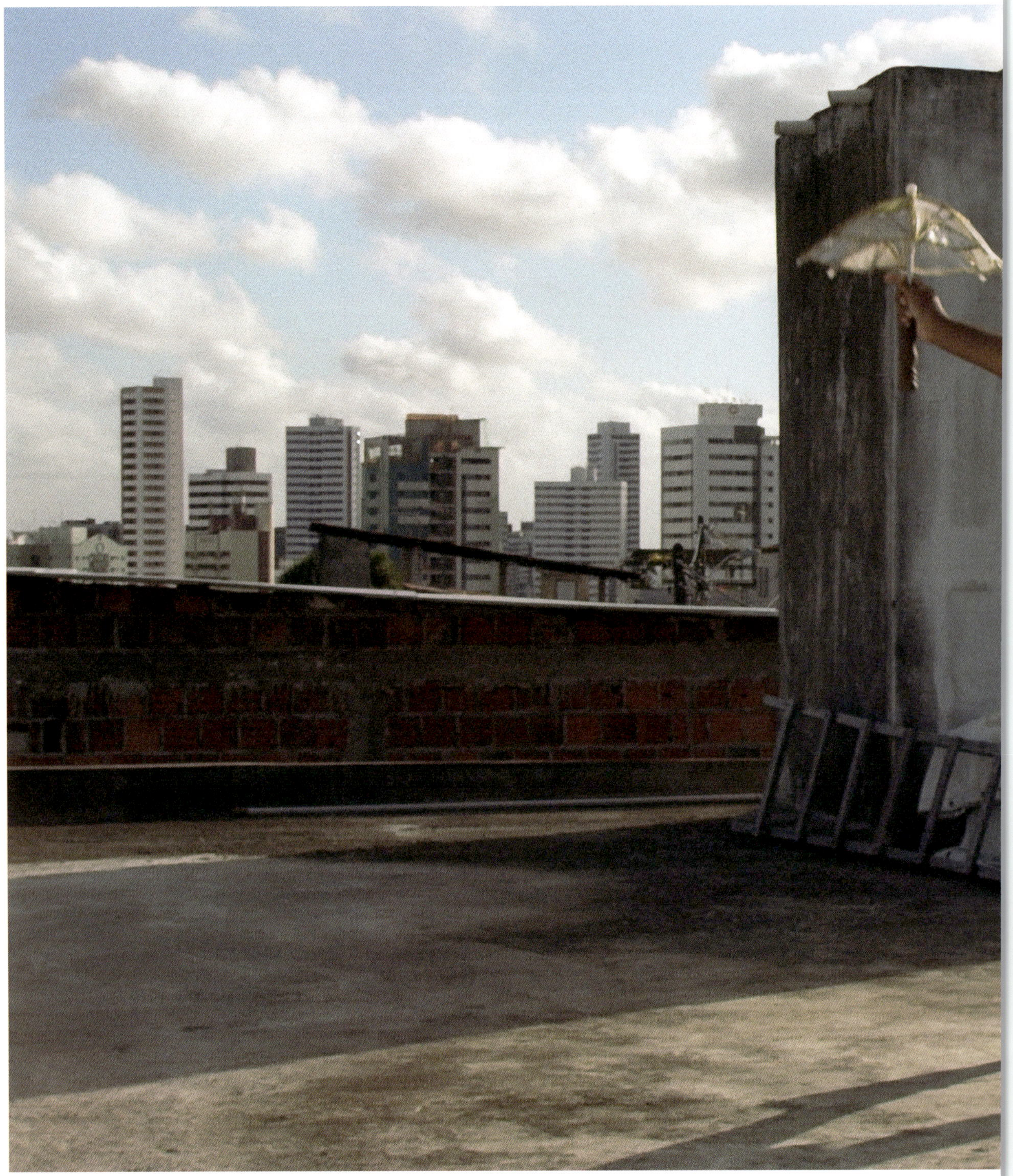

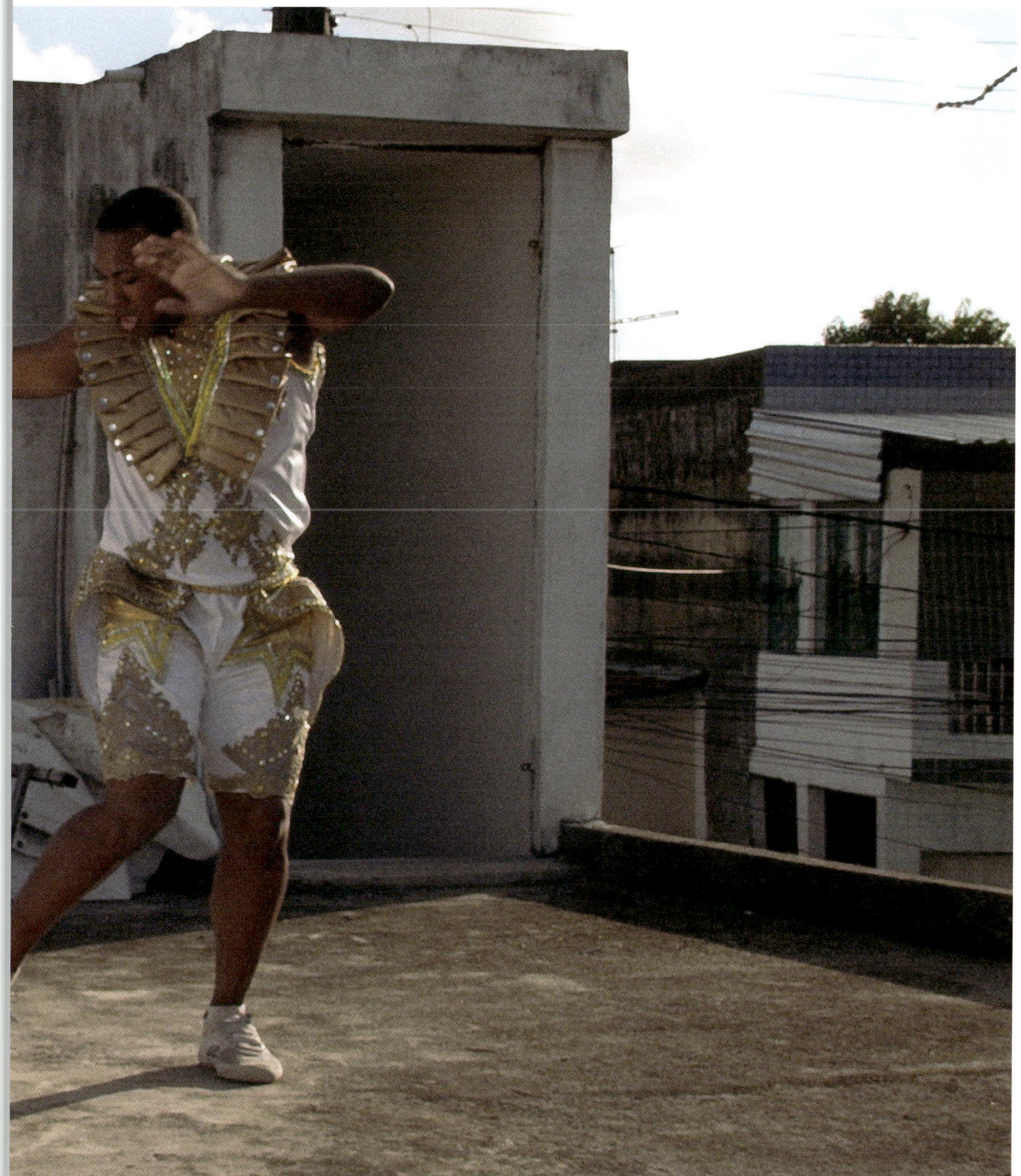

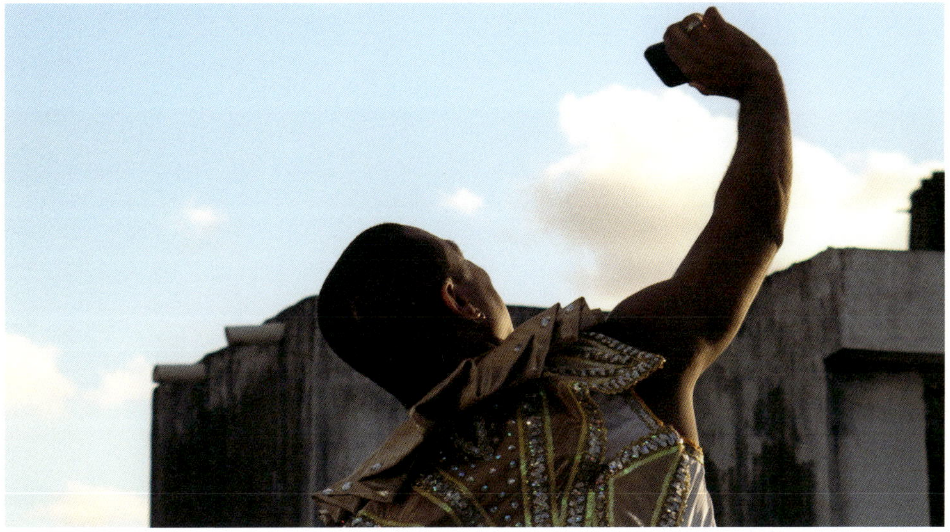

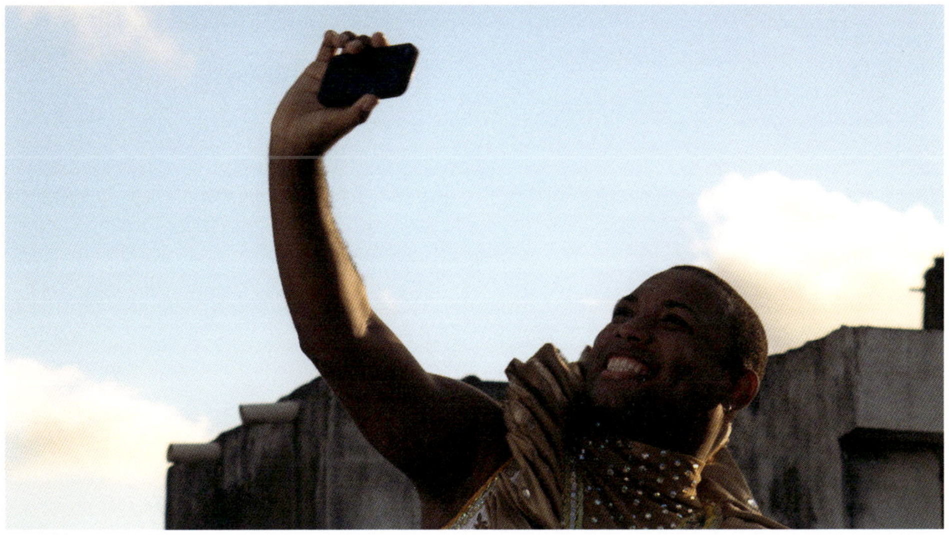

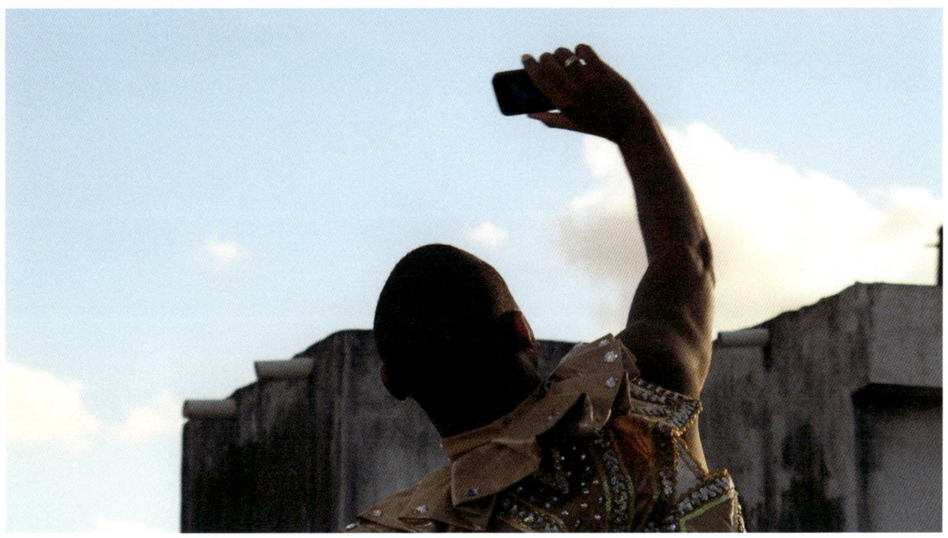

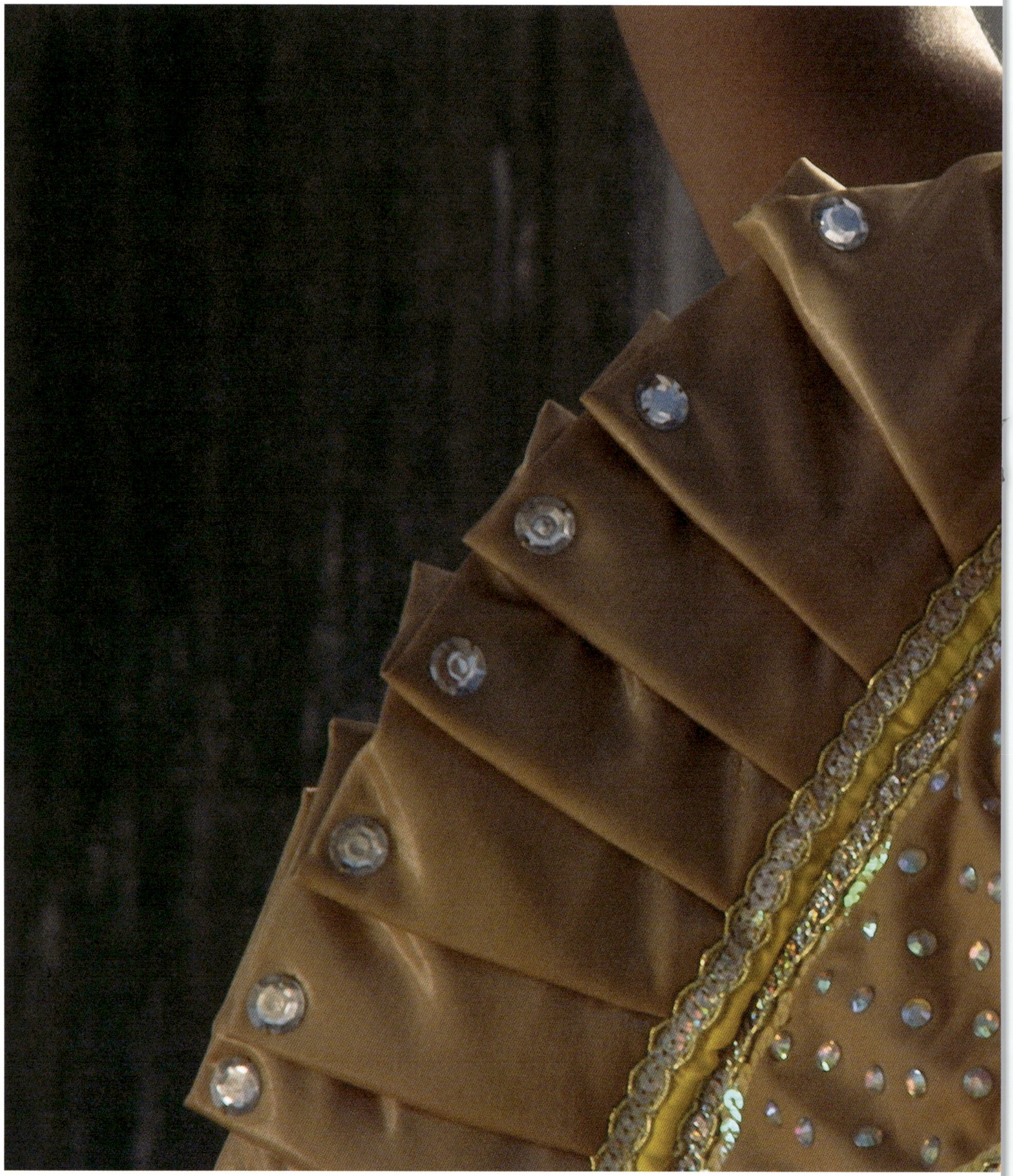

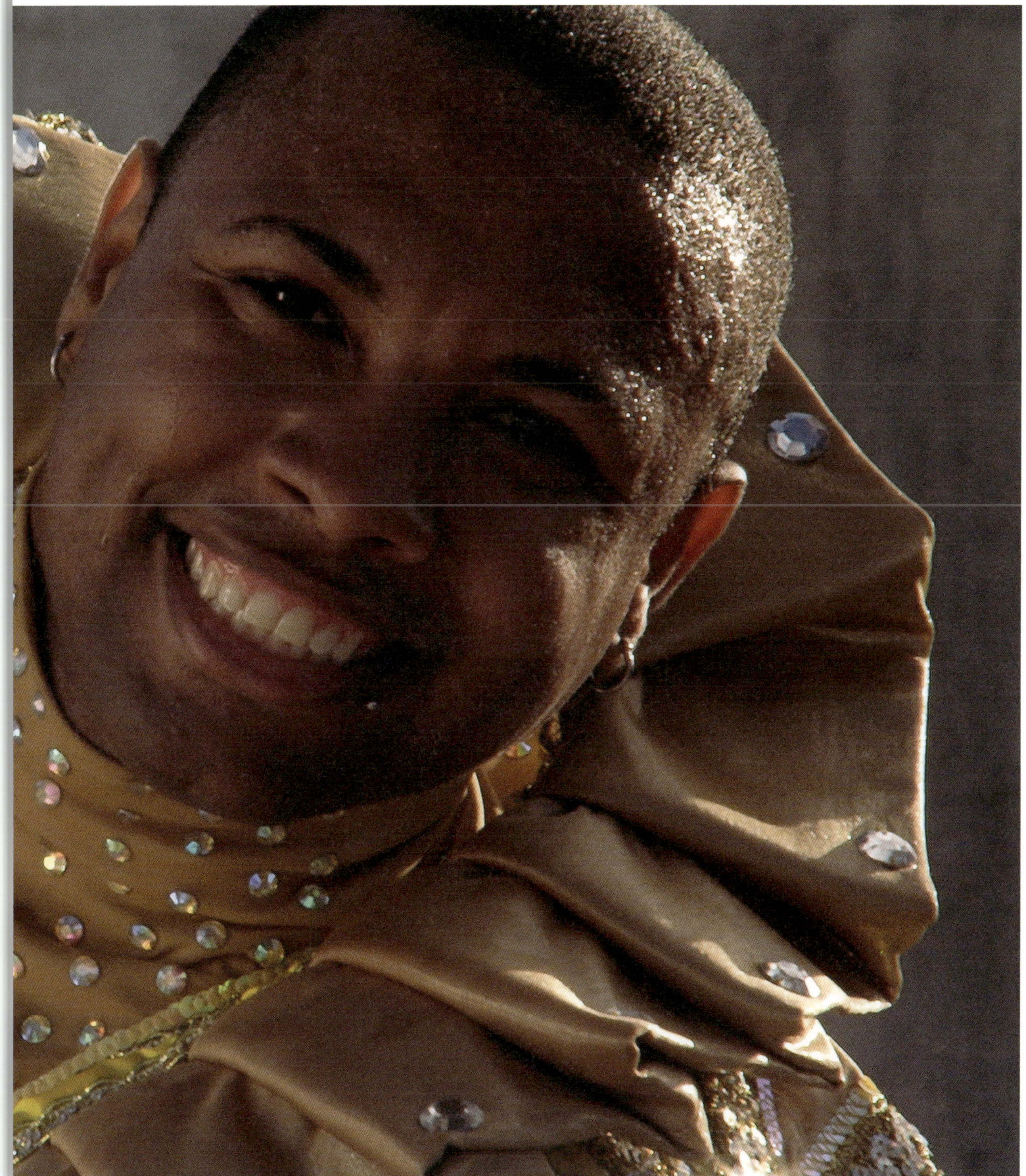

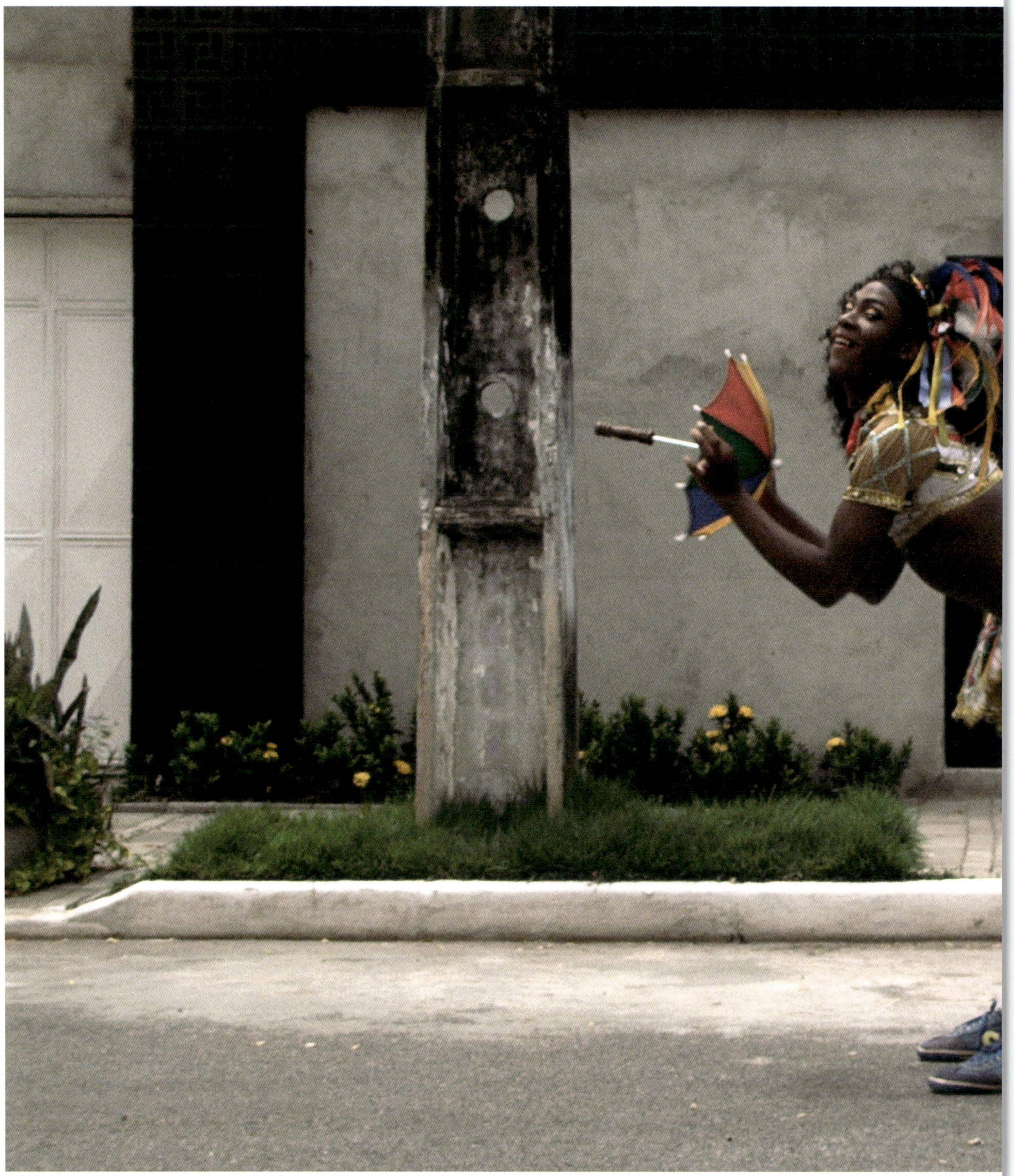

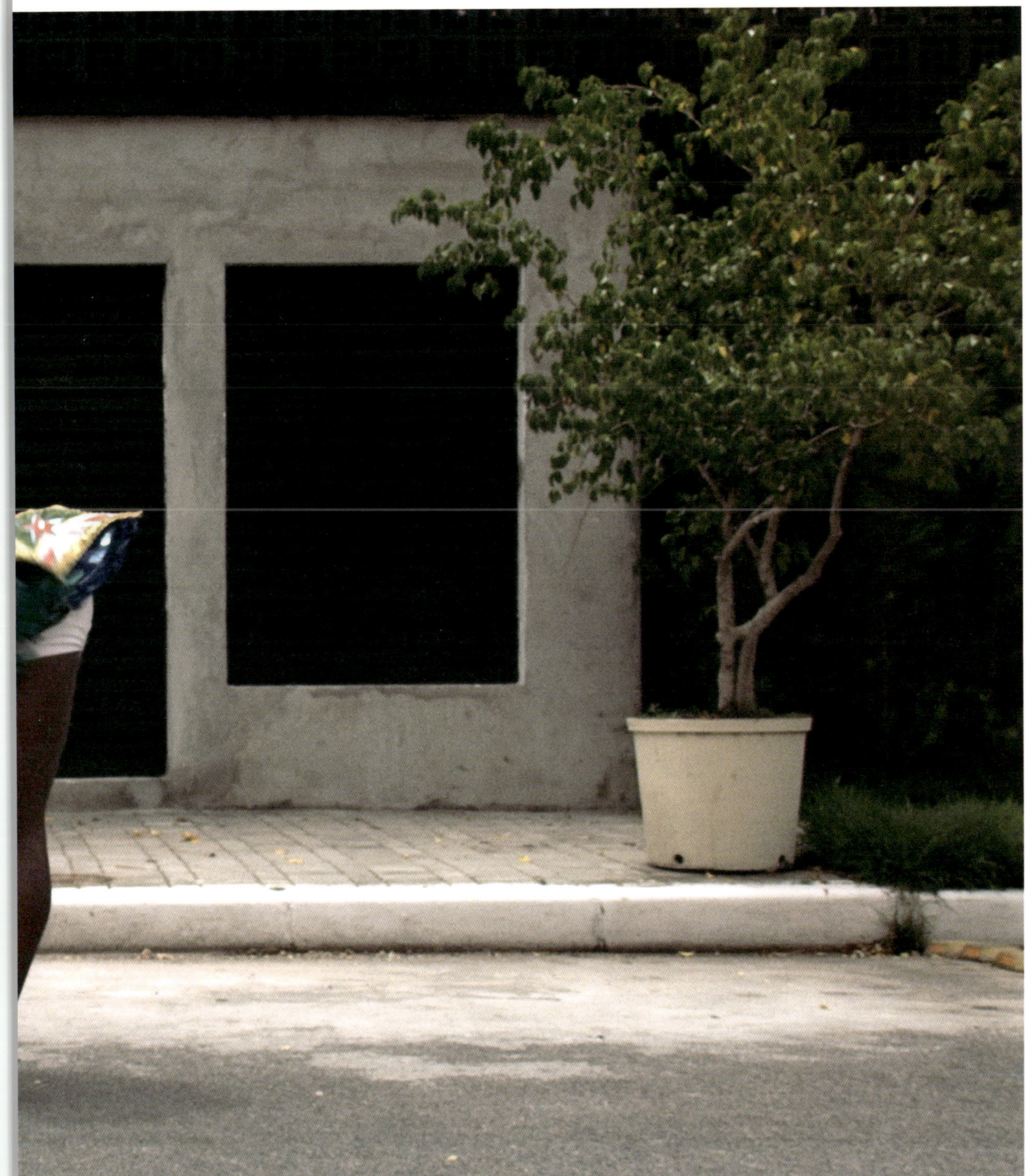

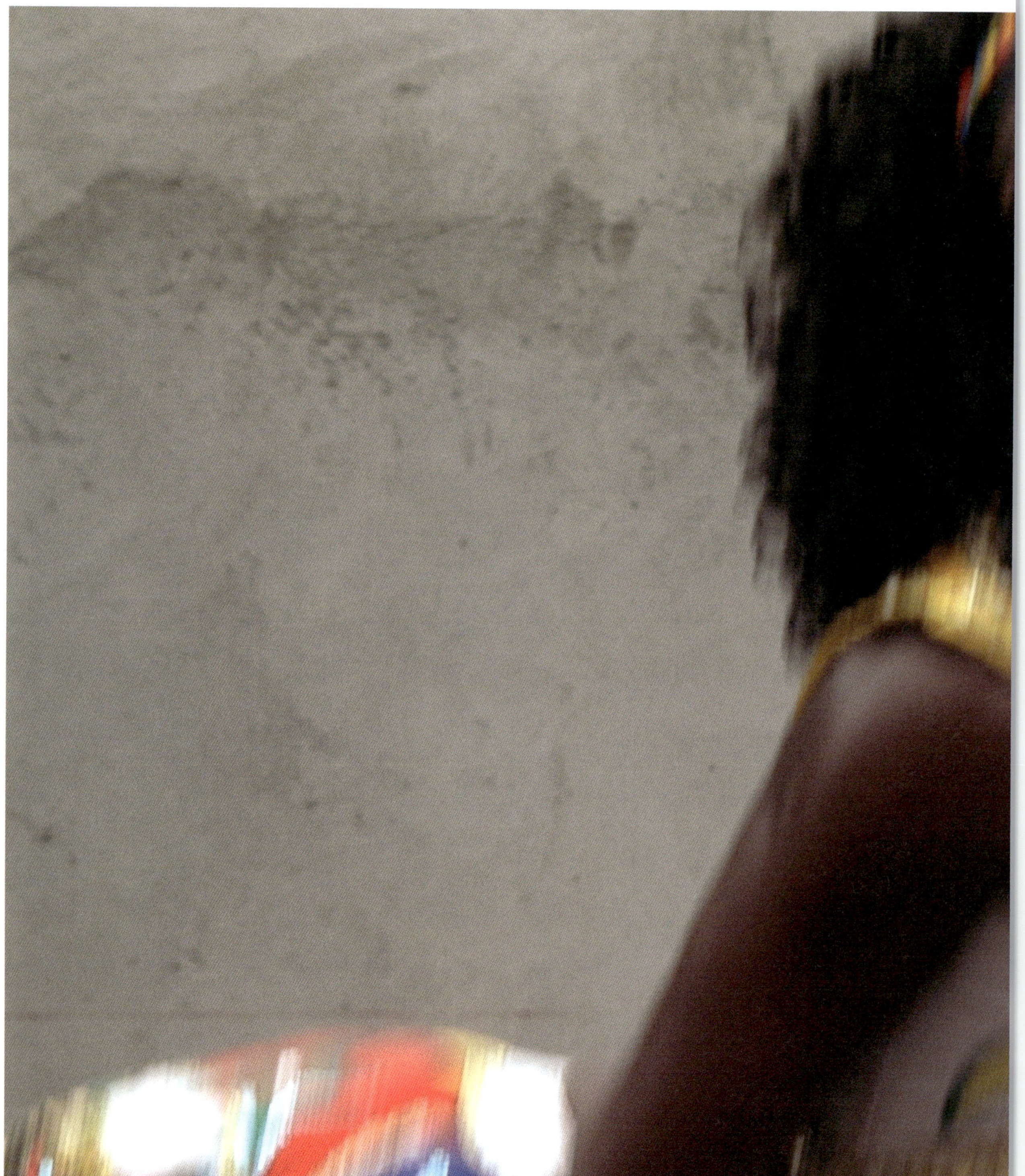

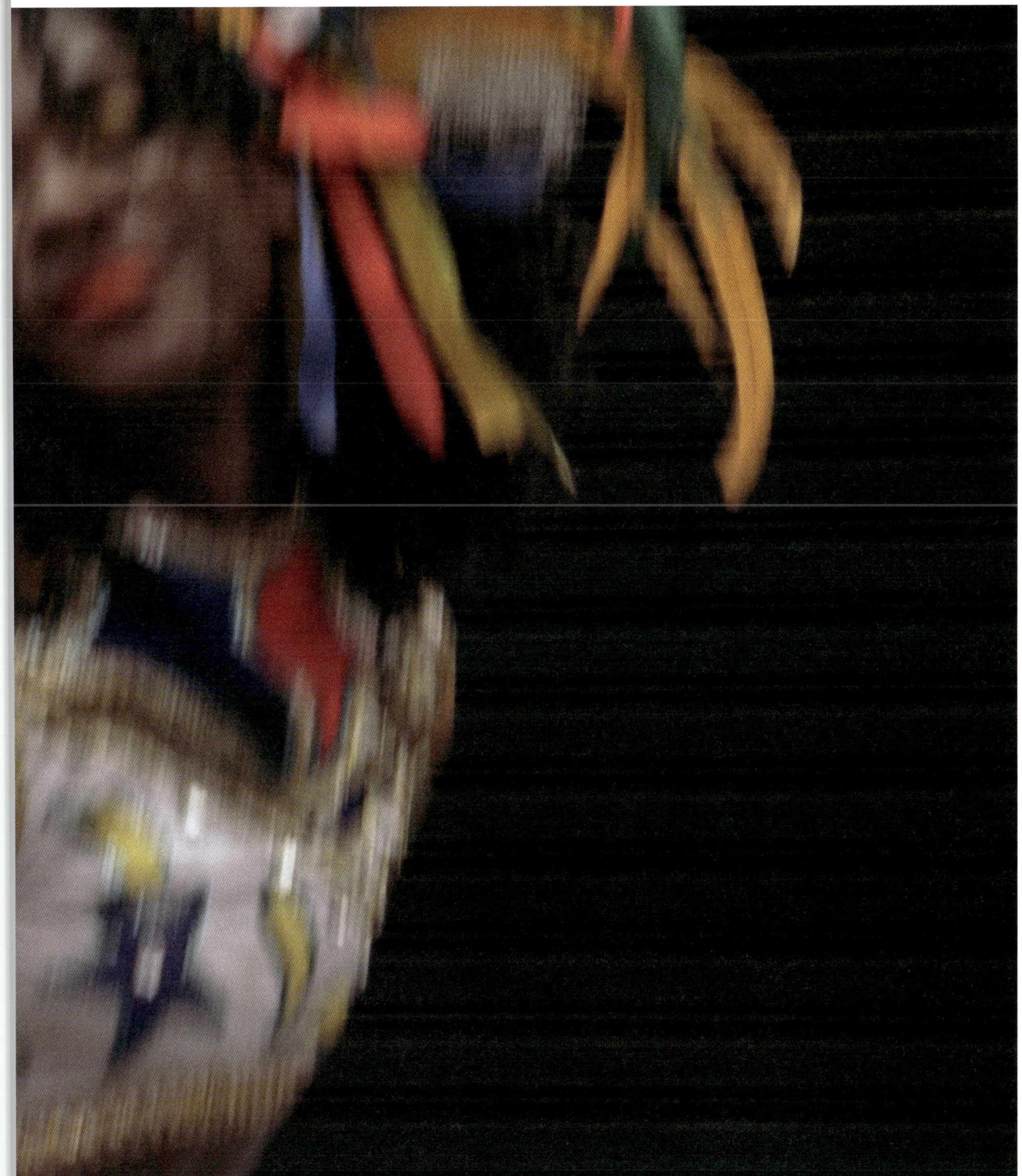

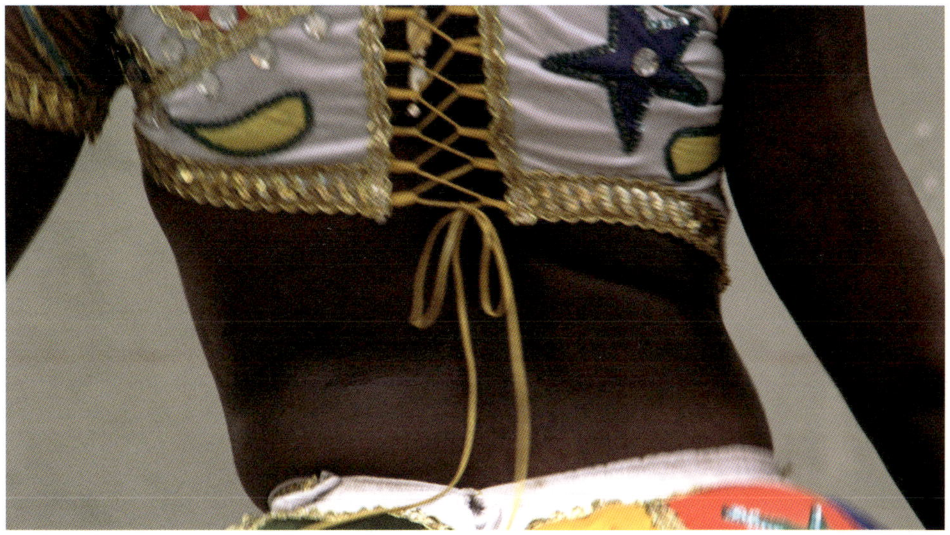
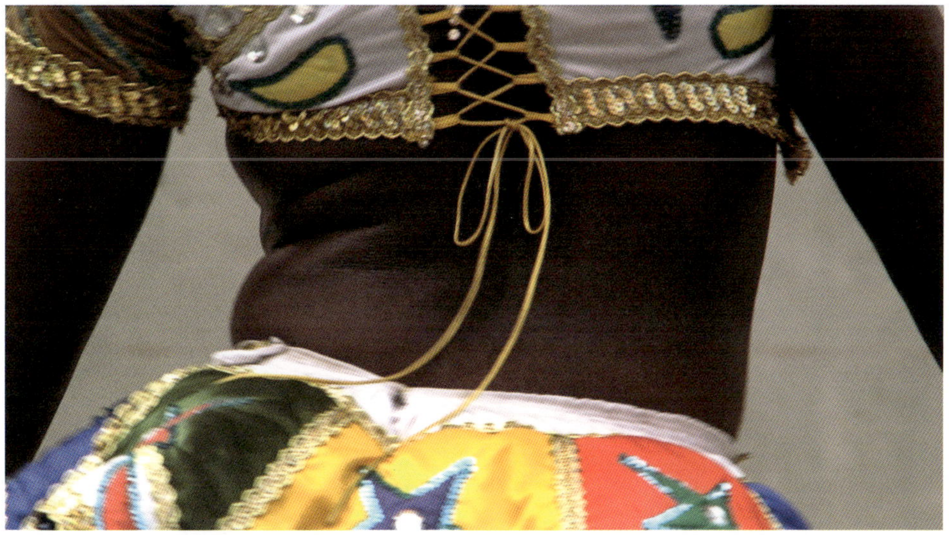
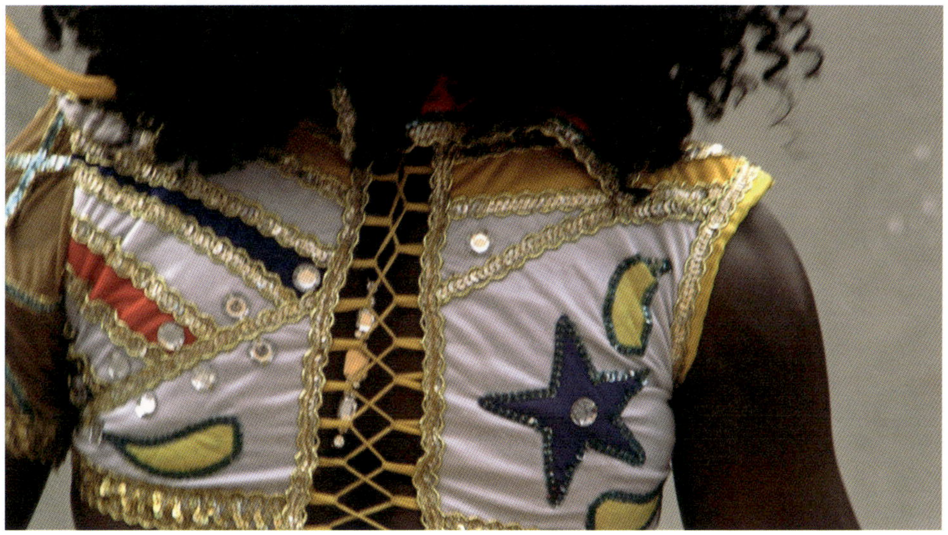

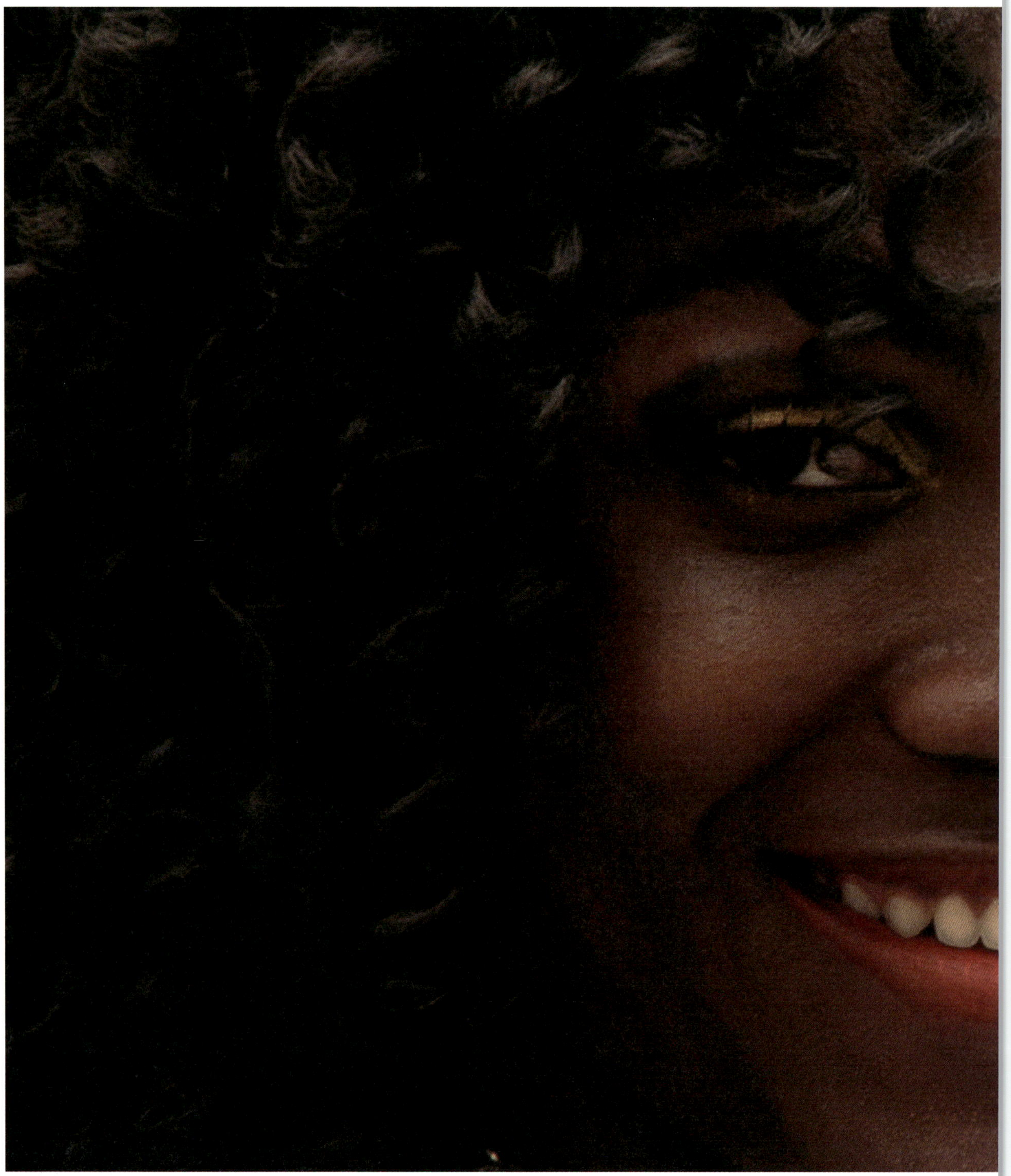

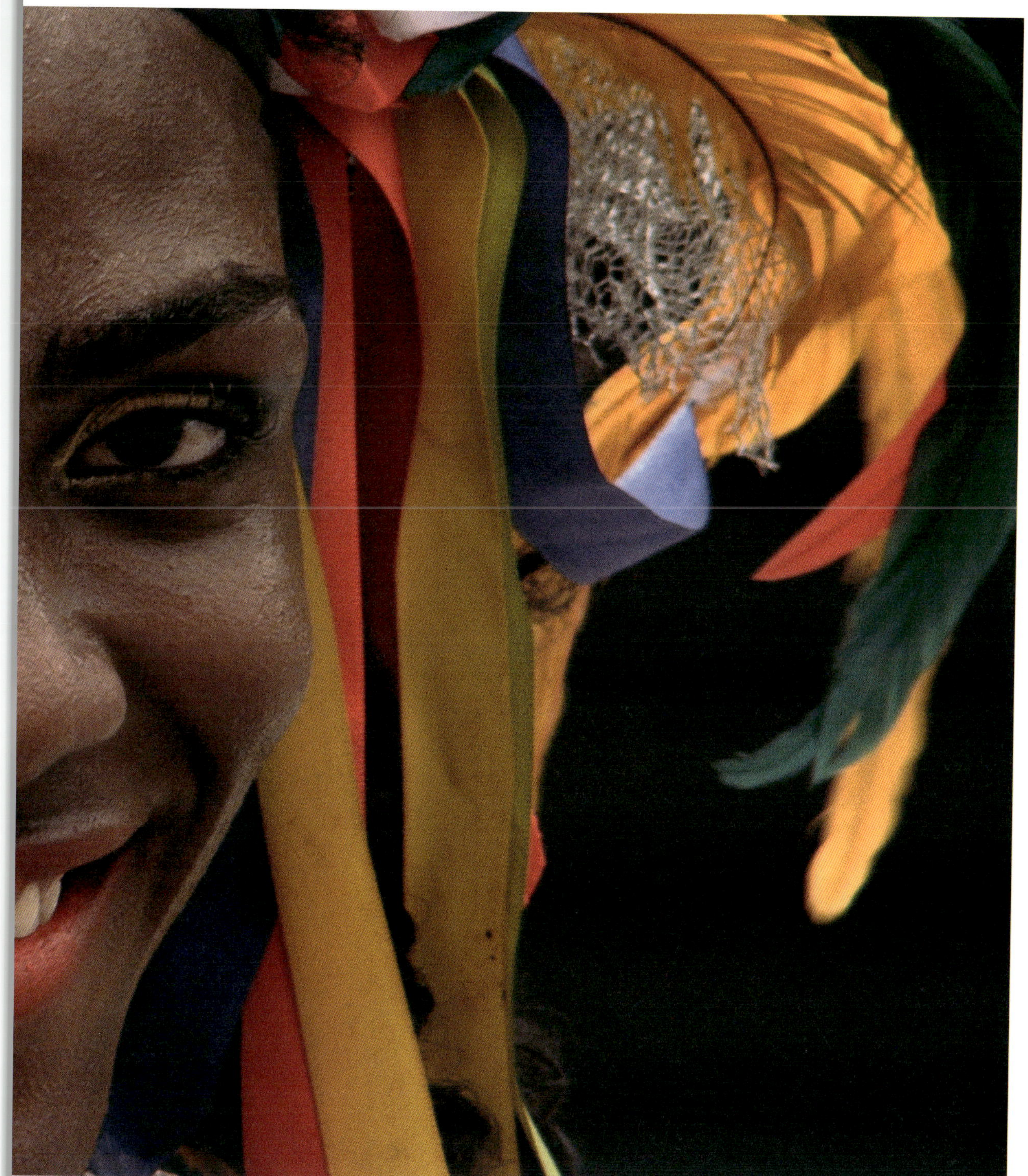

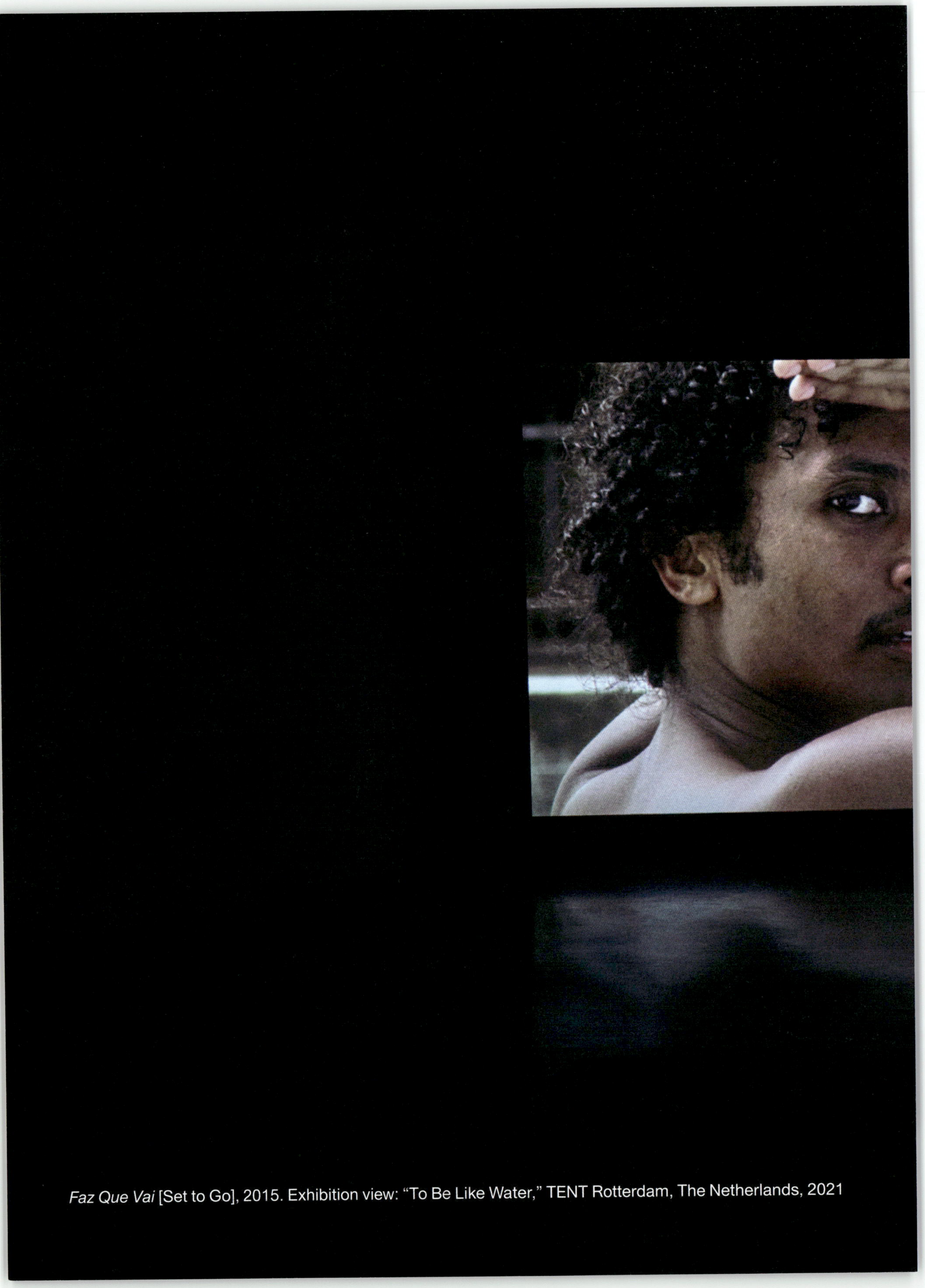

Faz Que Vai [Set to Go], 2015. Exhibition view: "To Be Like Water," TENT Rotterdam, The Netherlands, 2021

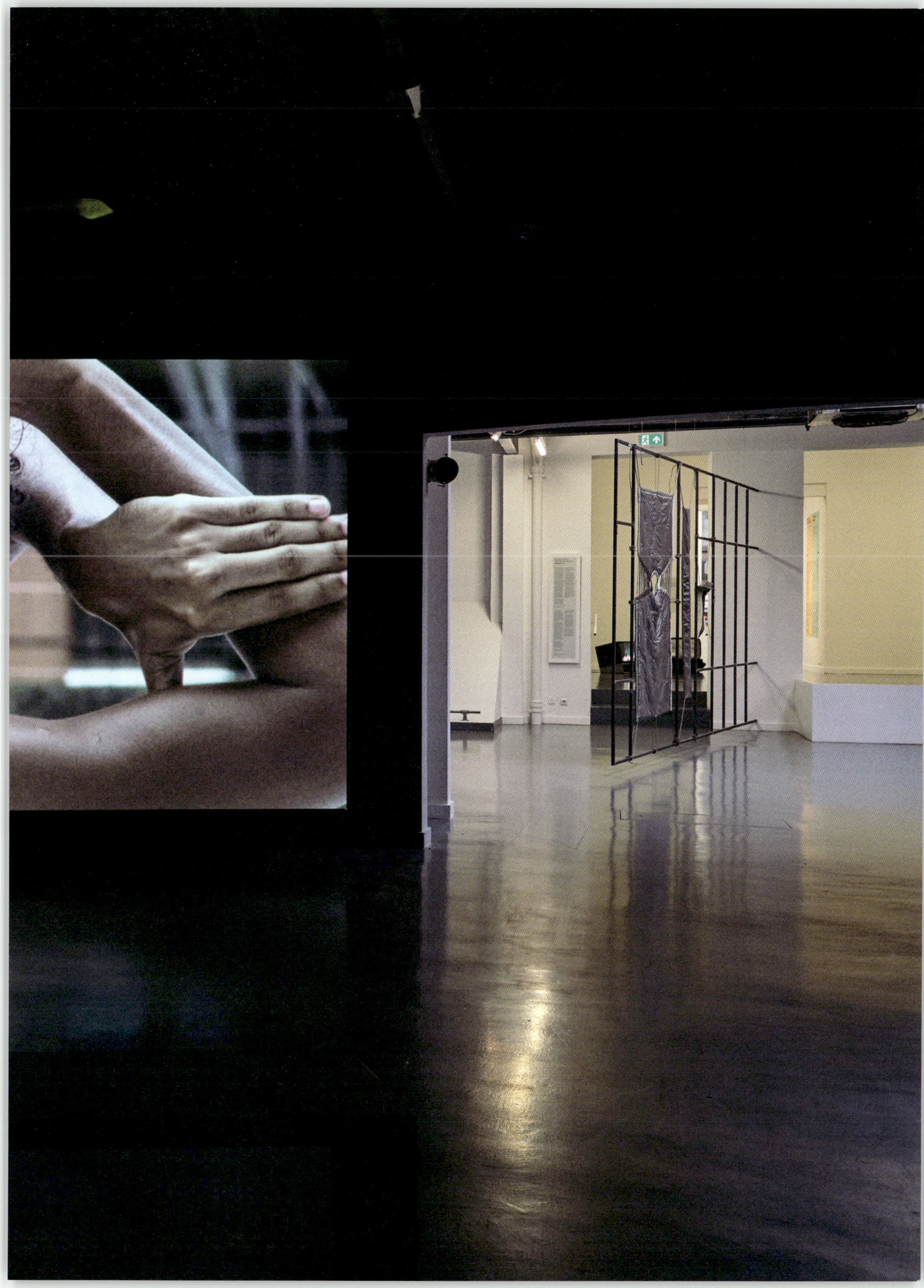

Estás Vendo Coisas
[You Are Seeing Things], 2016

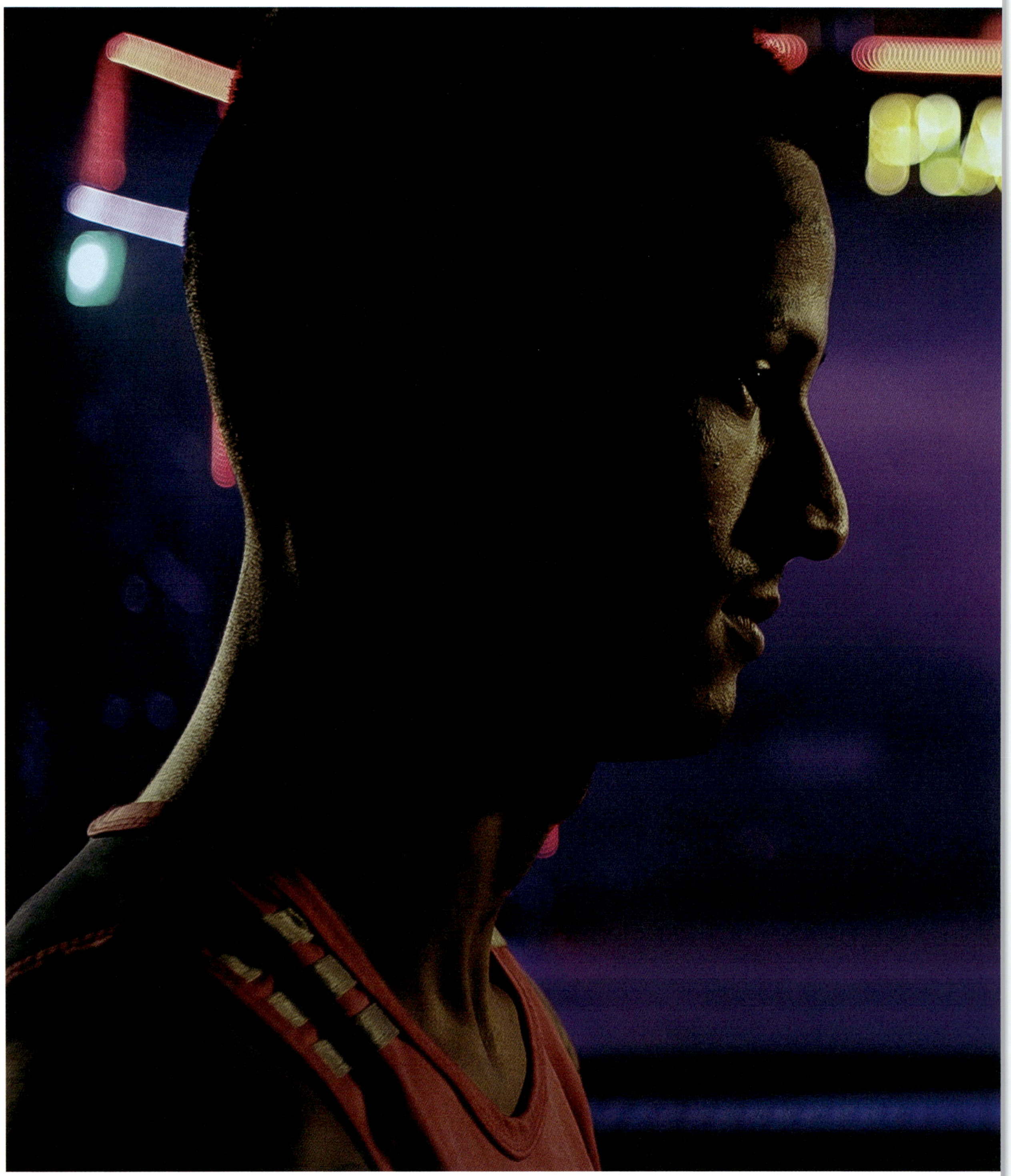

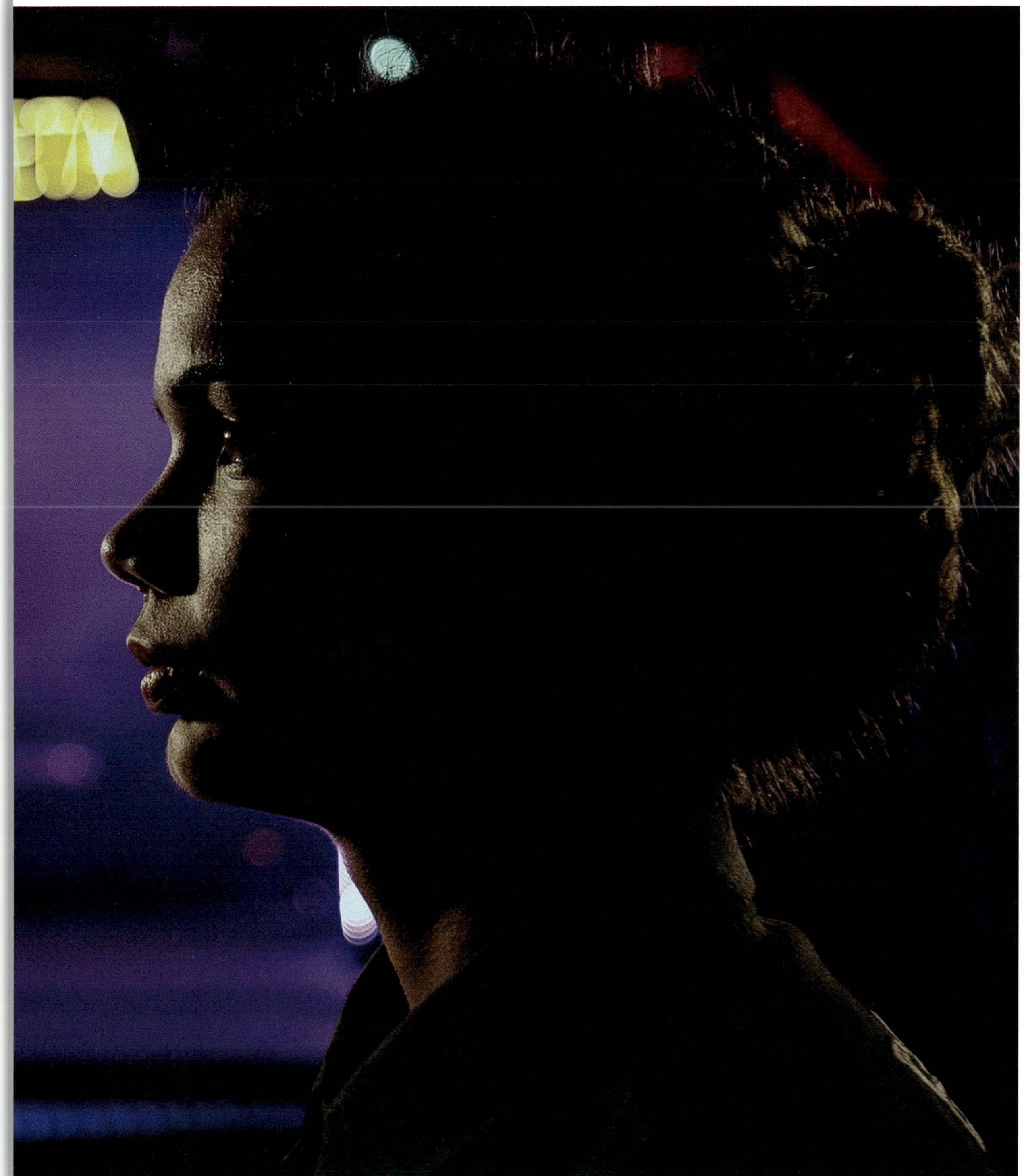

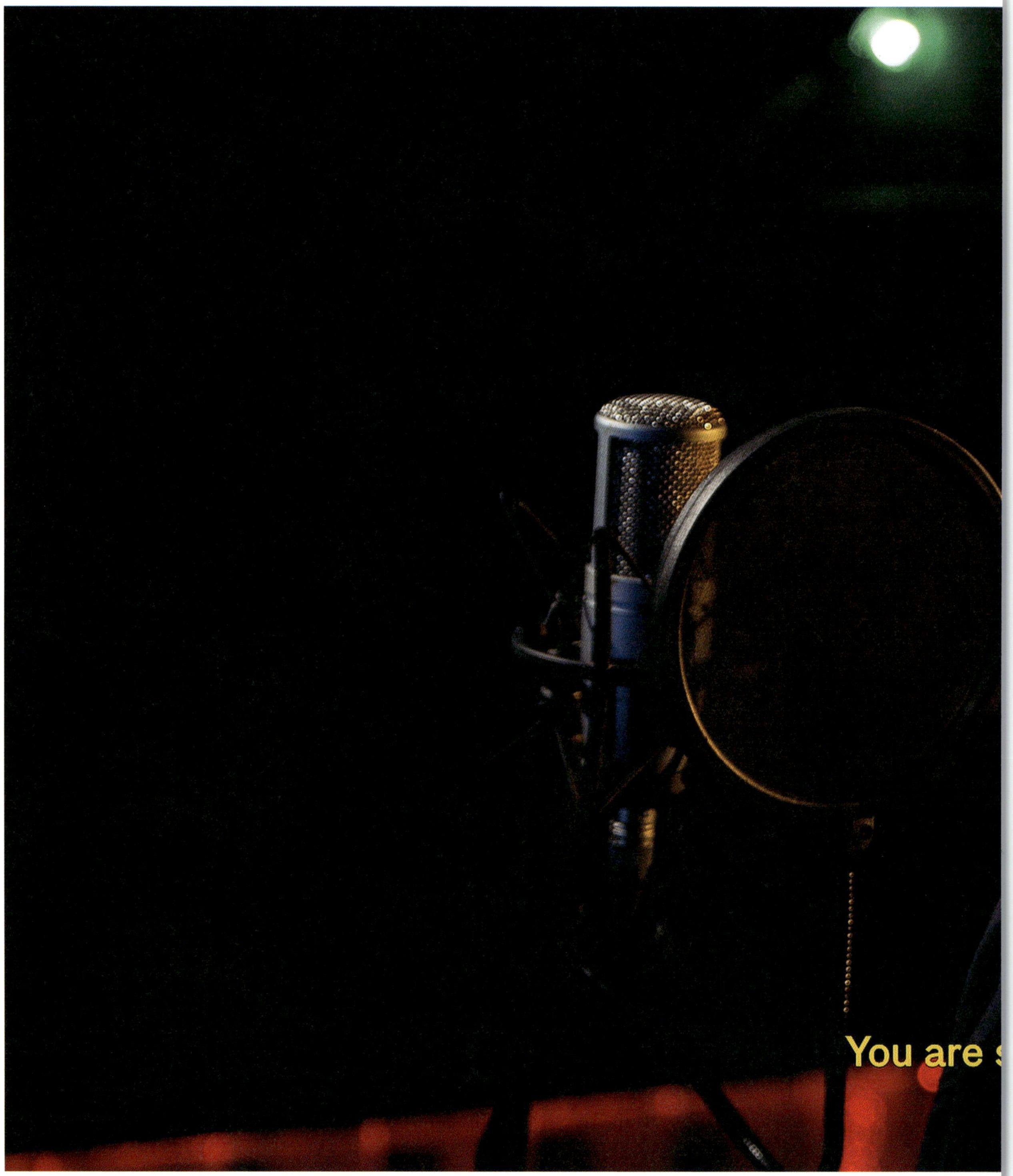
You are

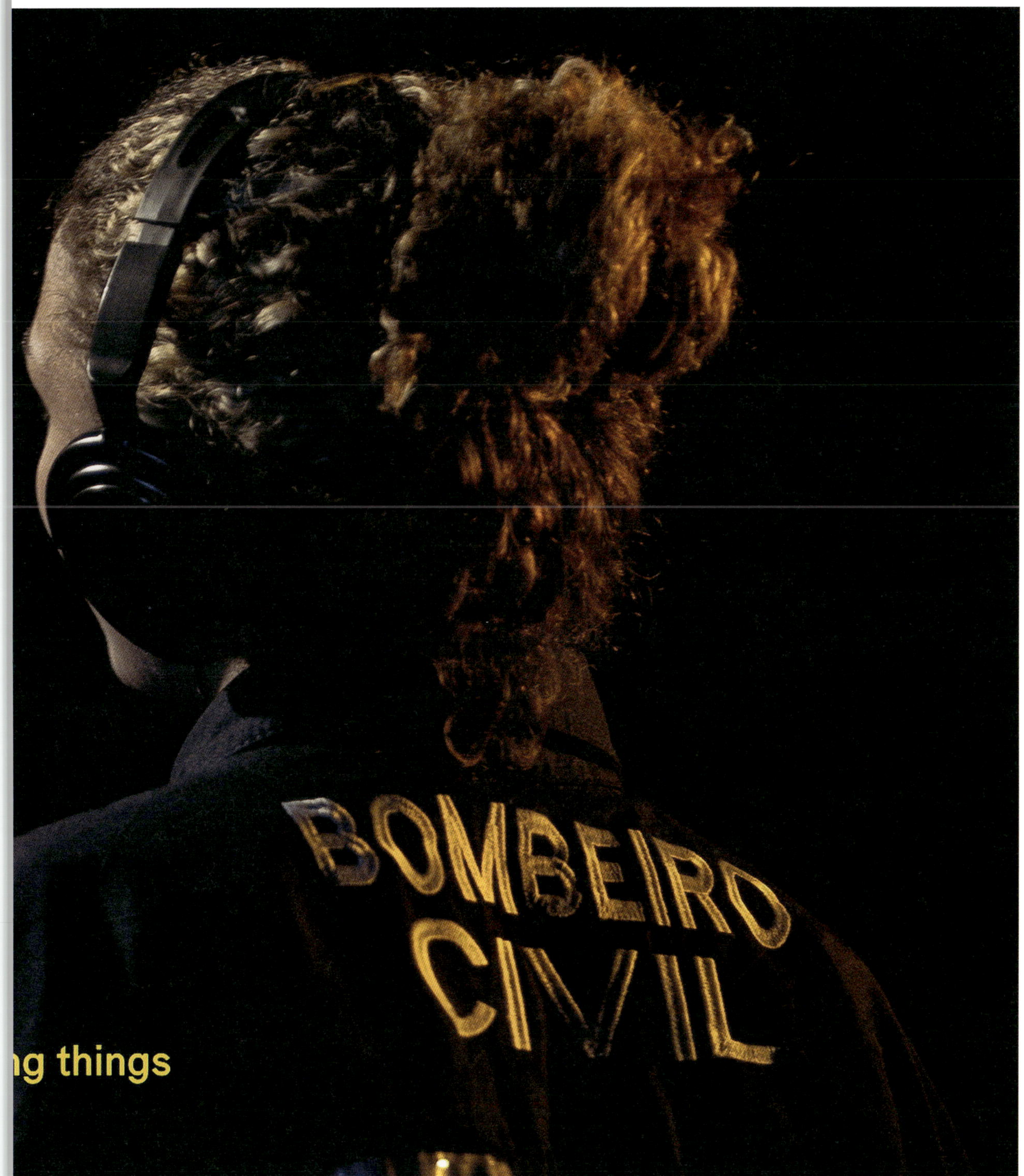

ng things

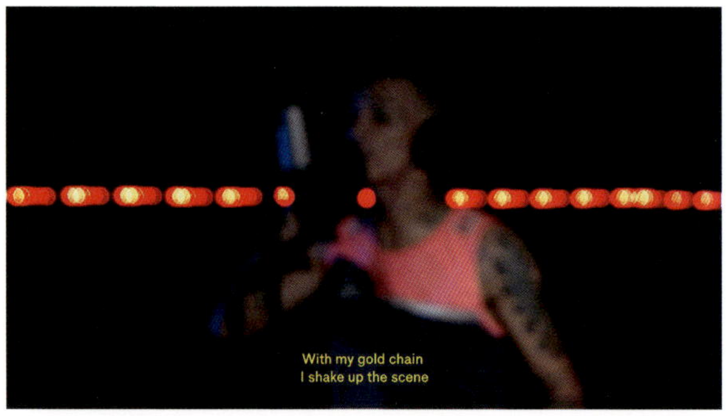
With my gold chain
I shake up the scene

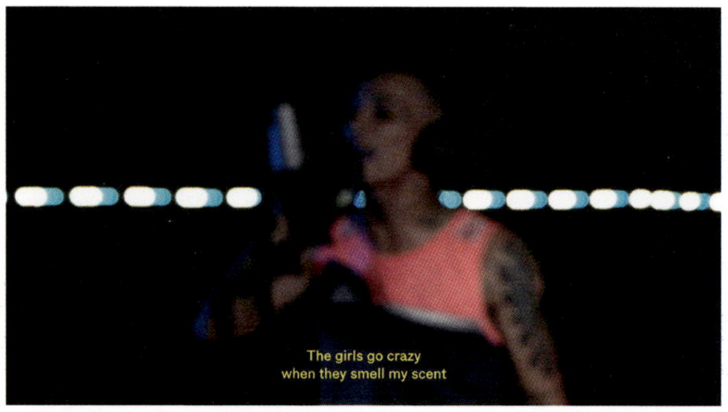
The girls go crazy
when they smell my scent

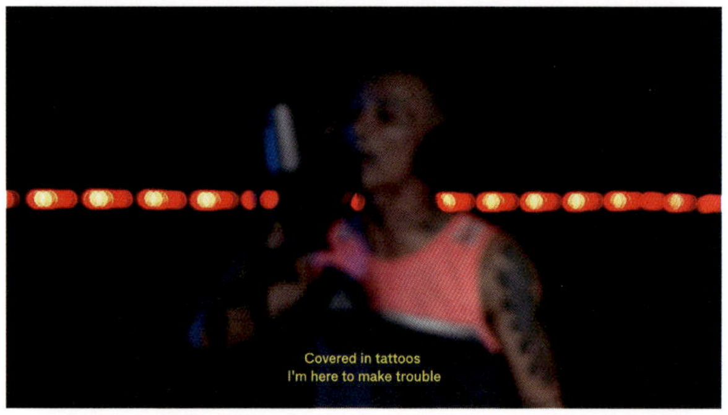
Covered in tattoos
I'm here to make trouble

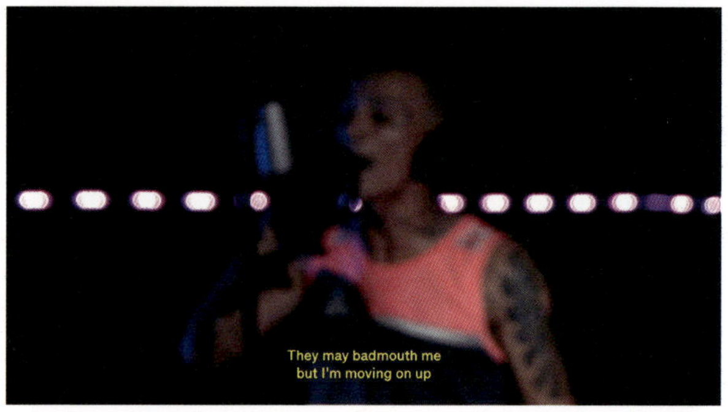
They may badmouth me
but I'm moving on up

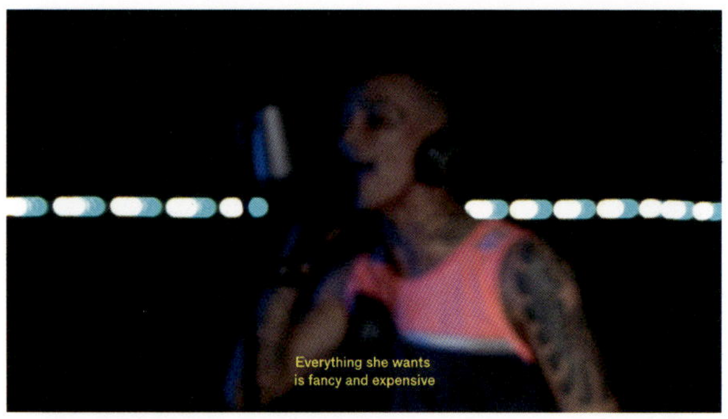
Everything she wants
is fancy and expensive

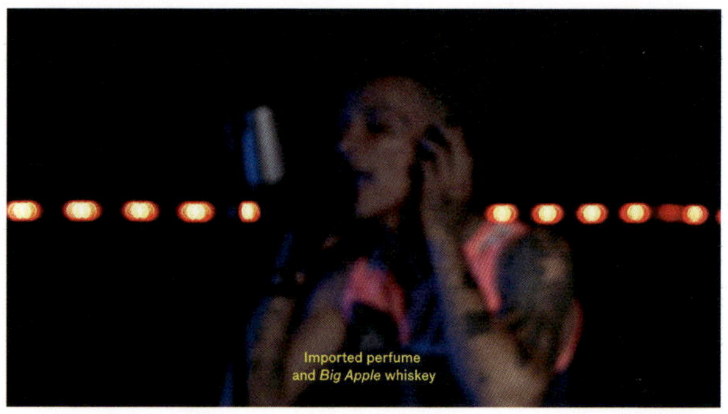
Imported perfume
and *Big Apple* whiskey

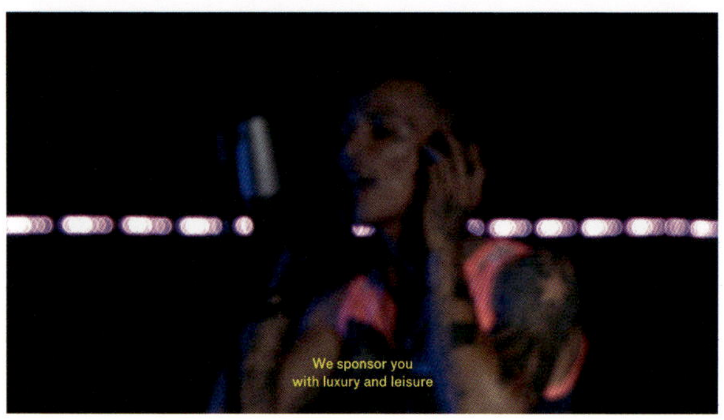
We sponsor you
with luxury and leisure

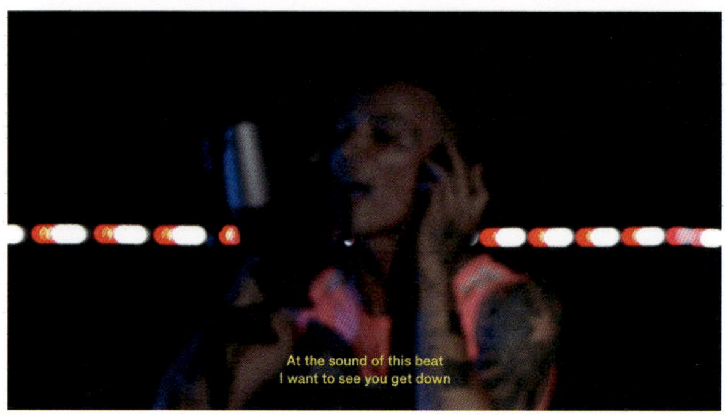
At the sound of this beat
I want to see you get down

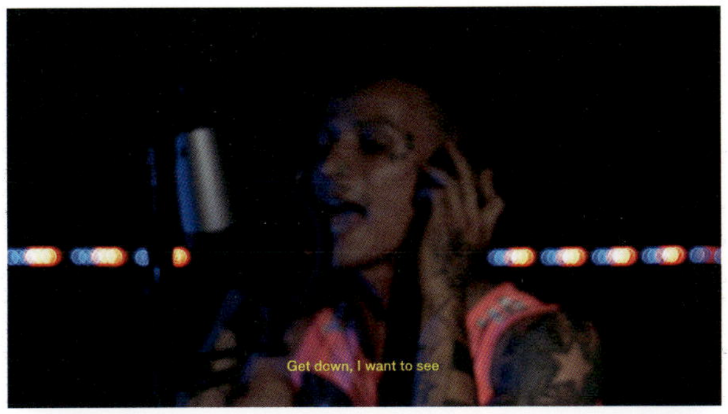
Get down, I want to see

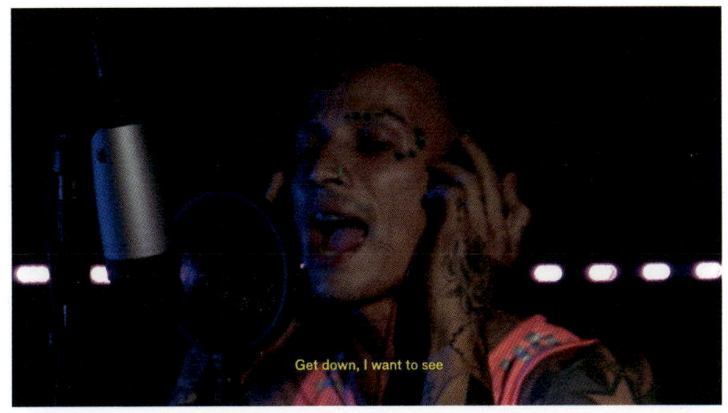
Get down, I want to see

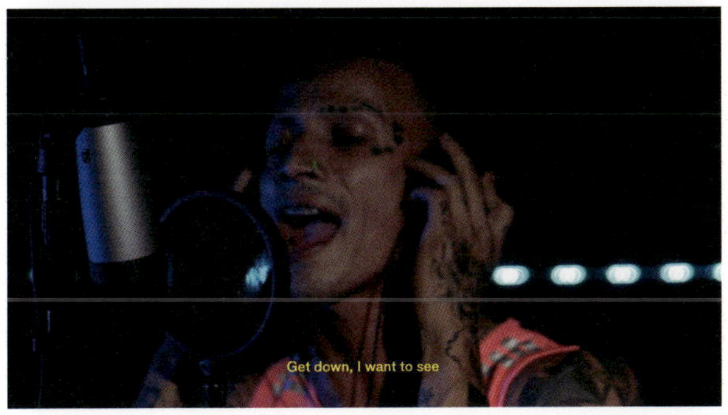
Get down, I want to see

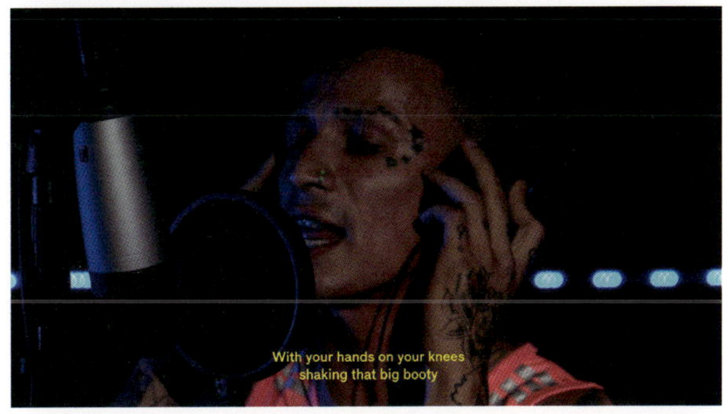
With your hands on your knees
shaking that big booty

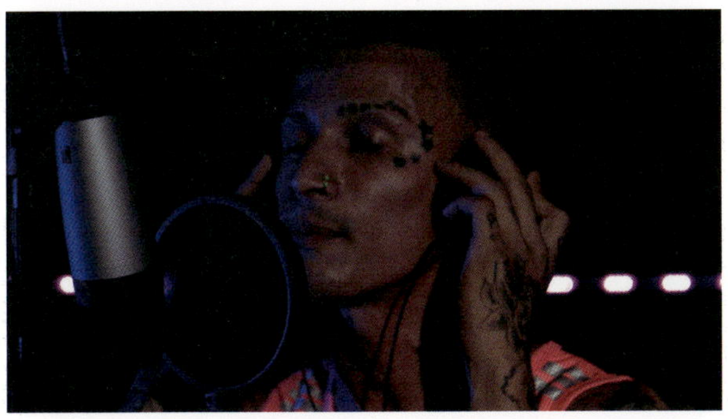

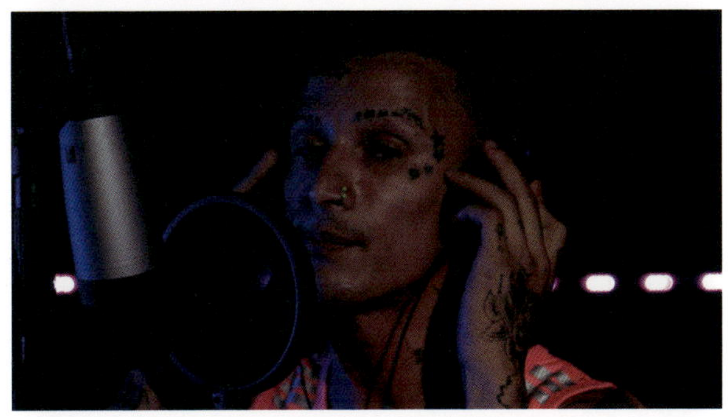

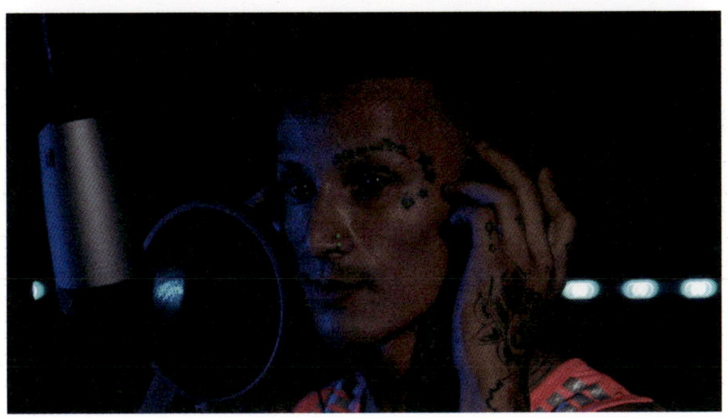

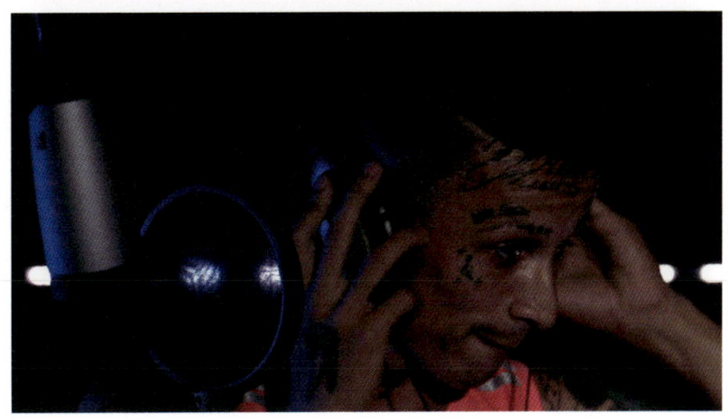

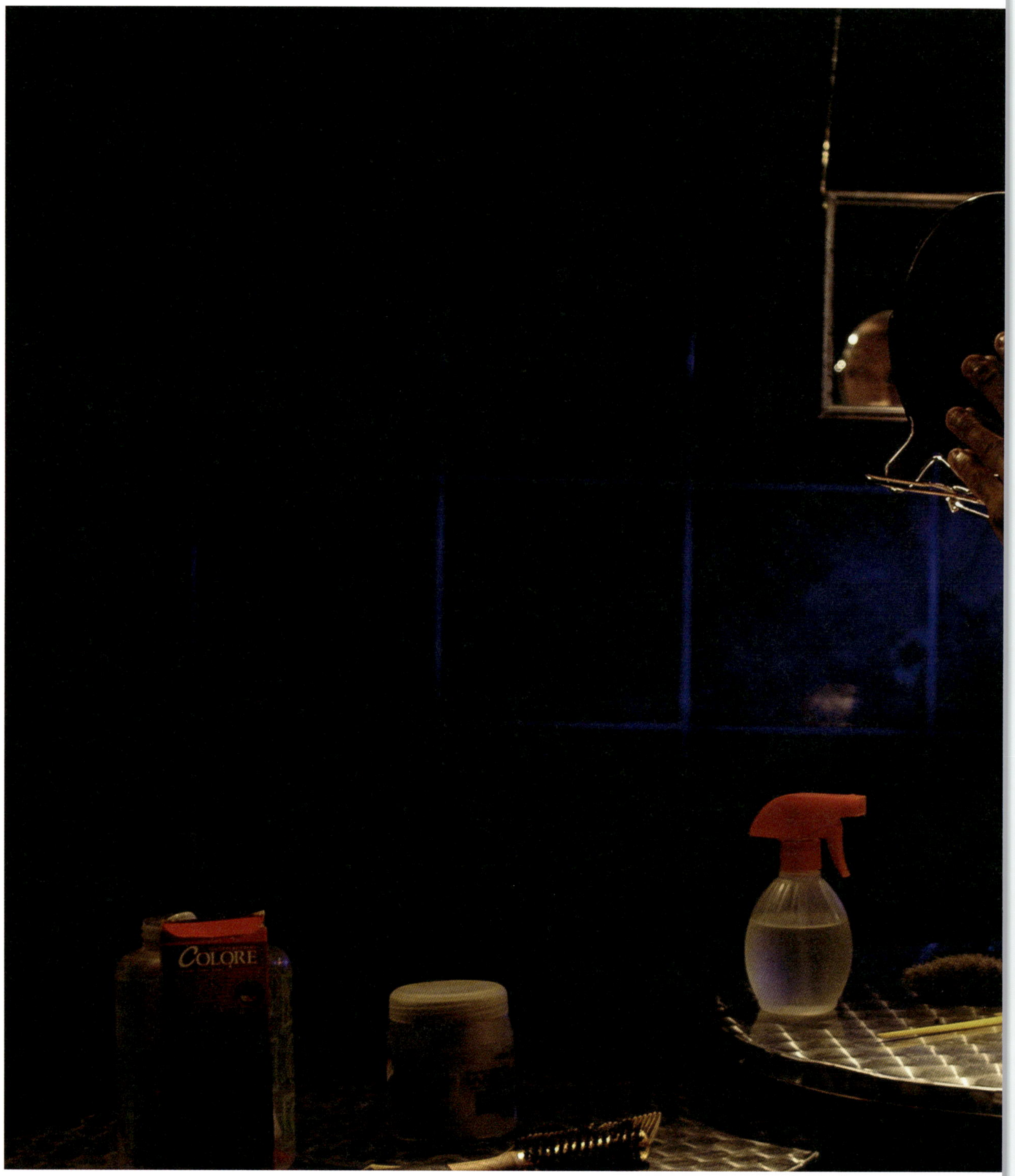
COLORE

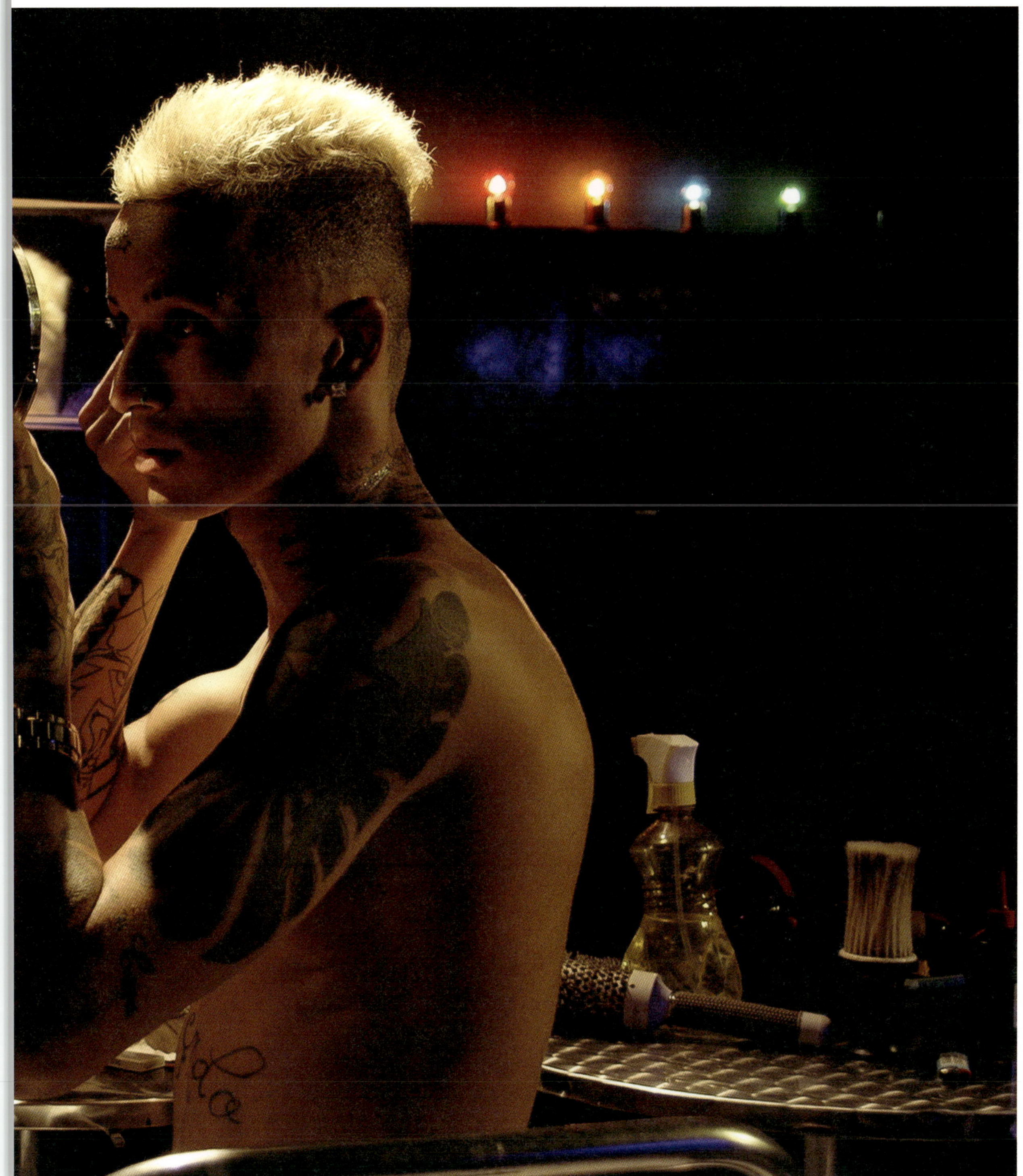

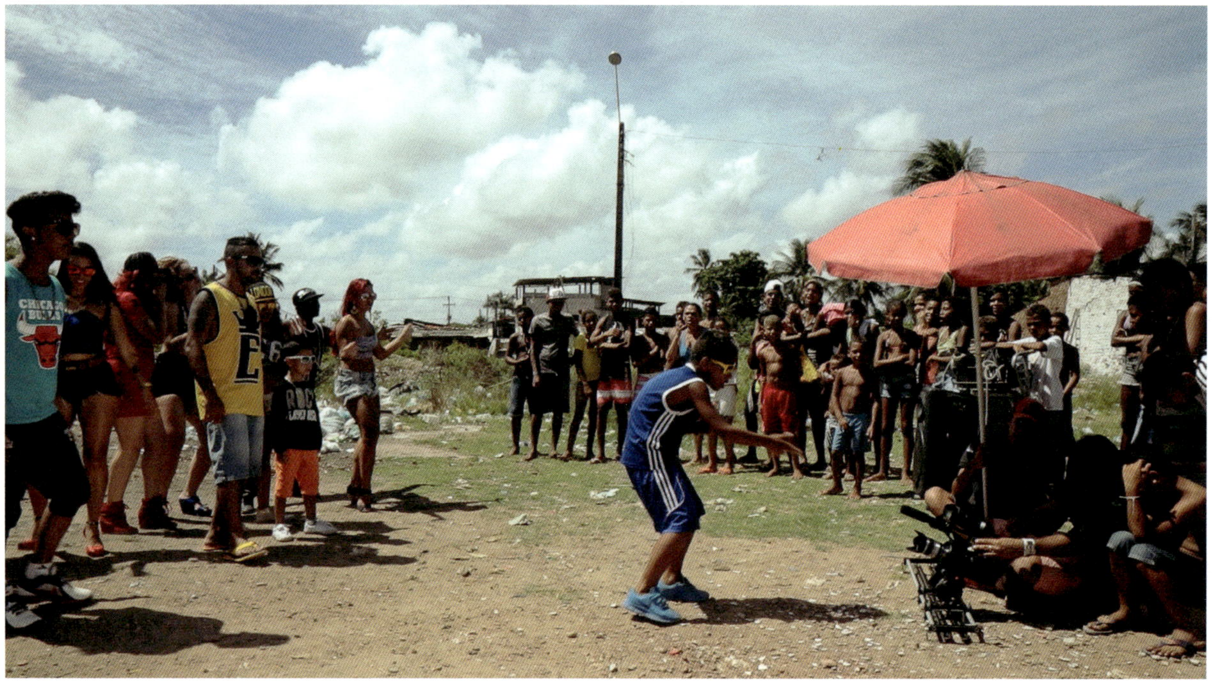

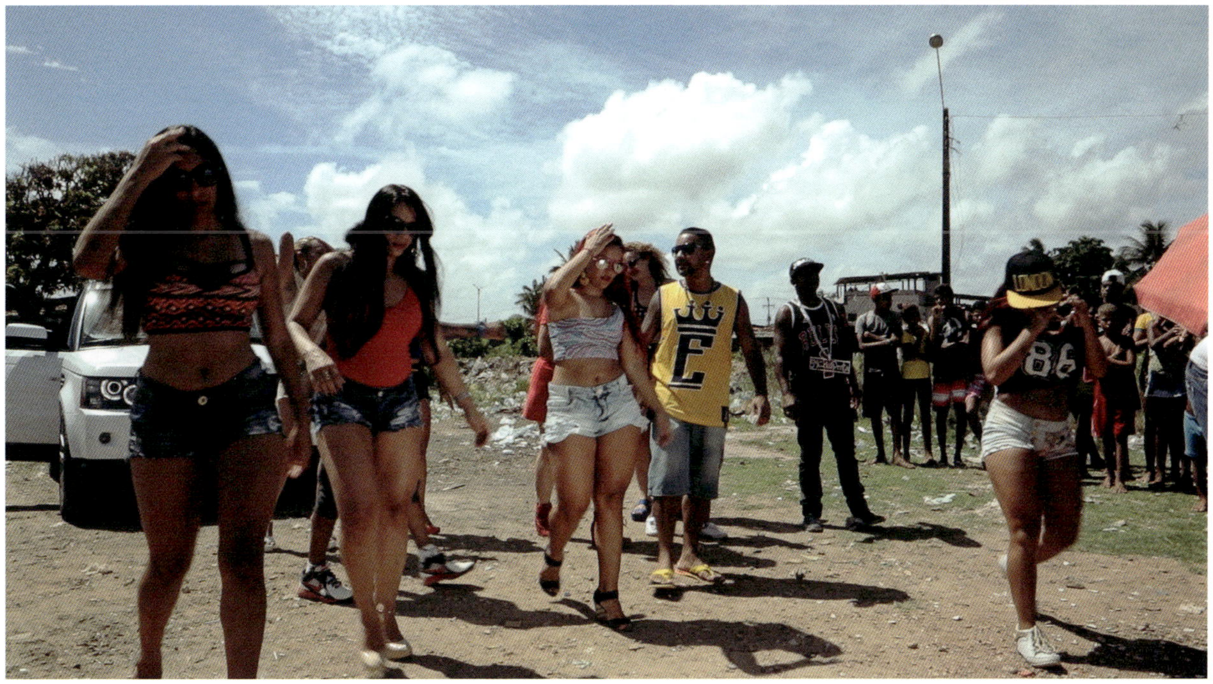

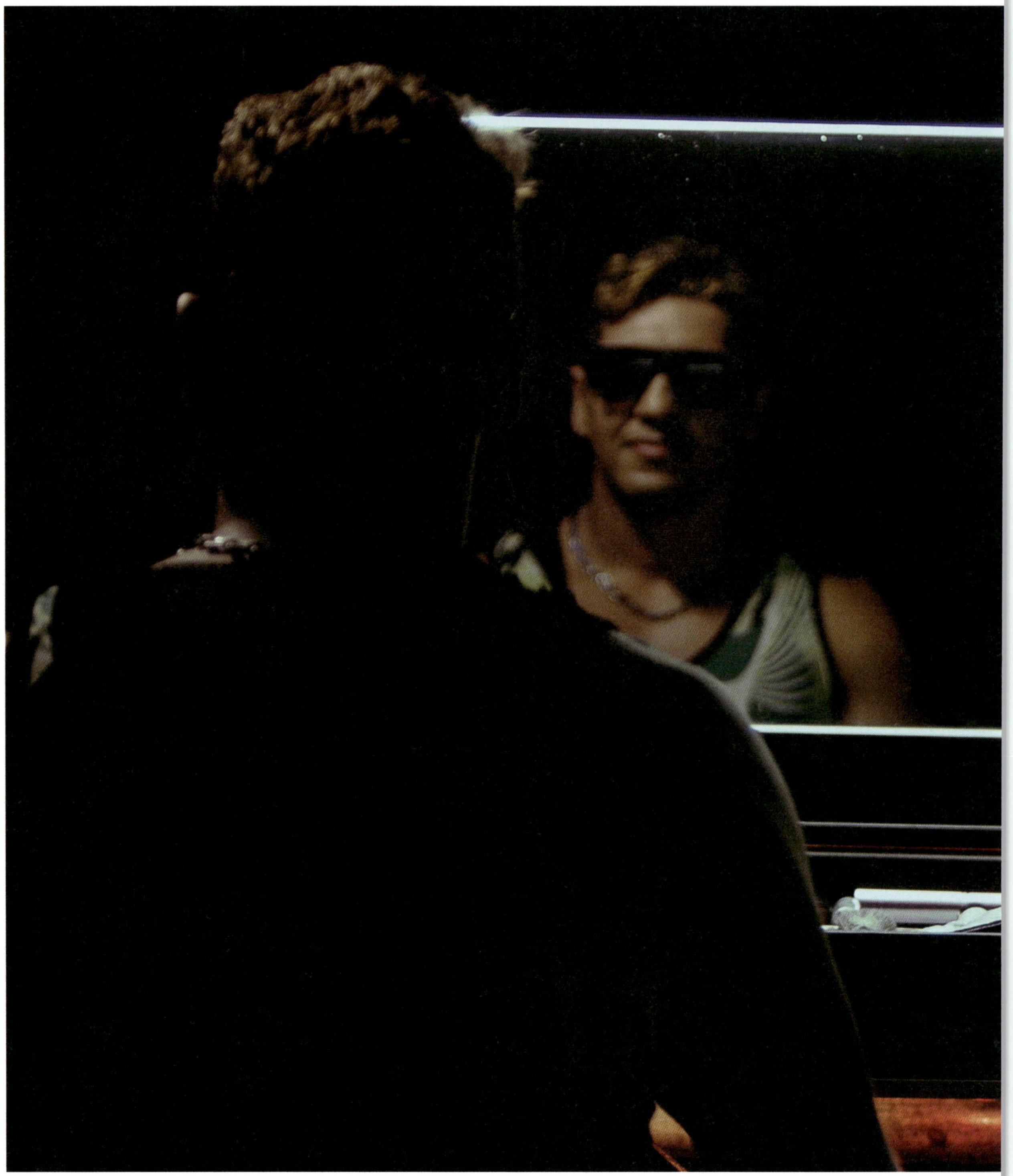

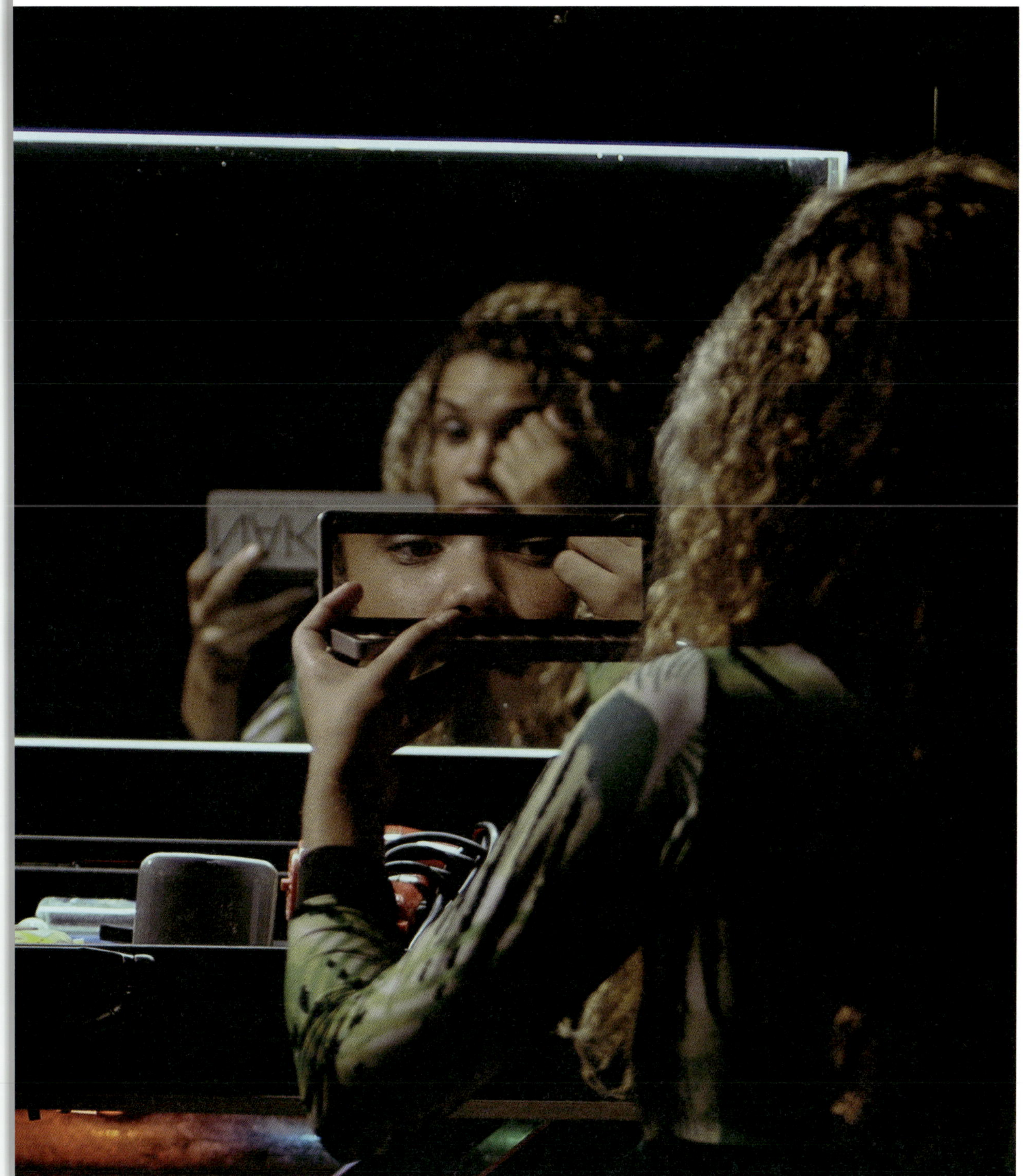

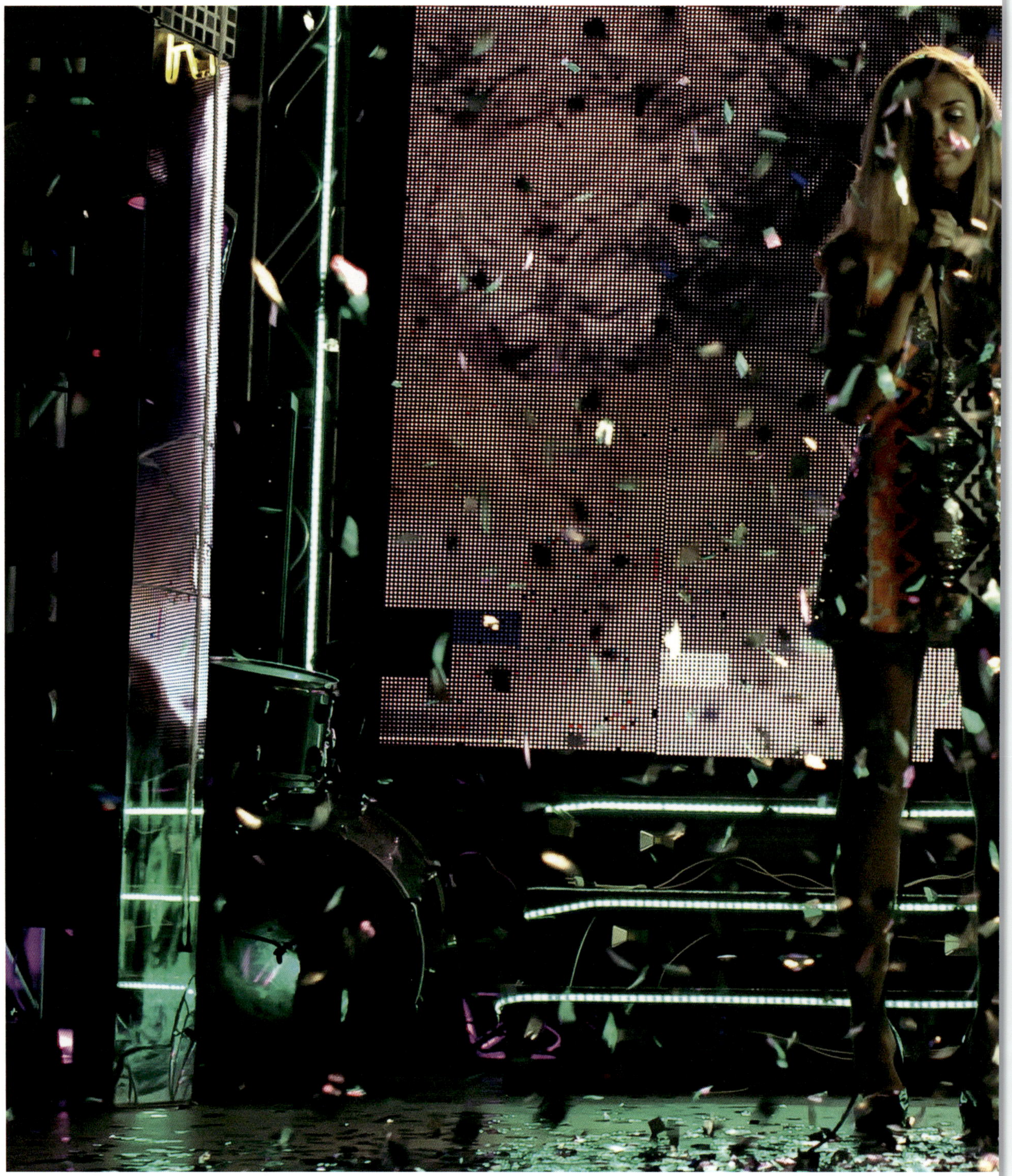

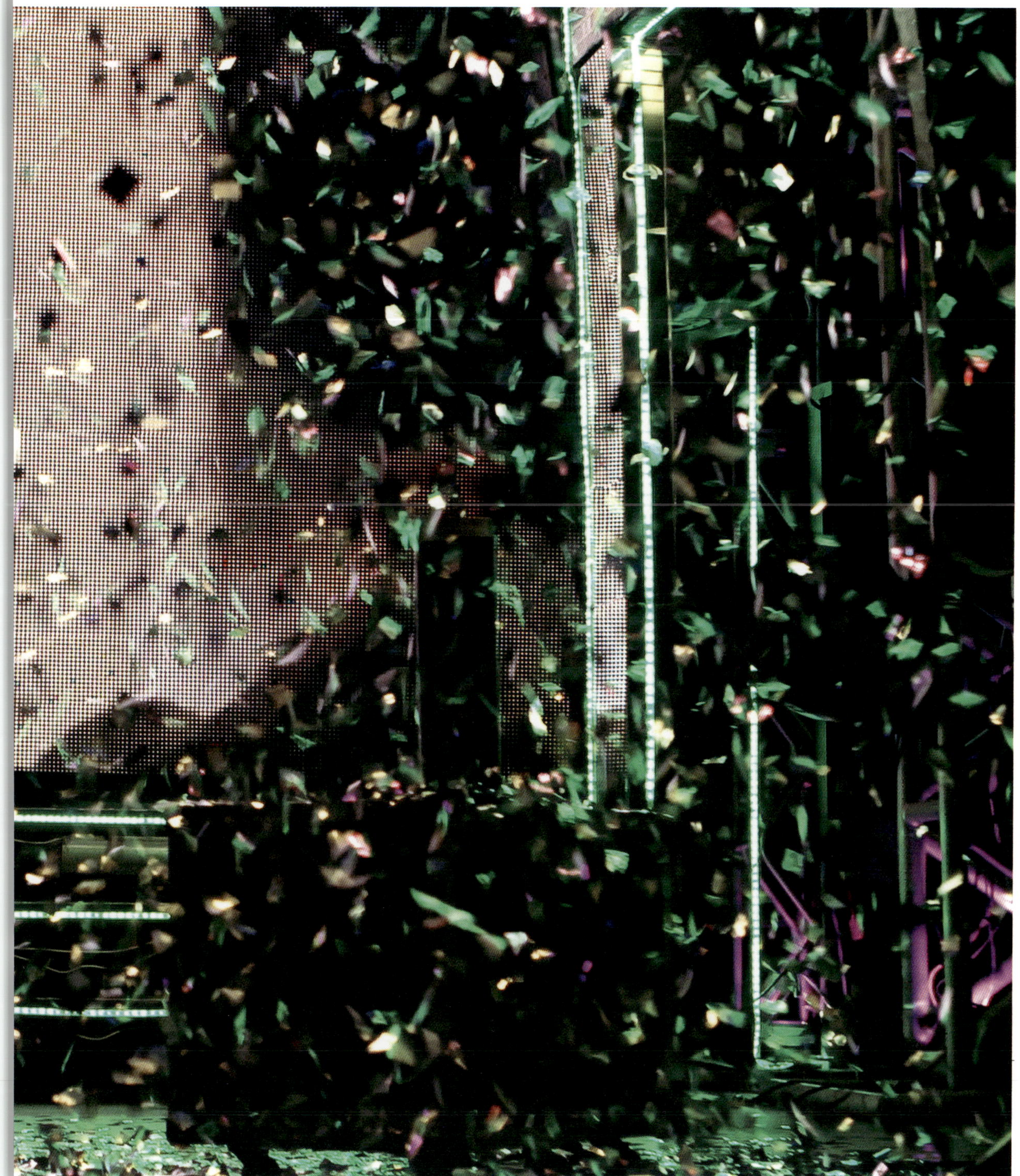

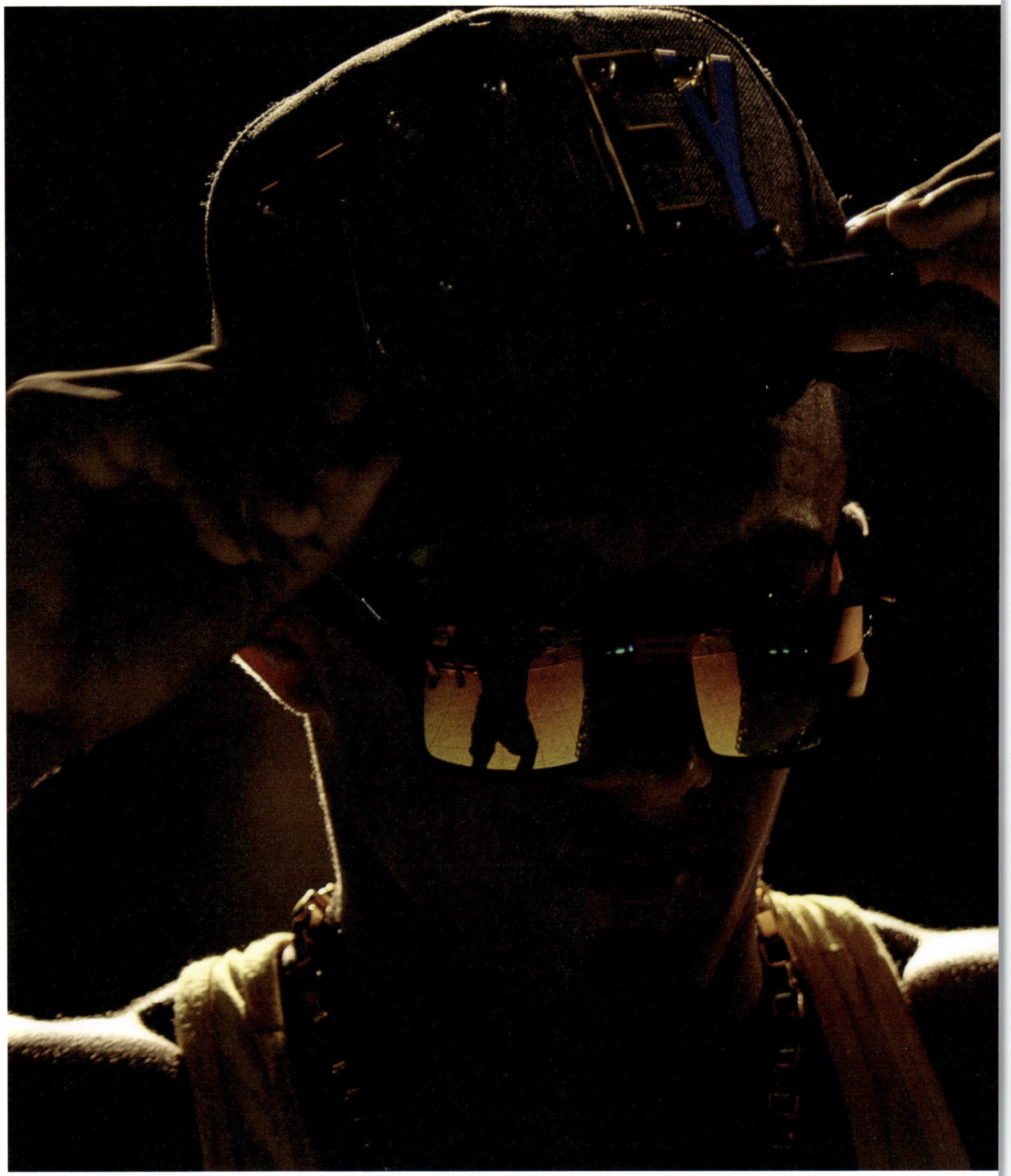

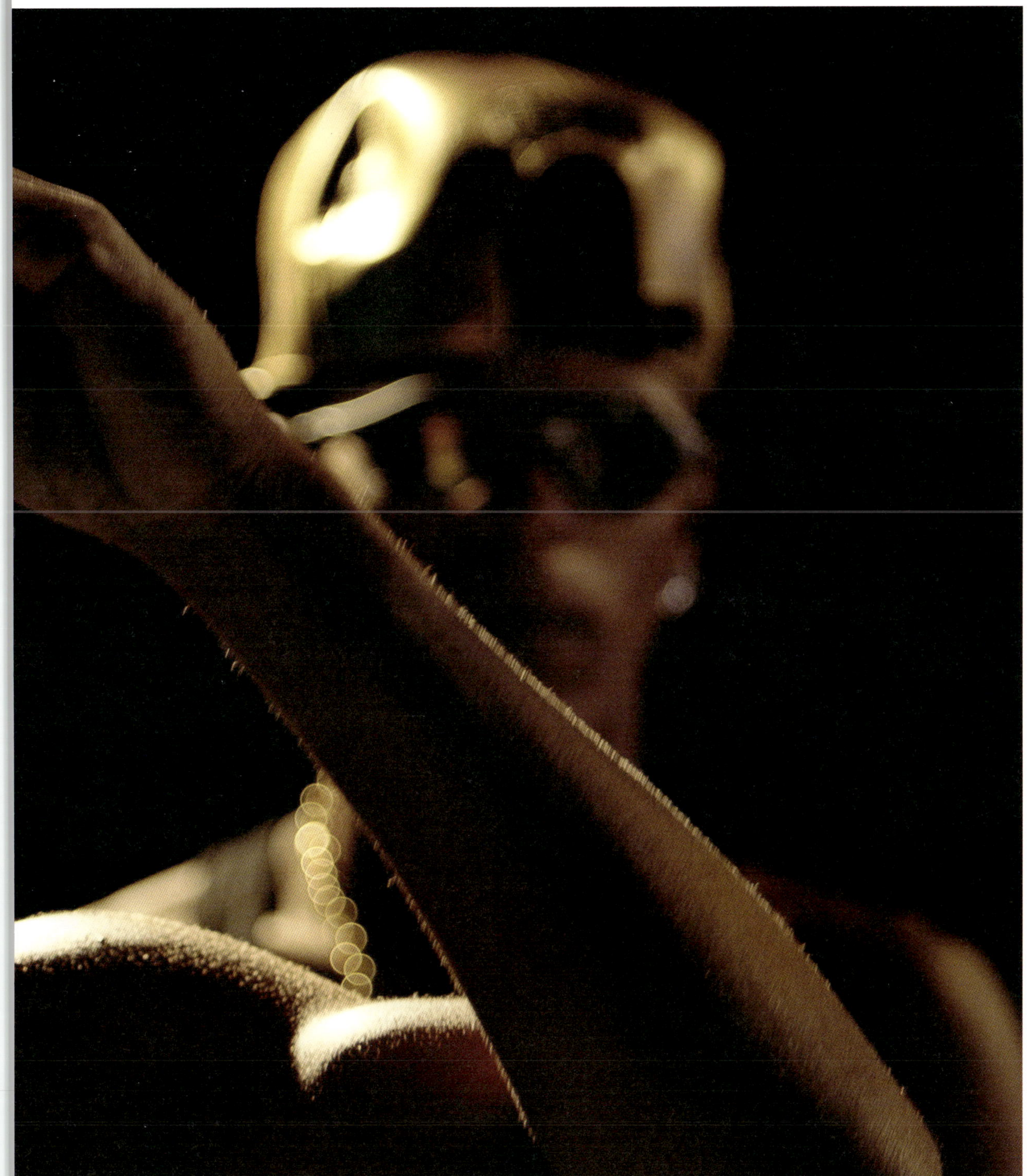

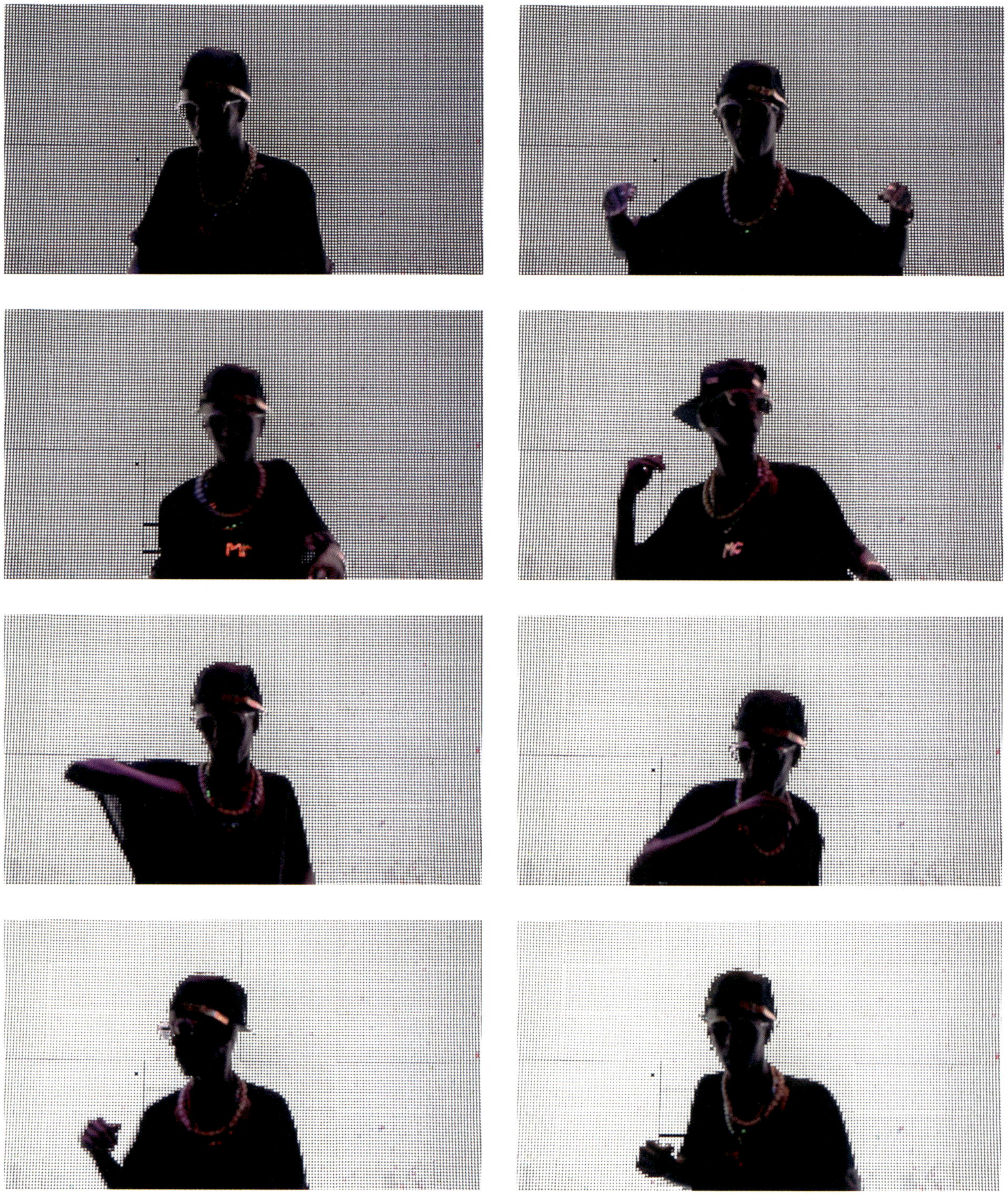

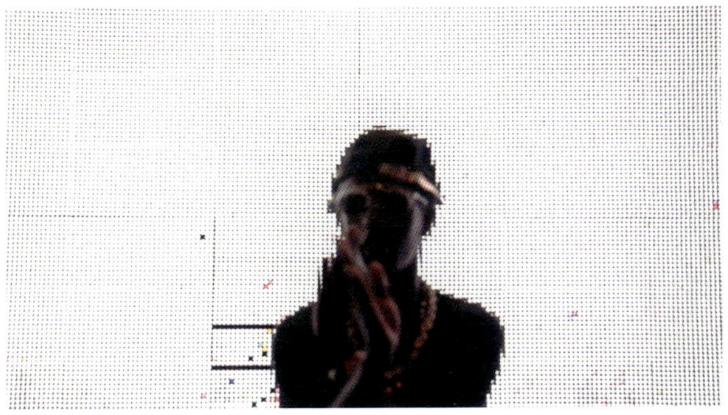

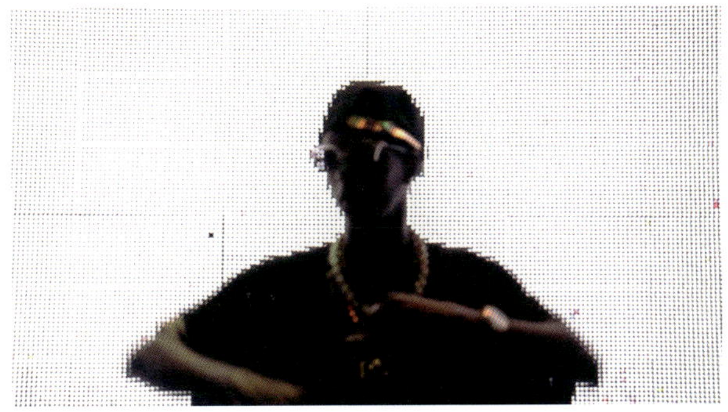

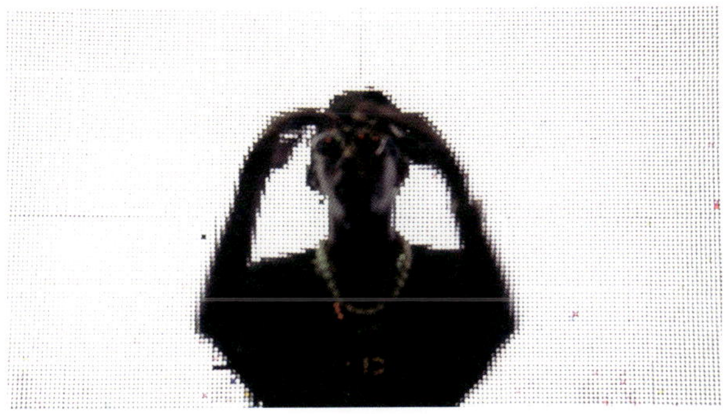

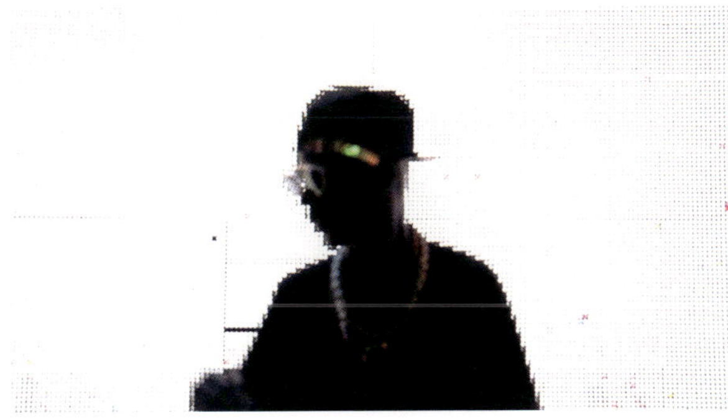

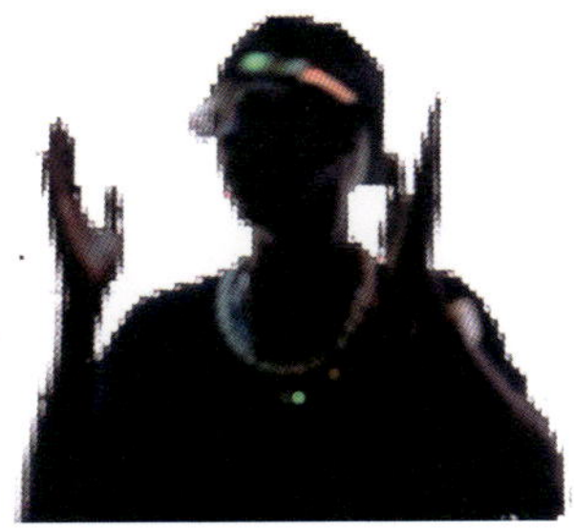

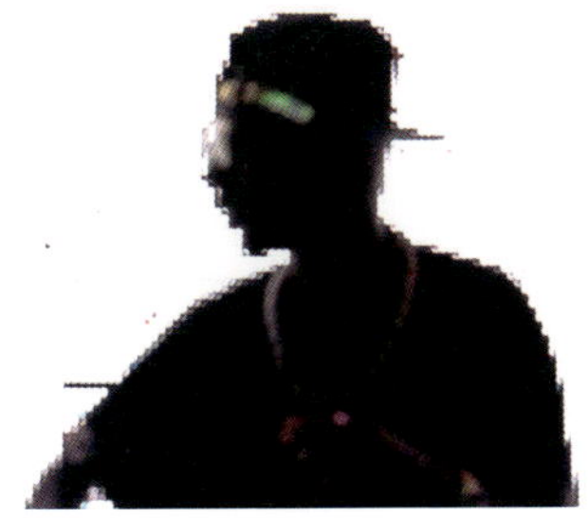

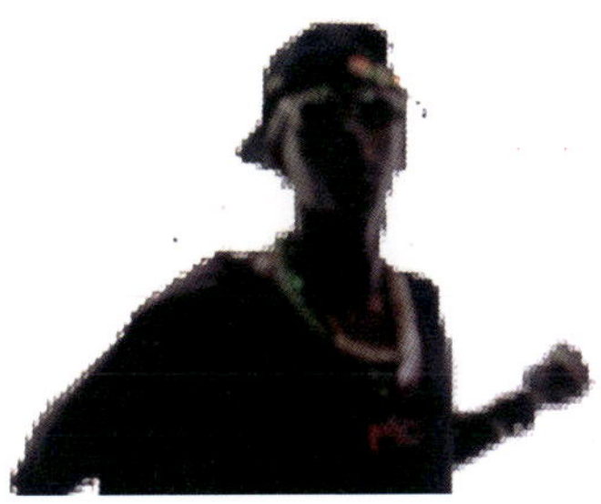

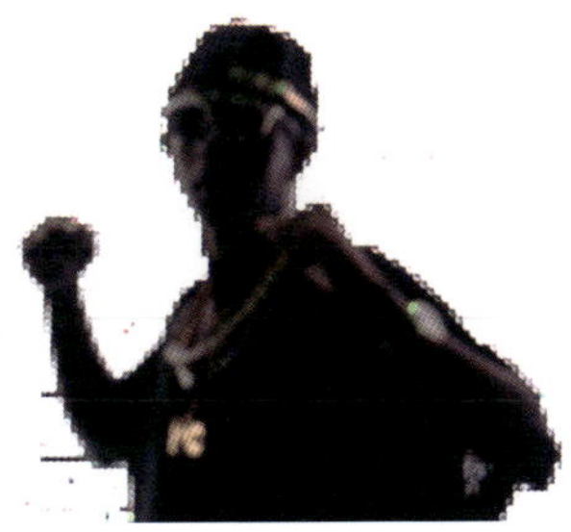

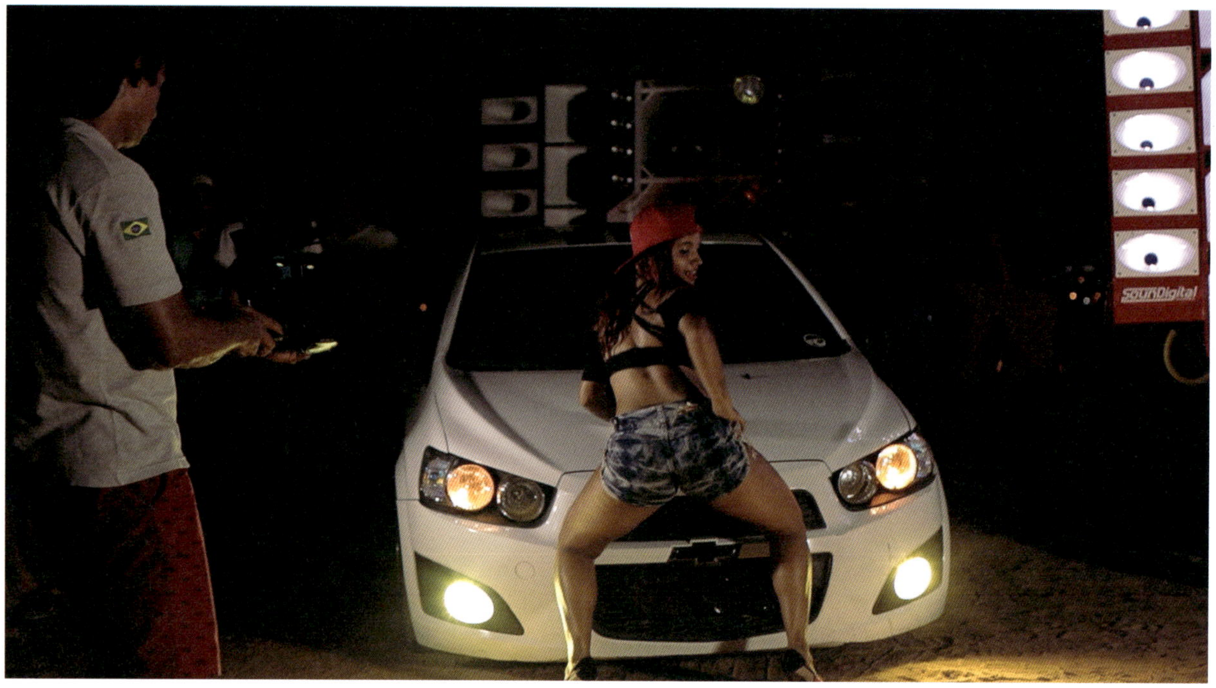
SounDigital

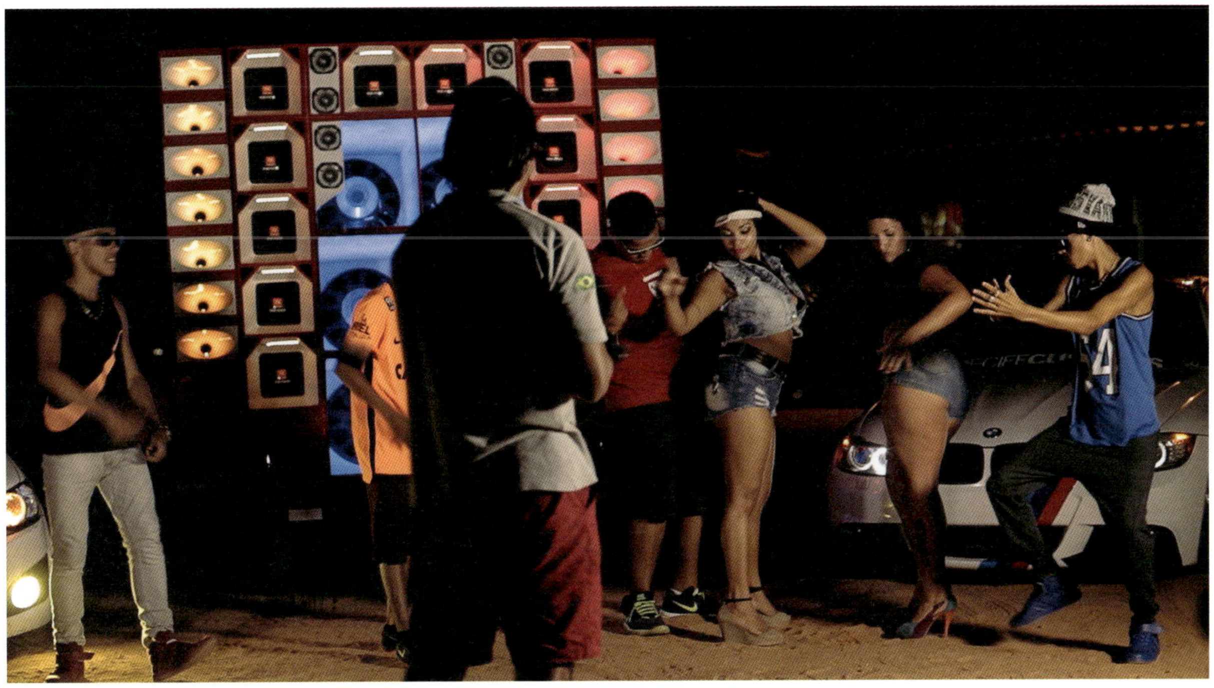

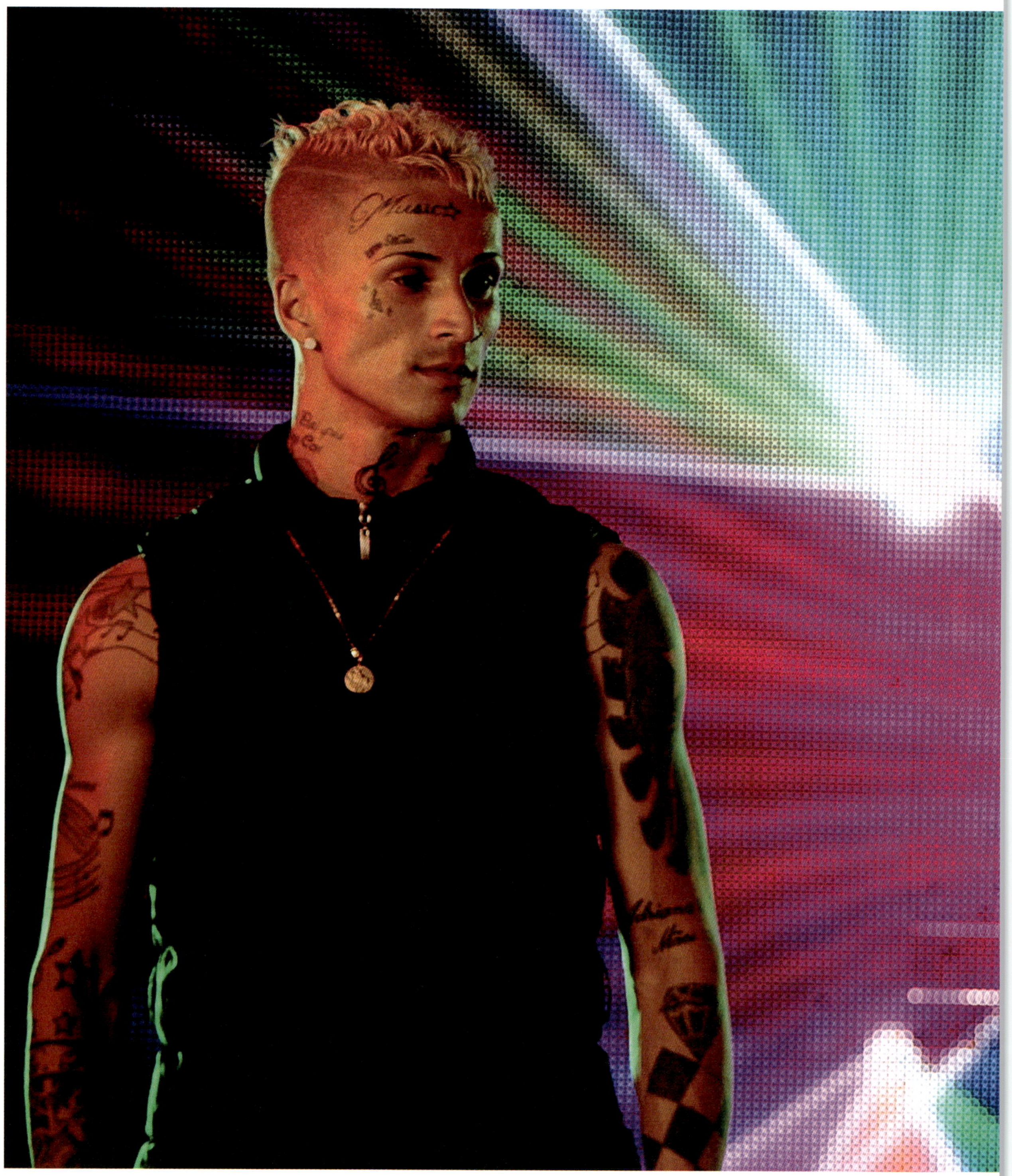

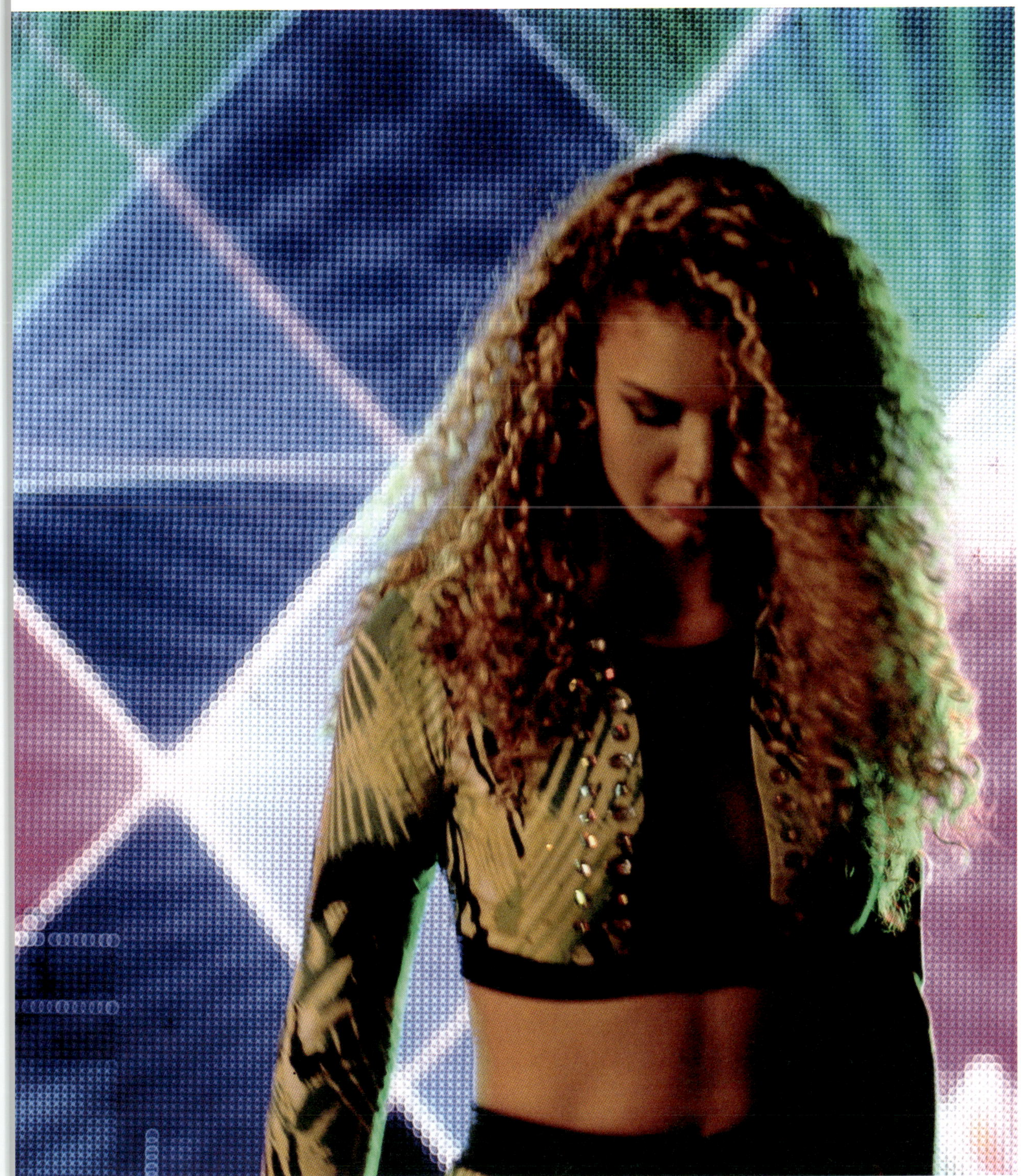

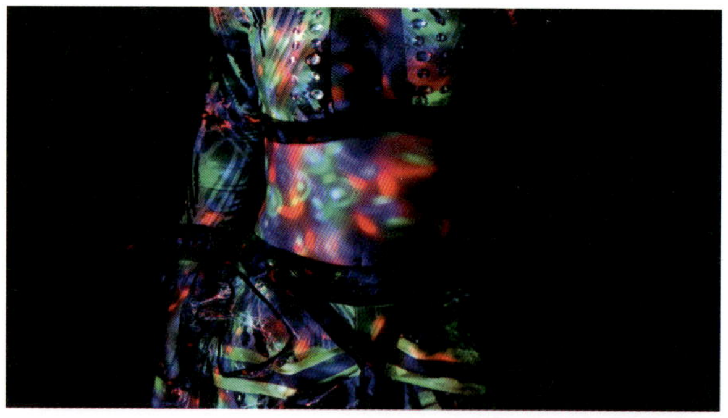
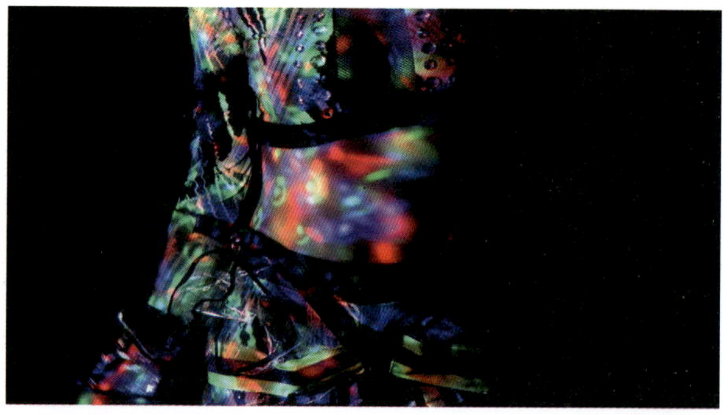
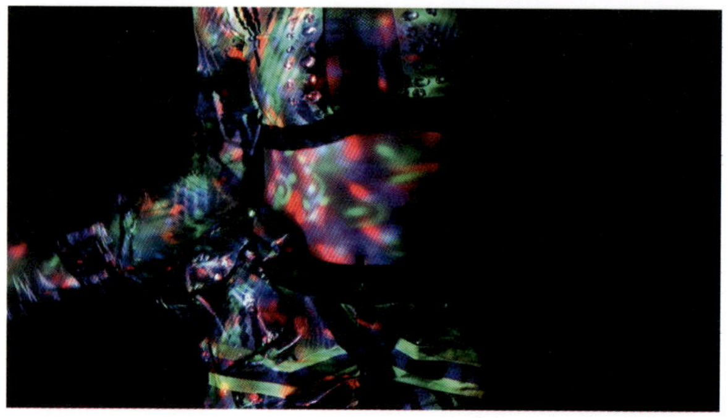
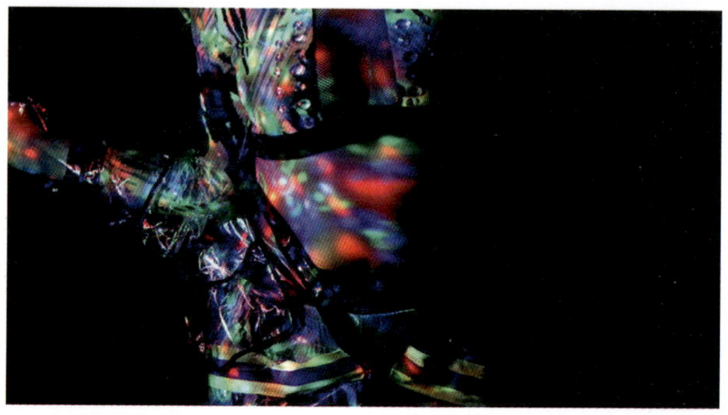
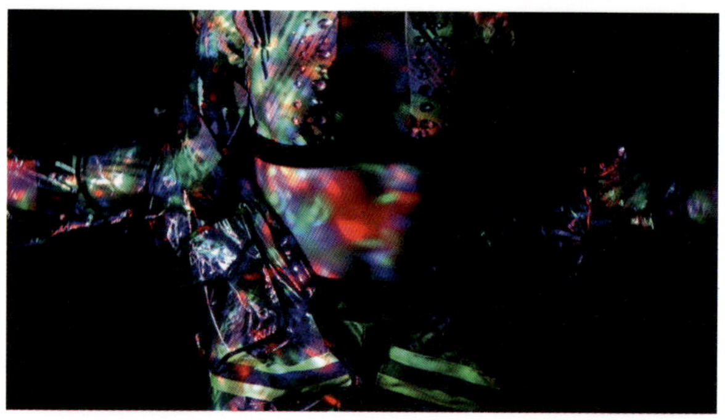
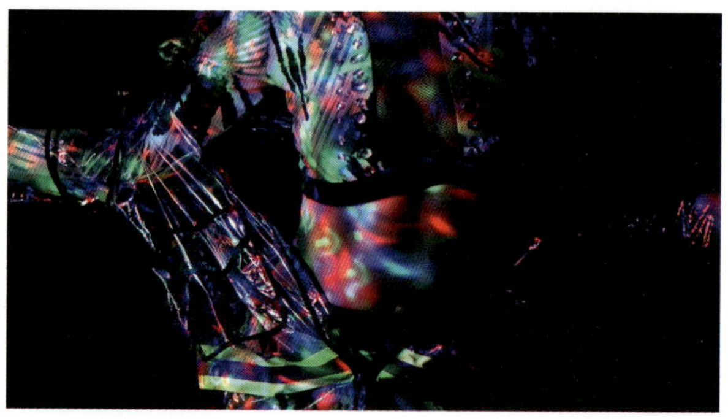
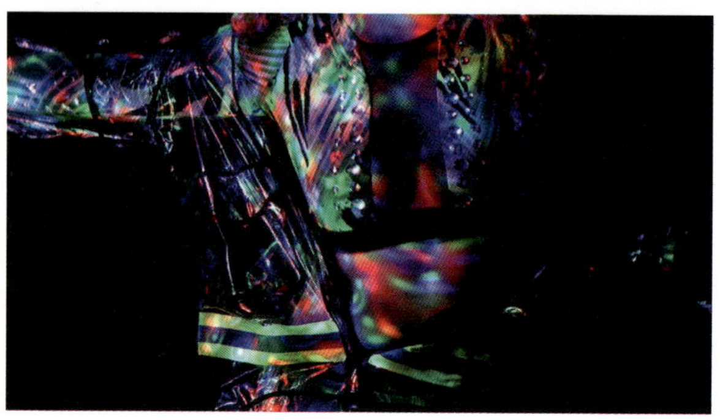
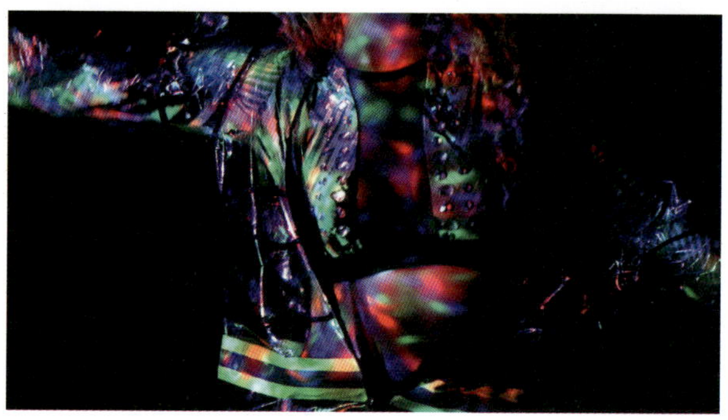

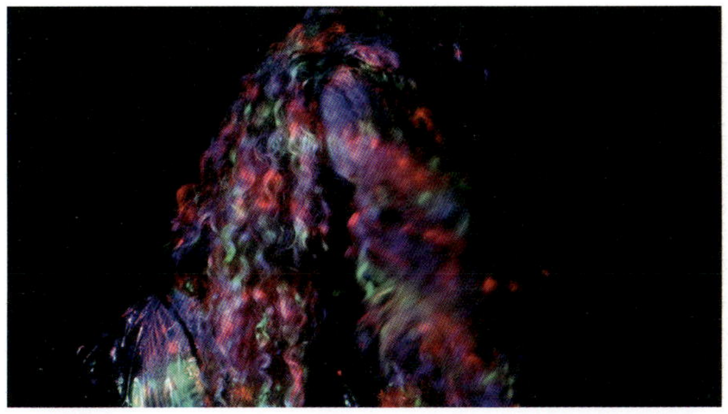
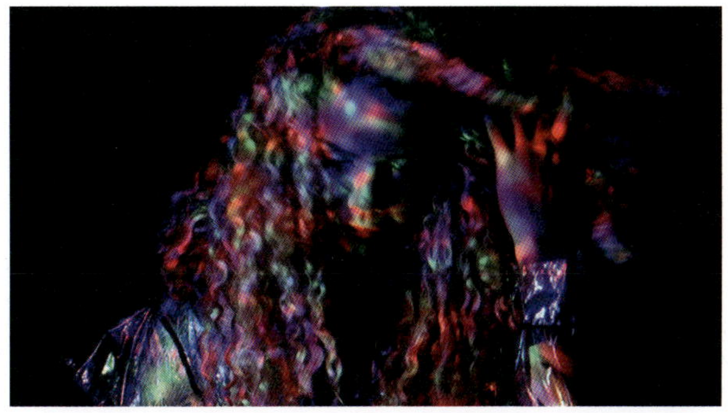
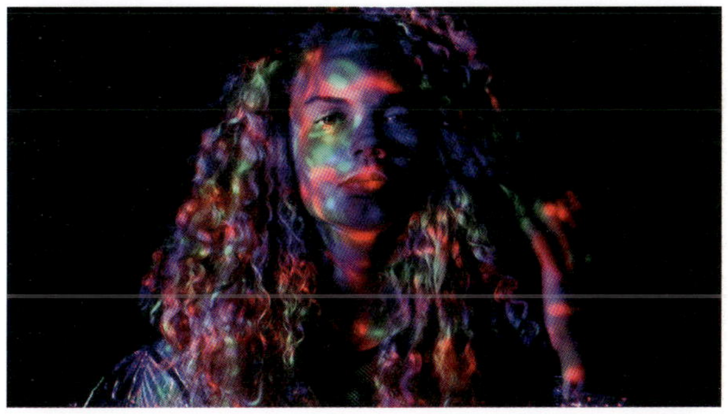
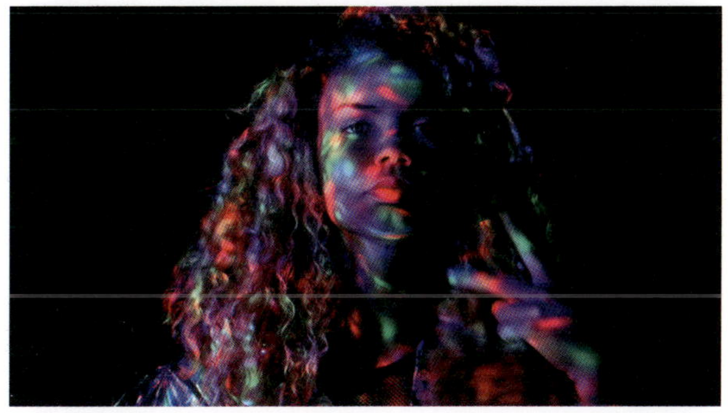
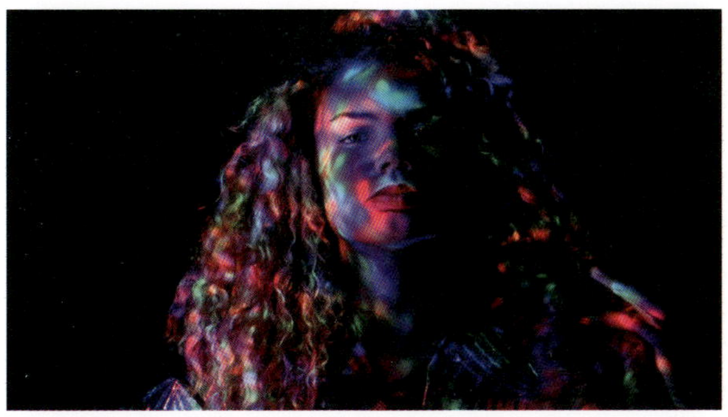
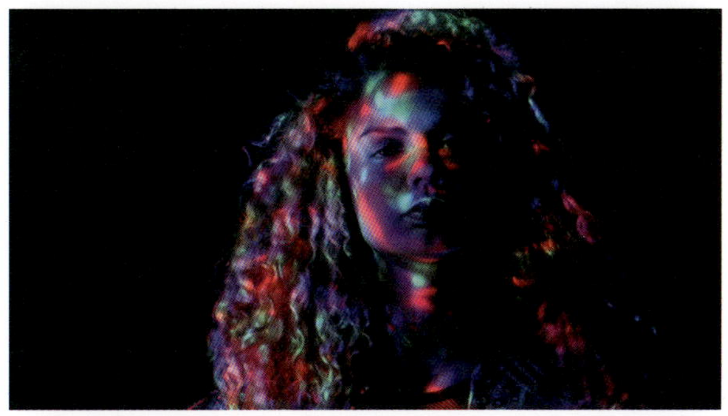
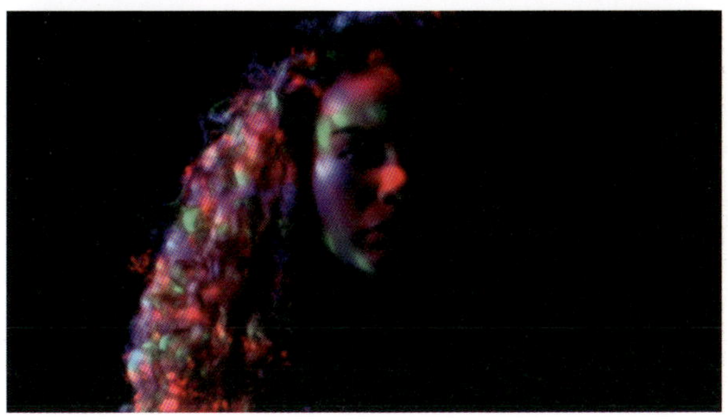
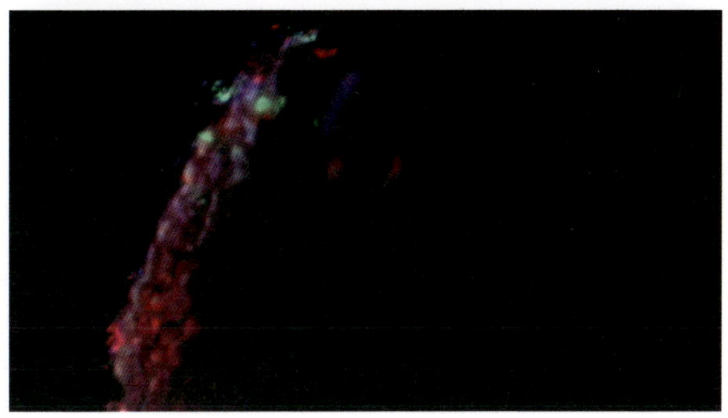

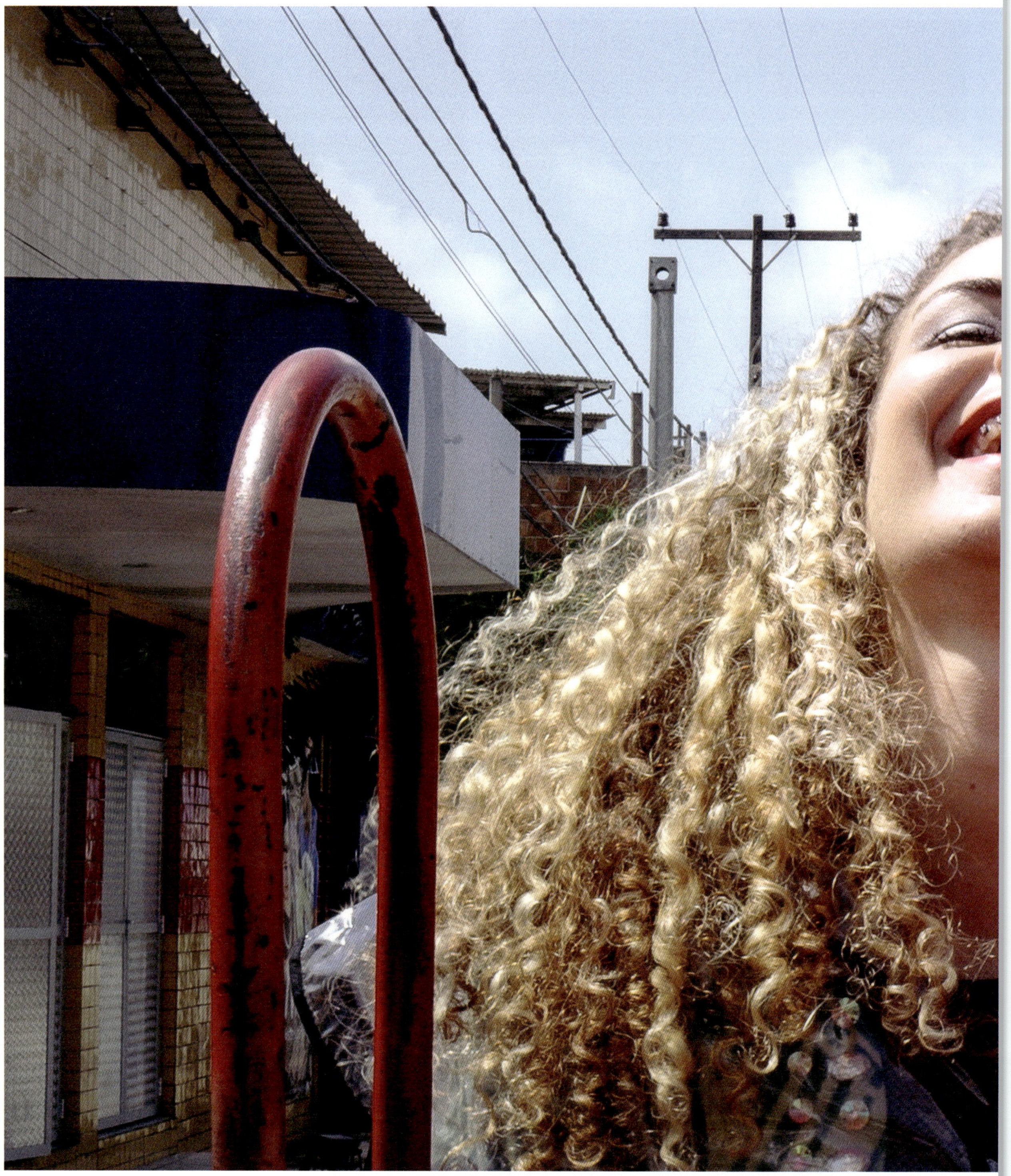

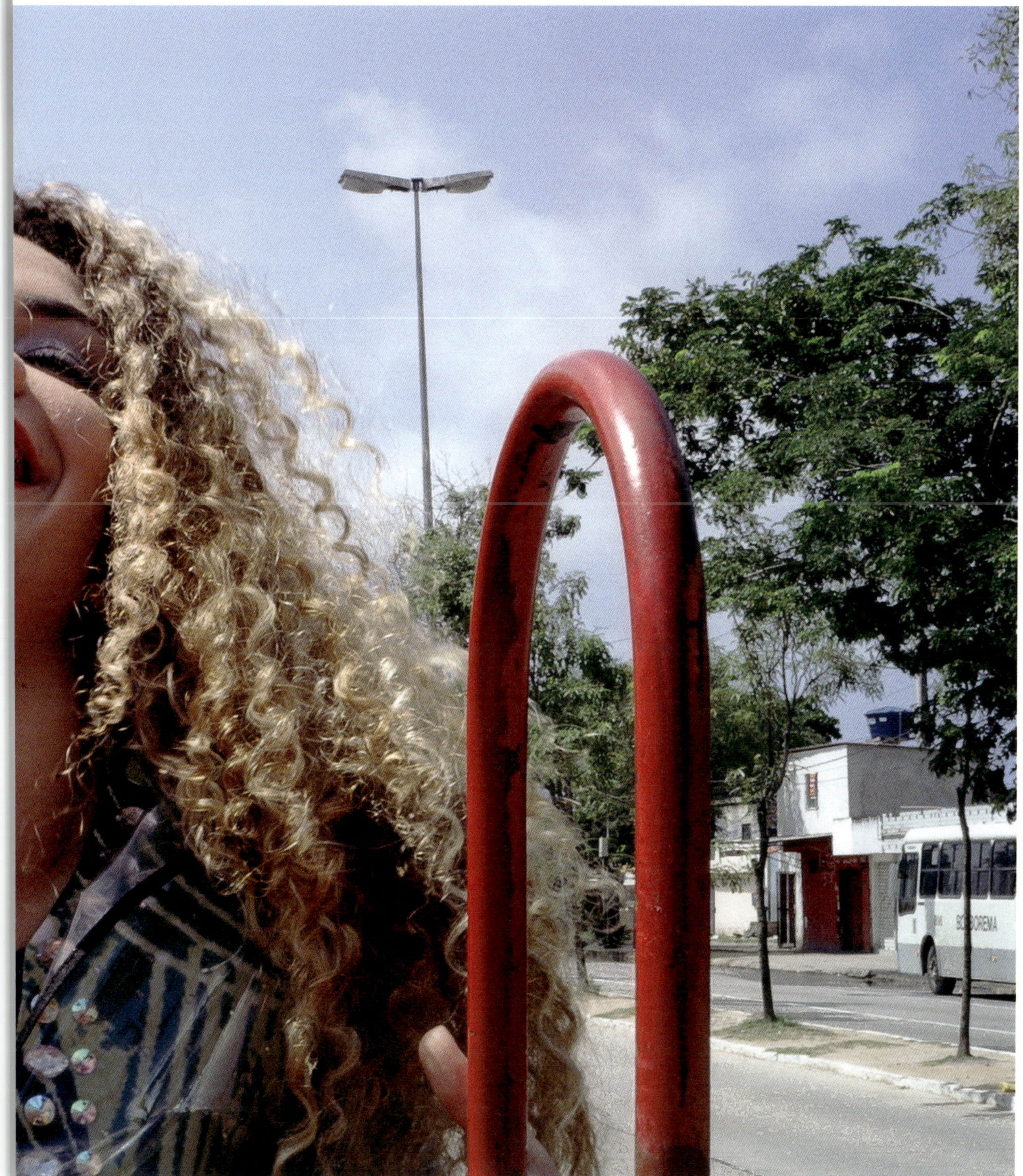

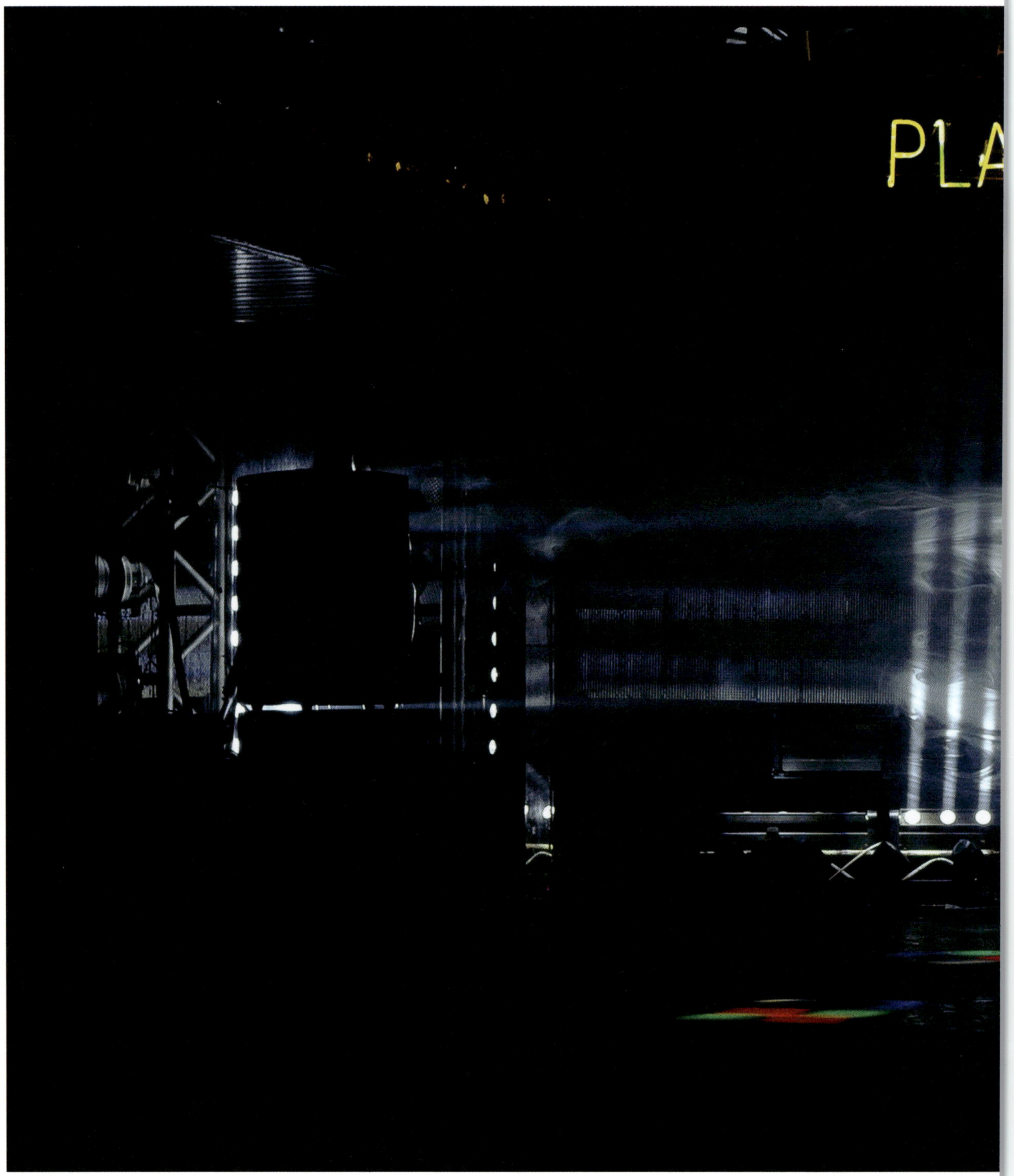

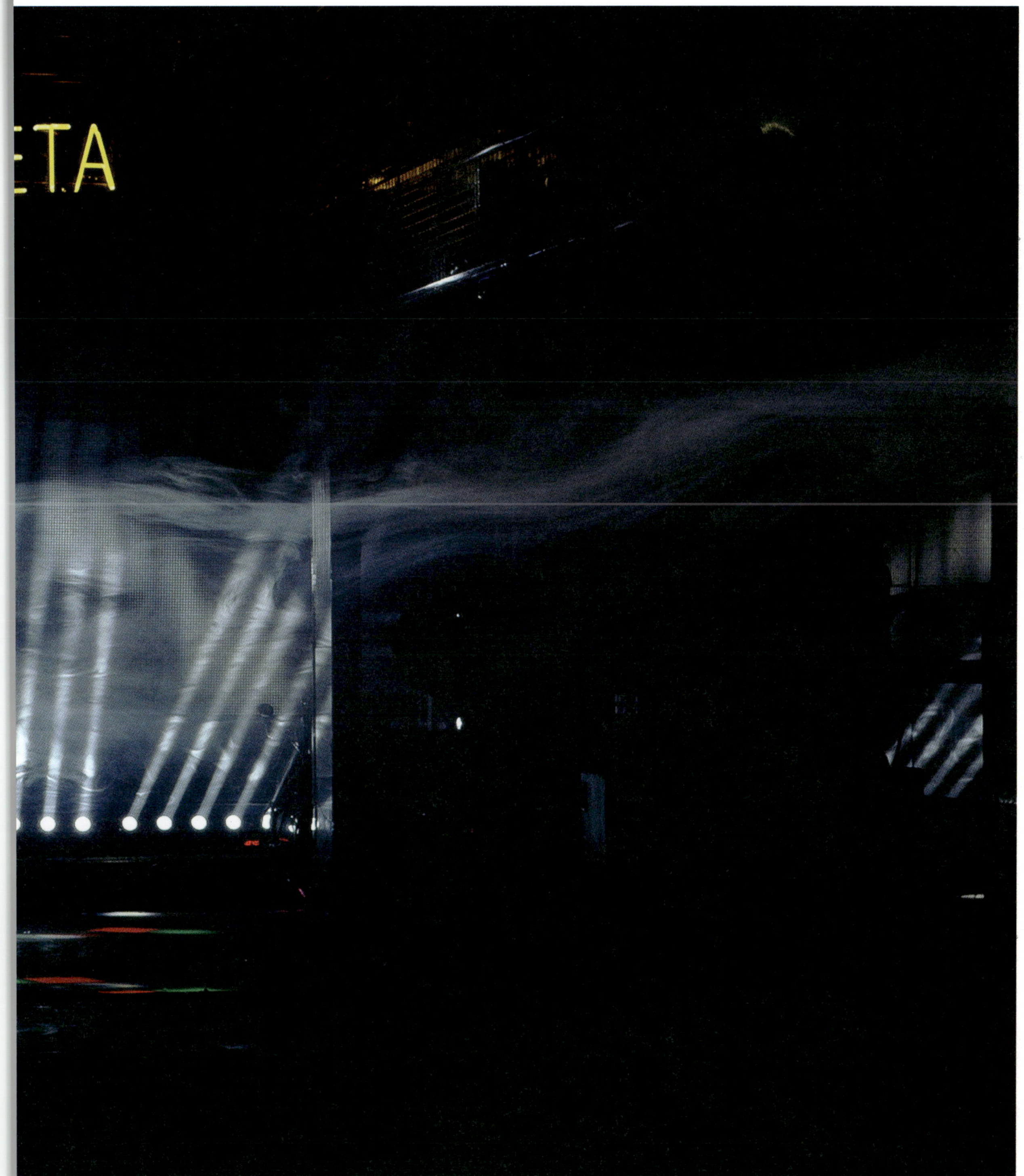
ETA

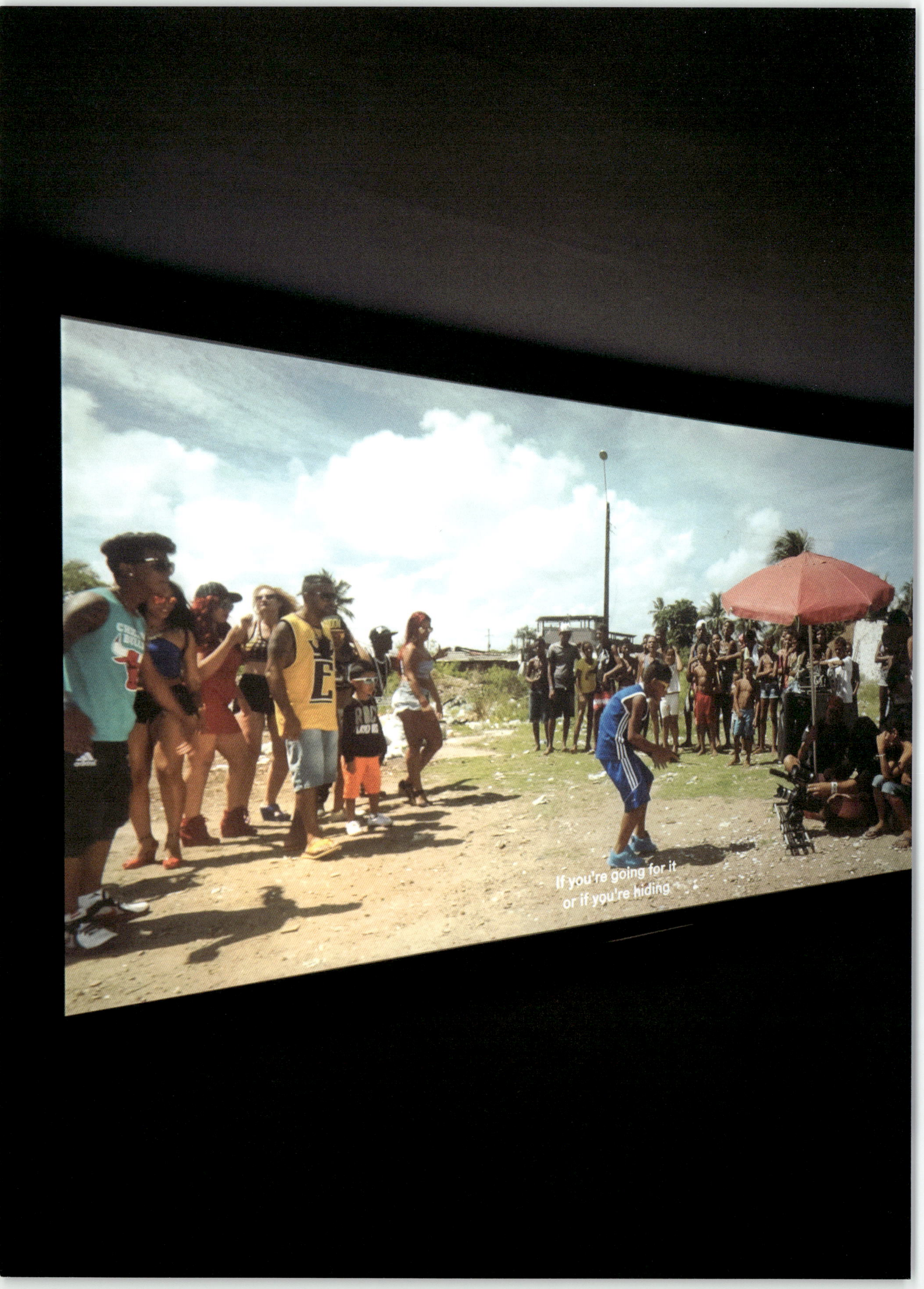
If you're going for it
or if you're hiding

Estás Vendo Coisas [You Are Seeing Things], 2016. Exhibition view: "Incerteza Viva" [Live Uncertainty], 32nd São Paulo Biennial, 2016

Terremoto Santo [Holy Tremor], 2017

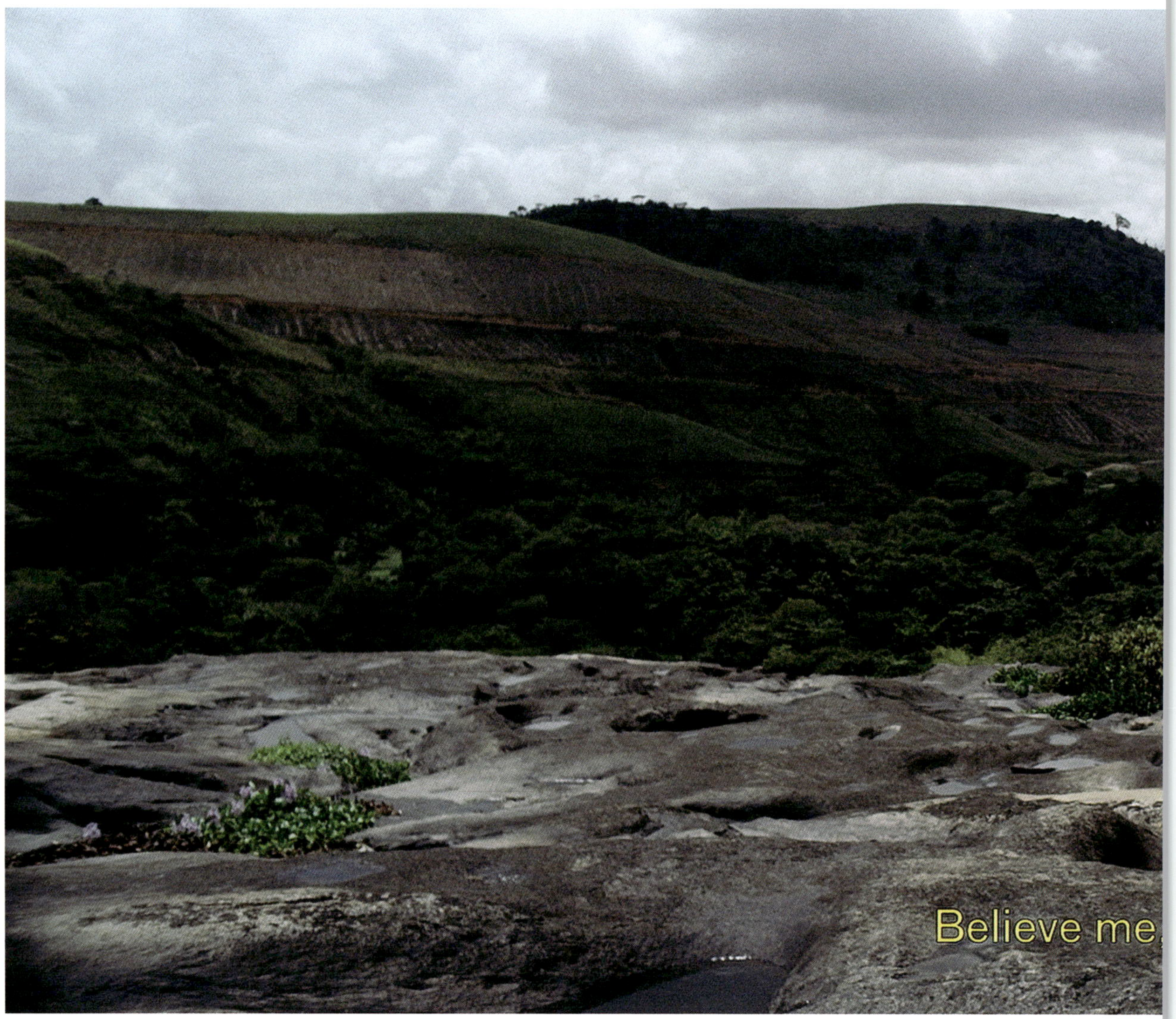
Believe me,

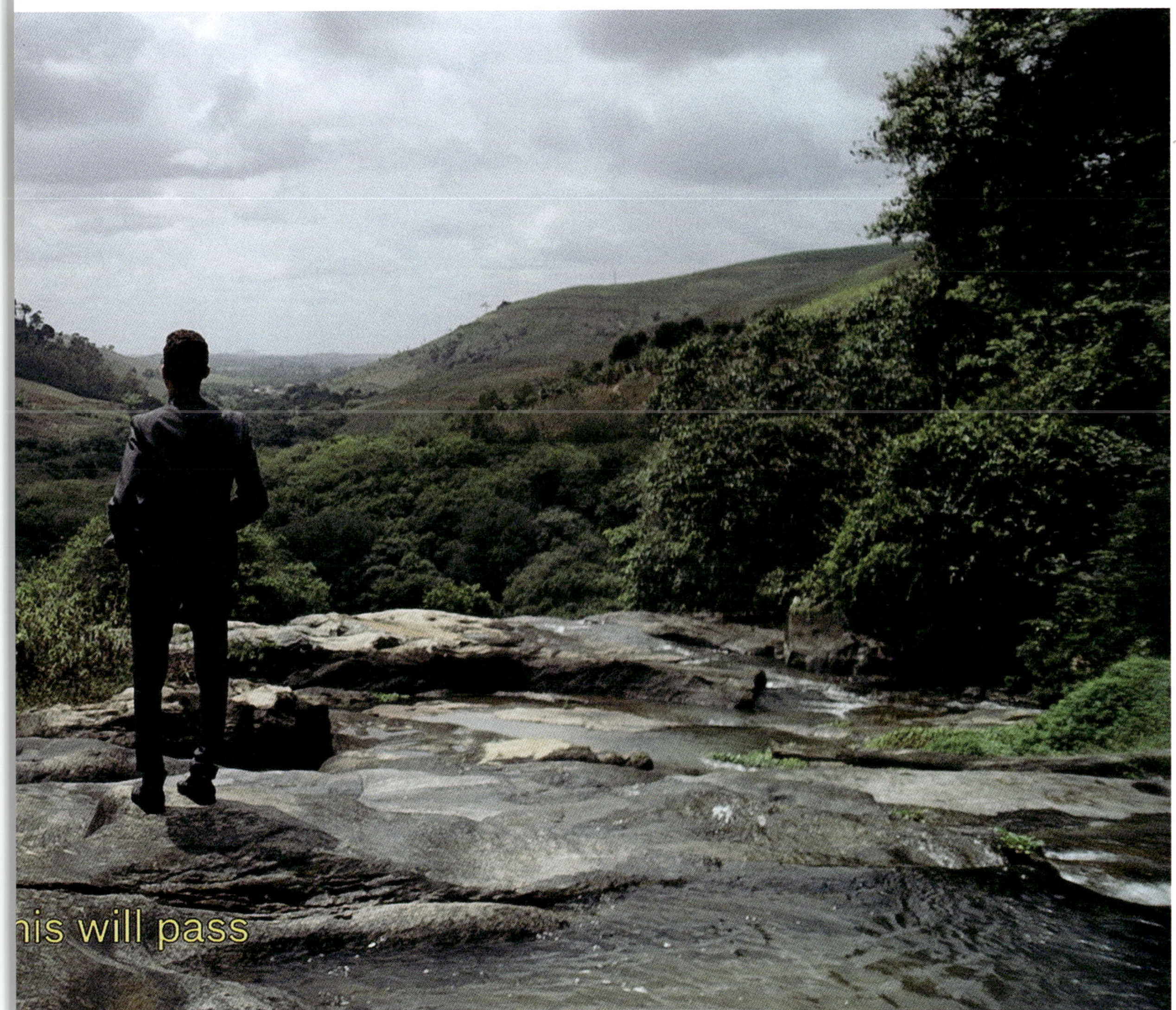
his will pass

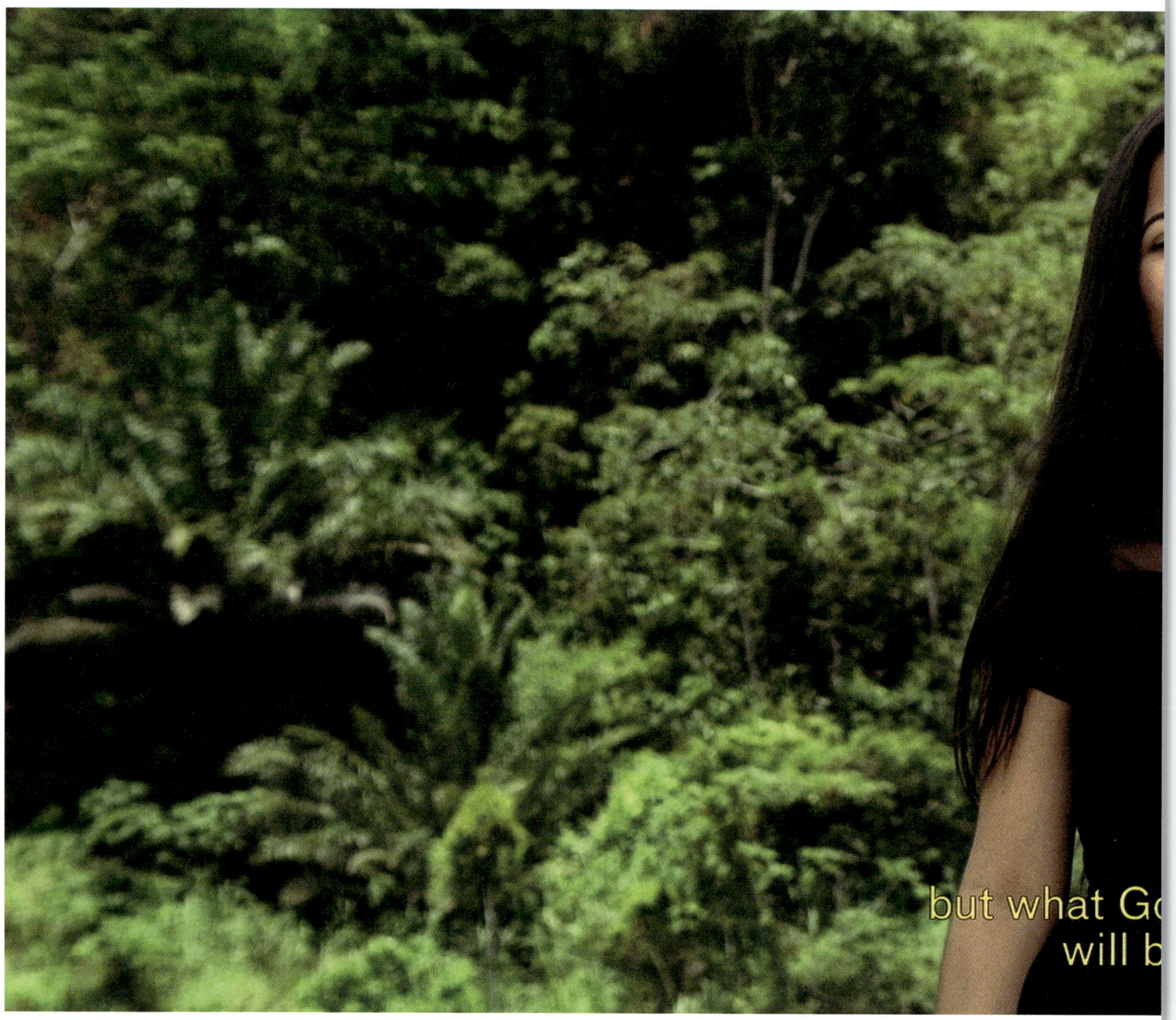
but what Go
will b

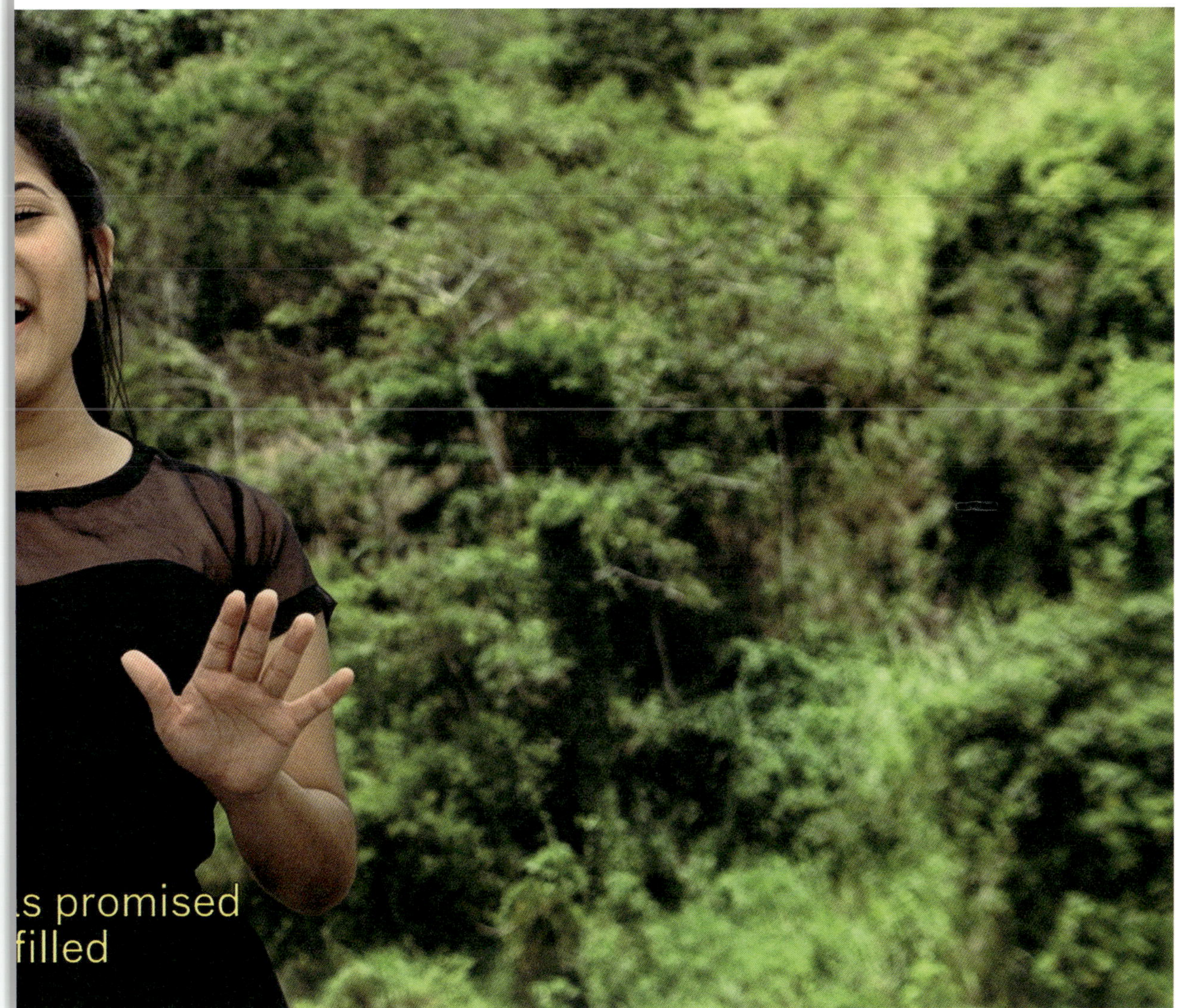
s promised
filled

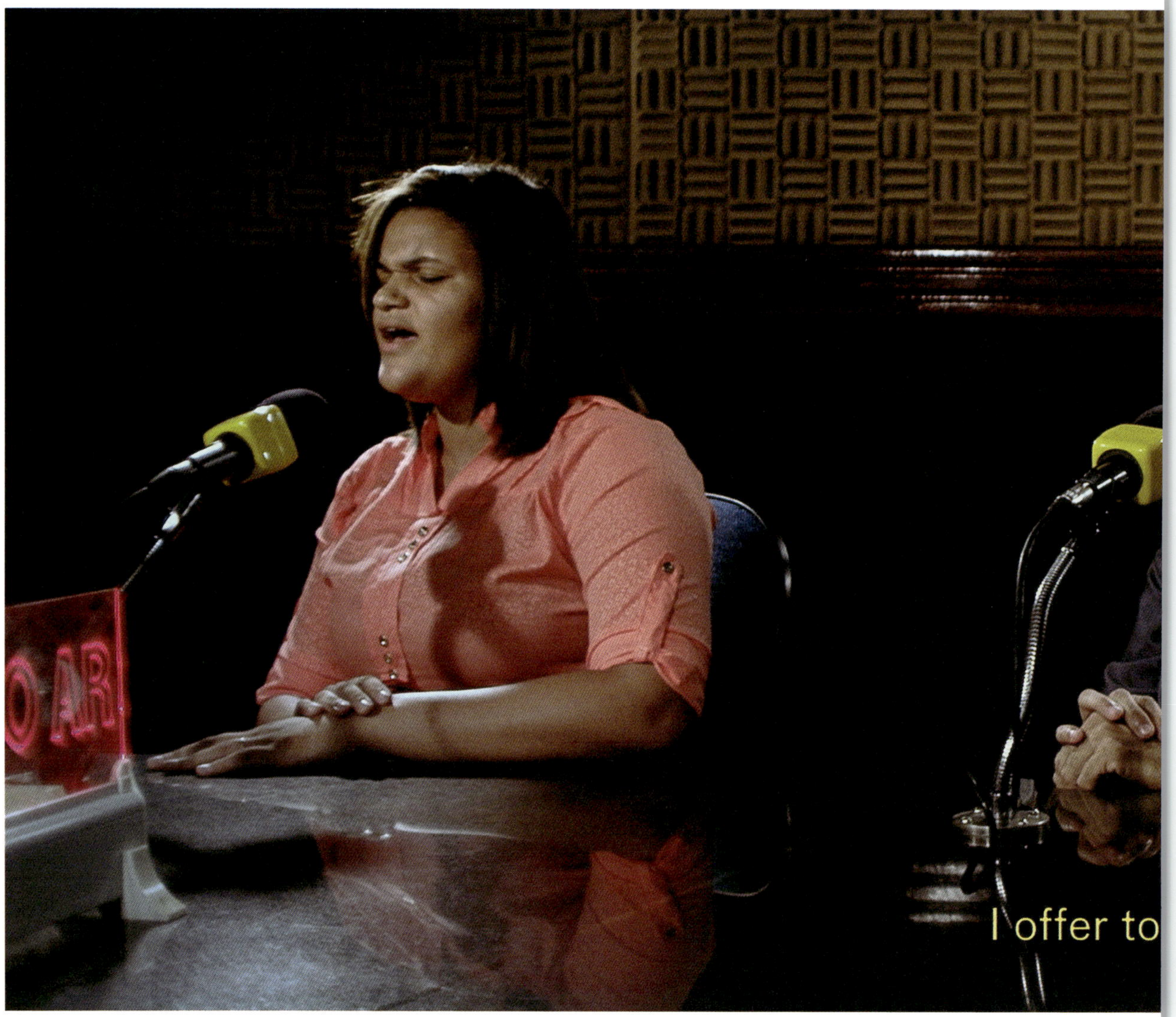
O AR
I offer to

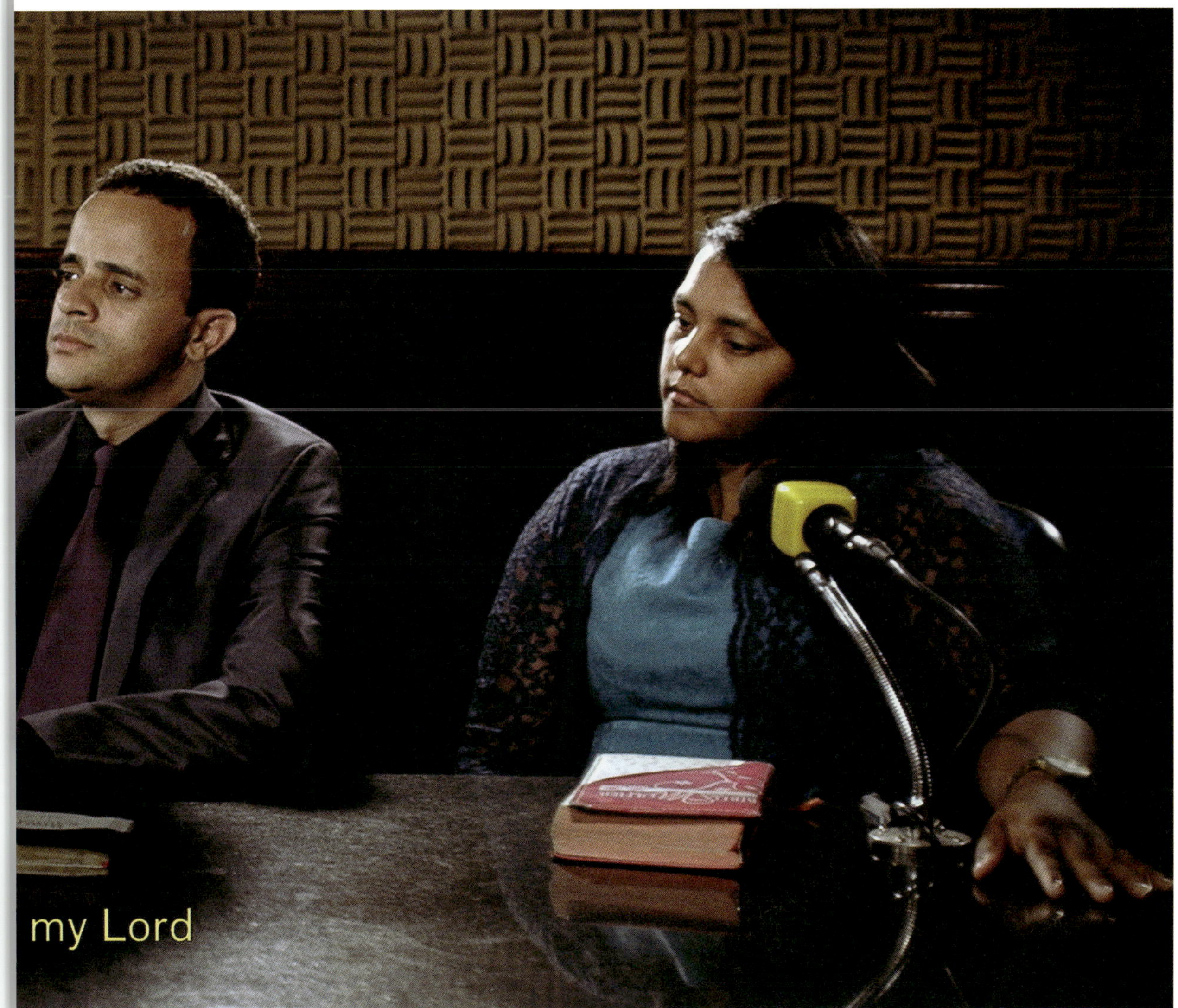
my Lord

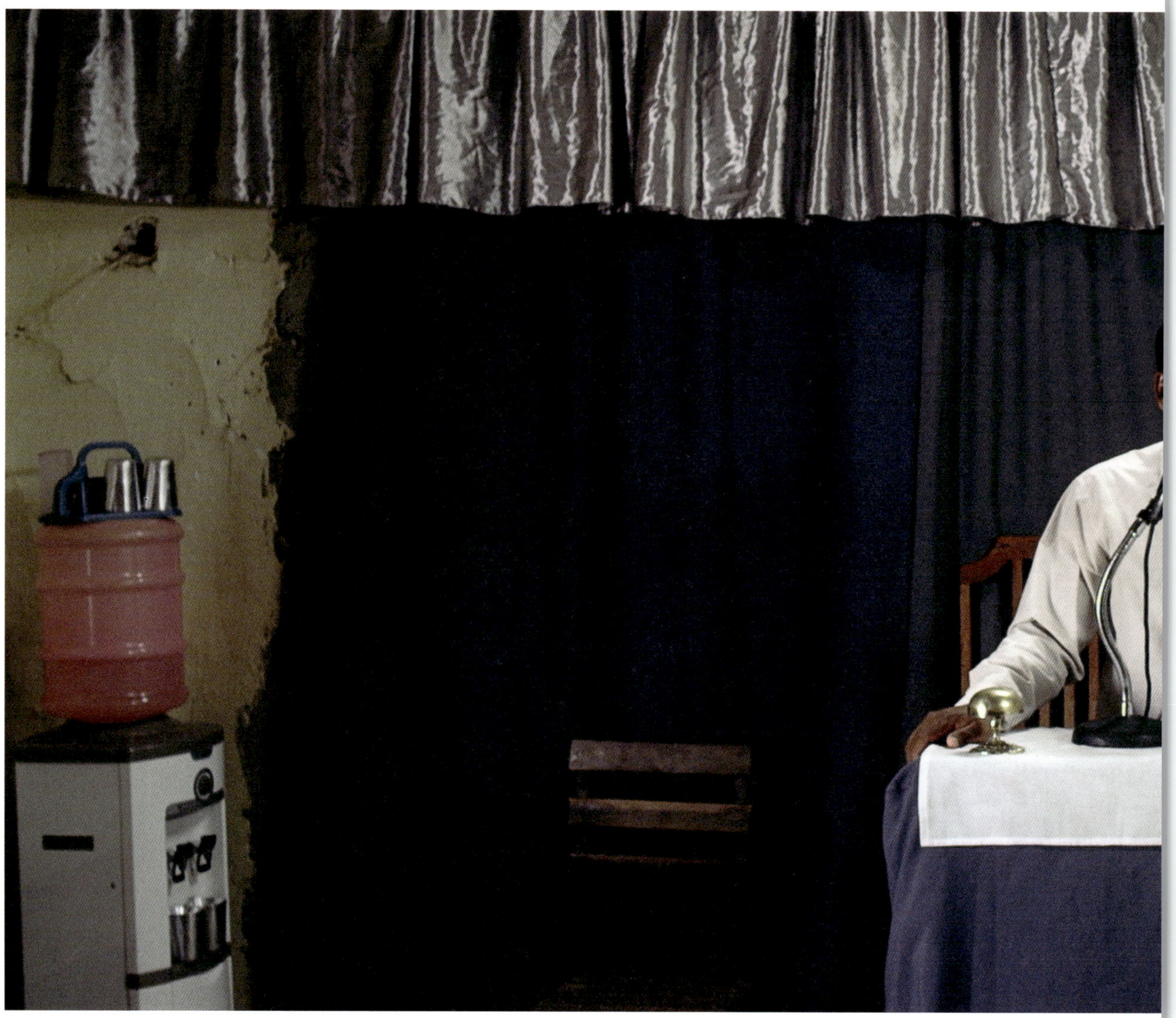

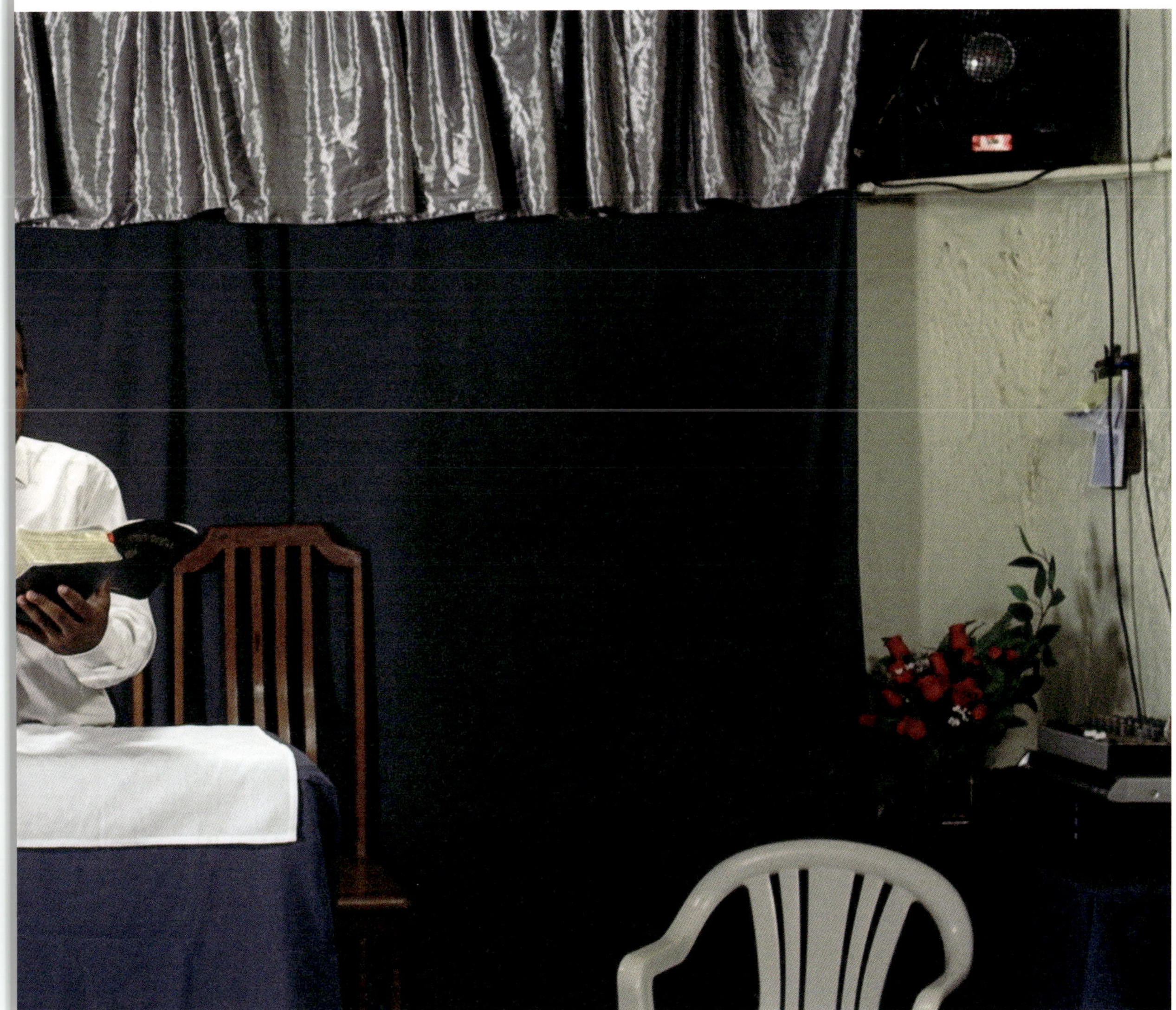

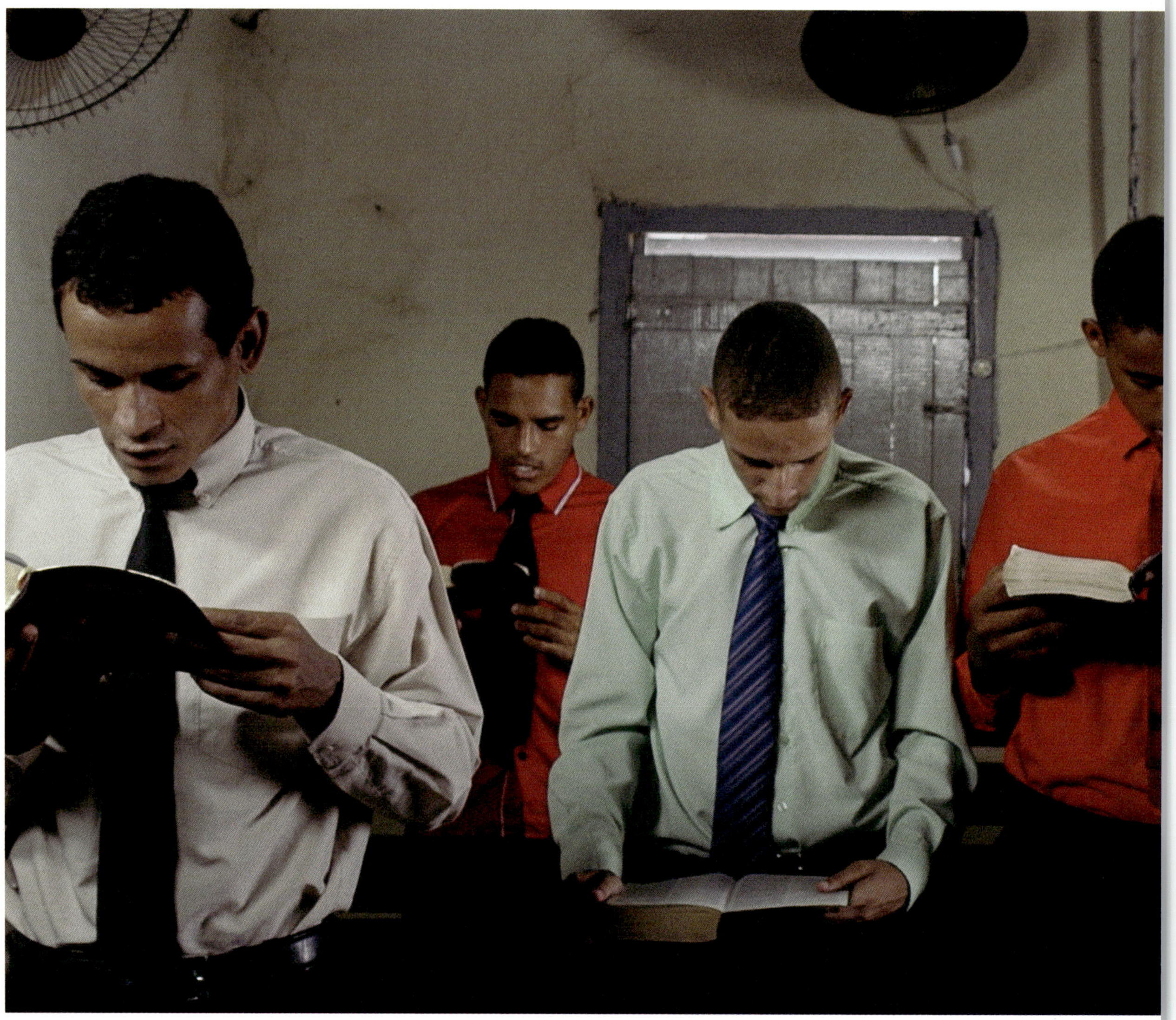

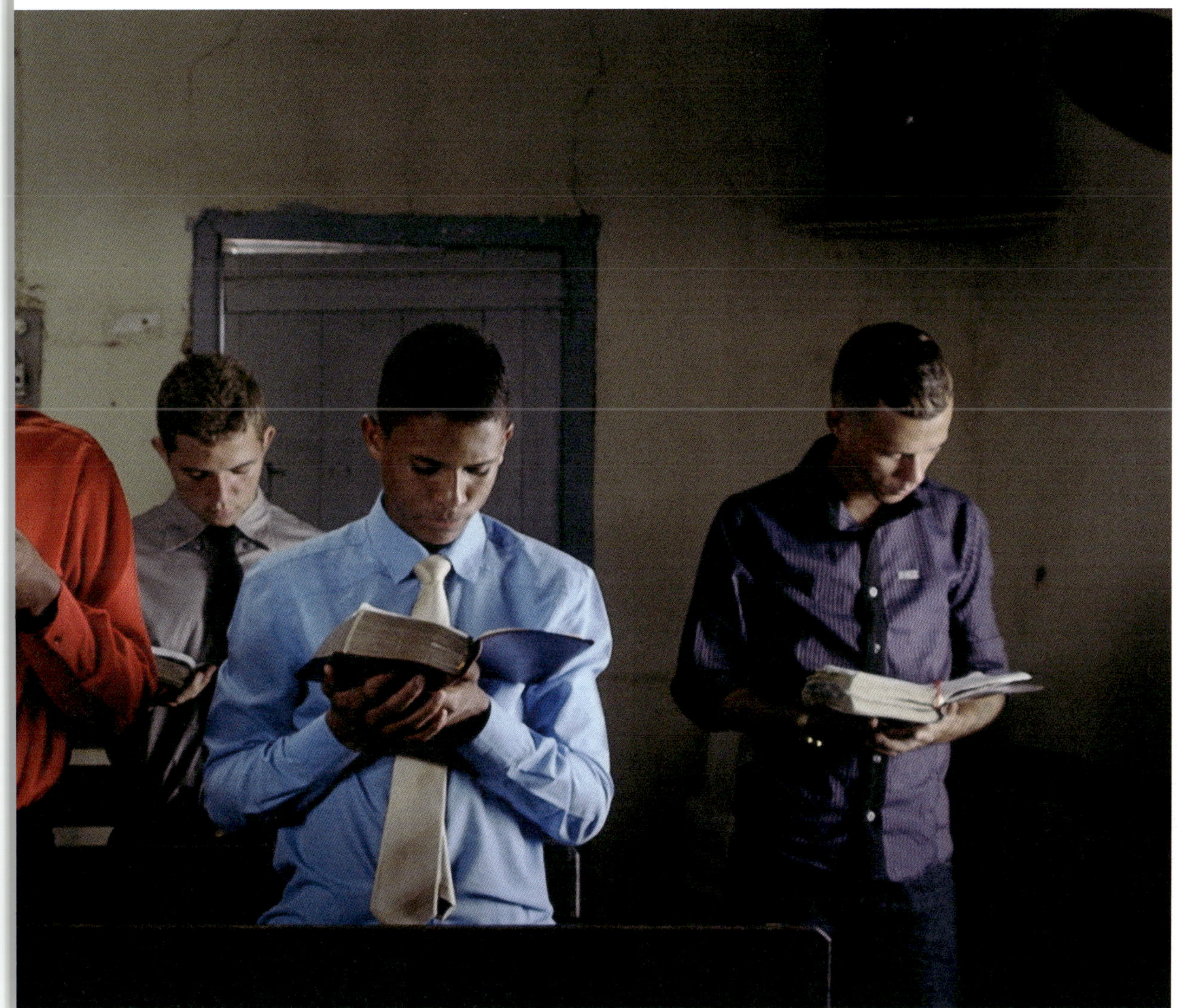

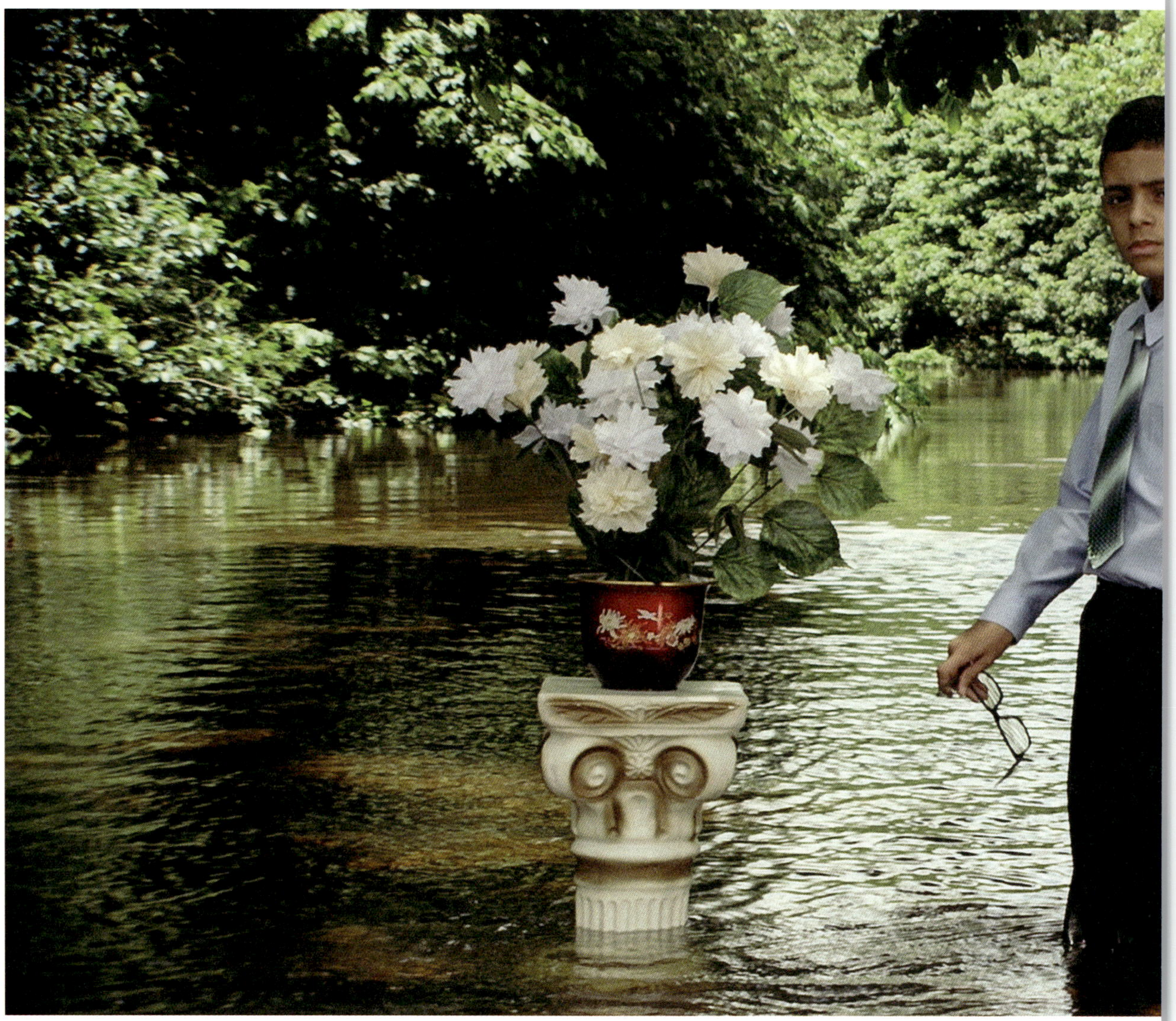

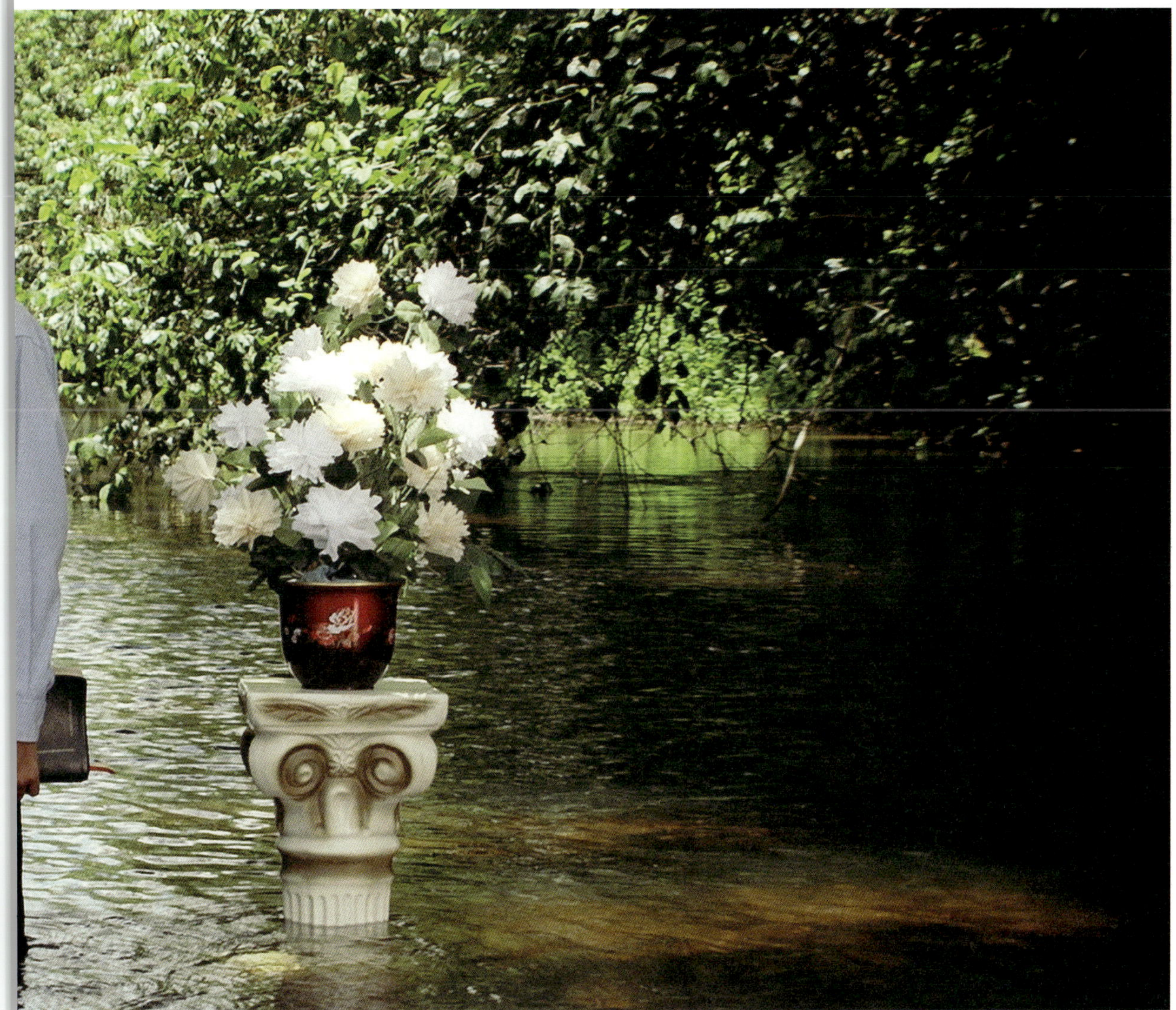

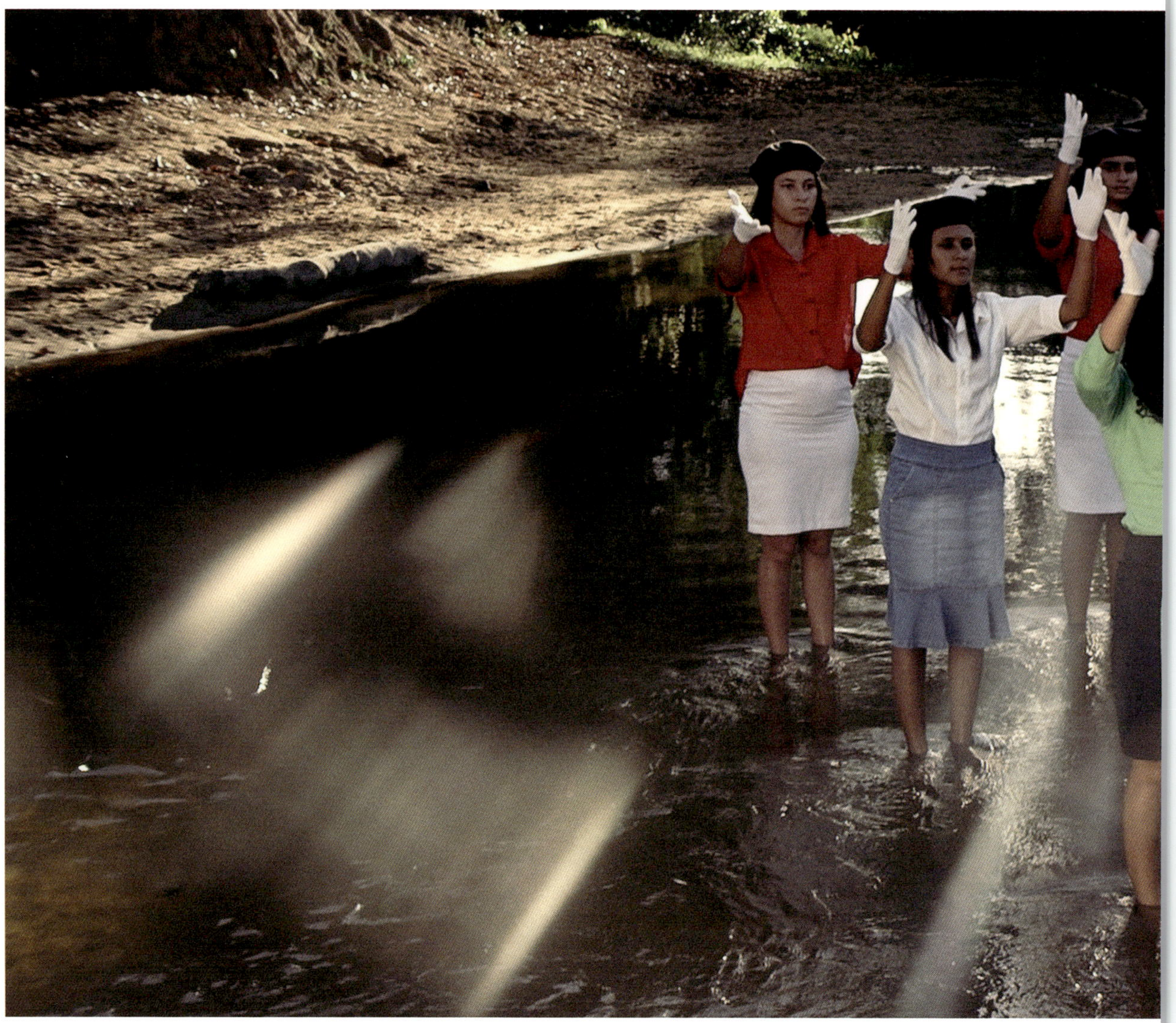

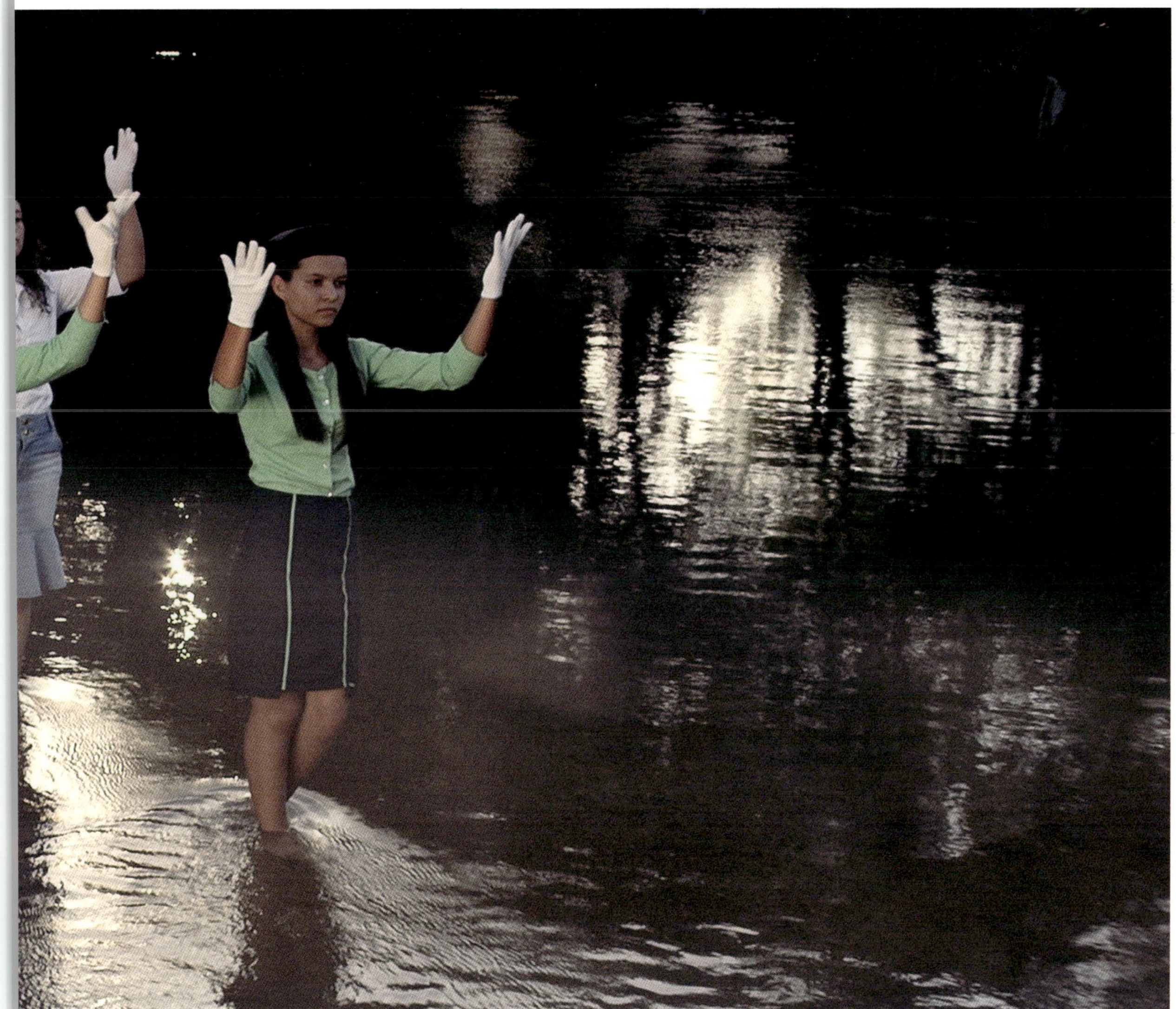

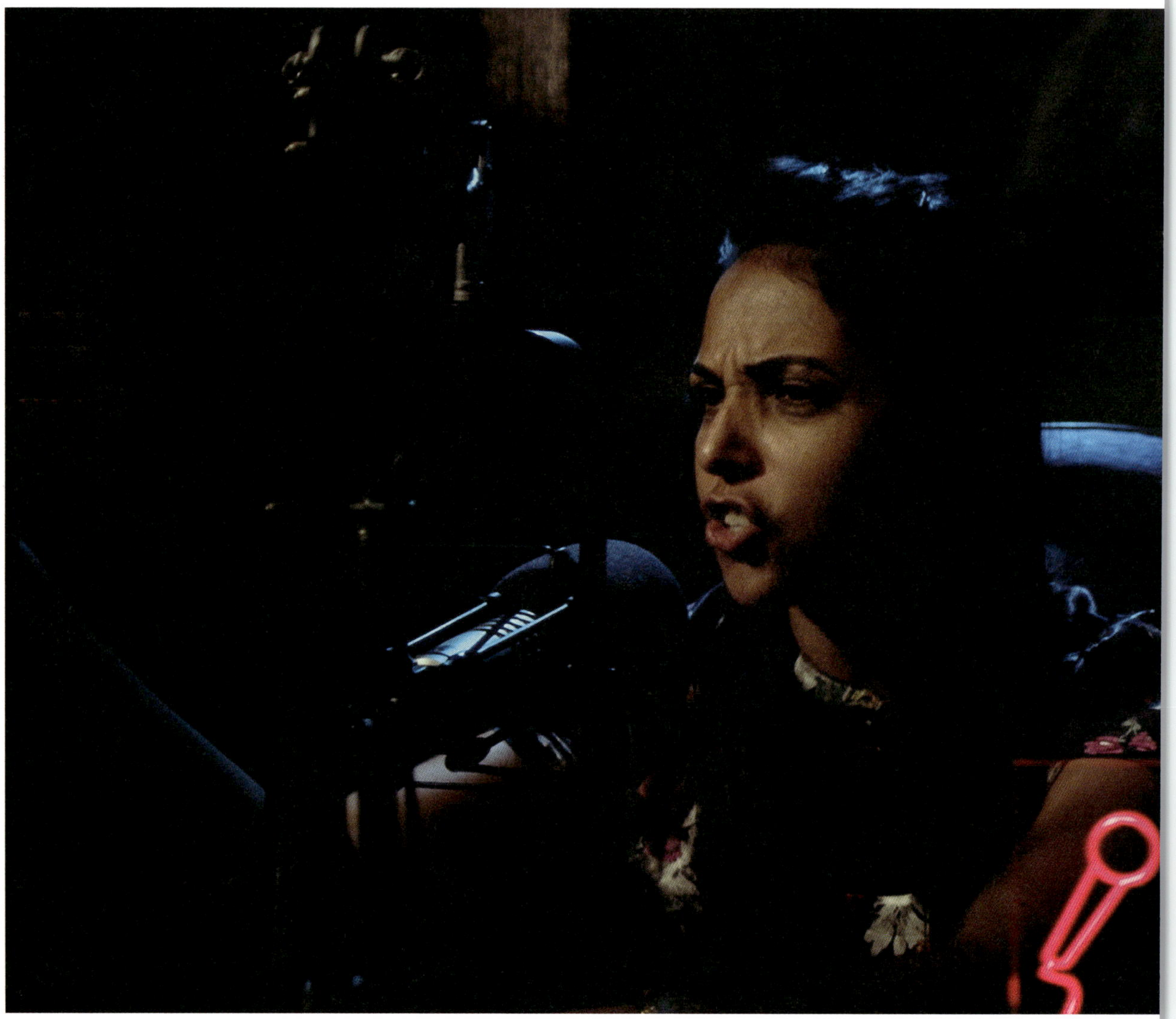

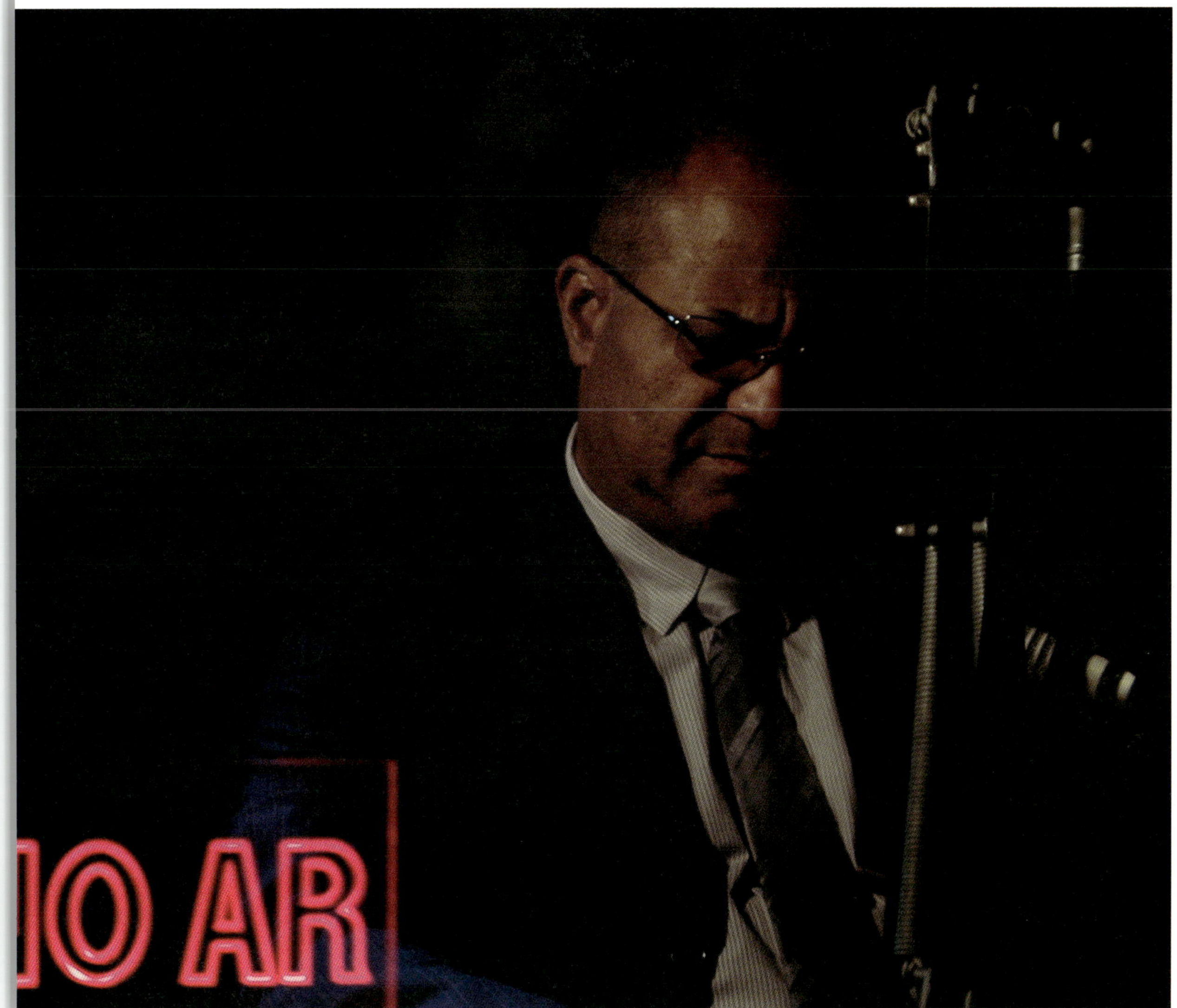
O AR

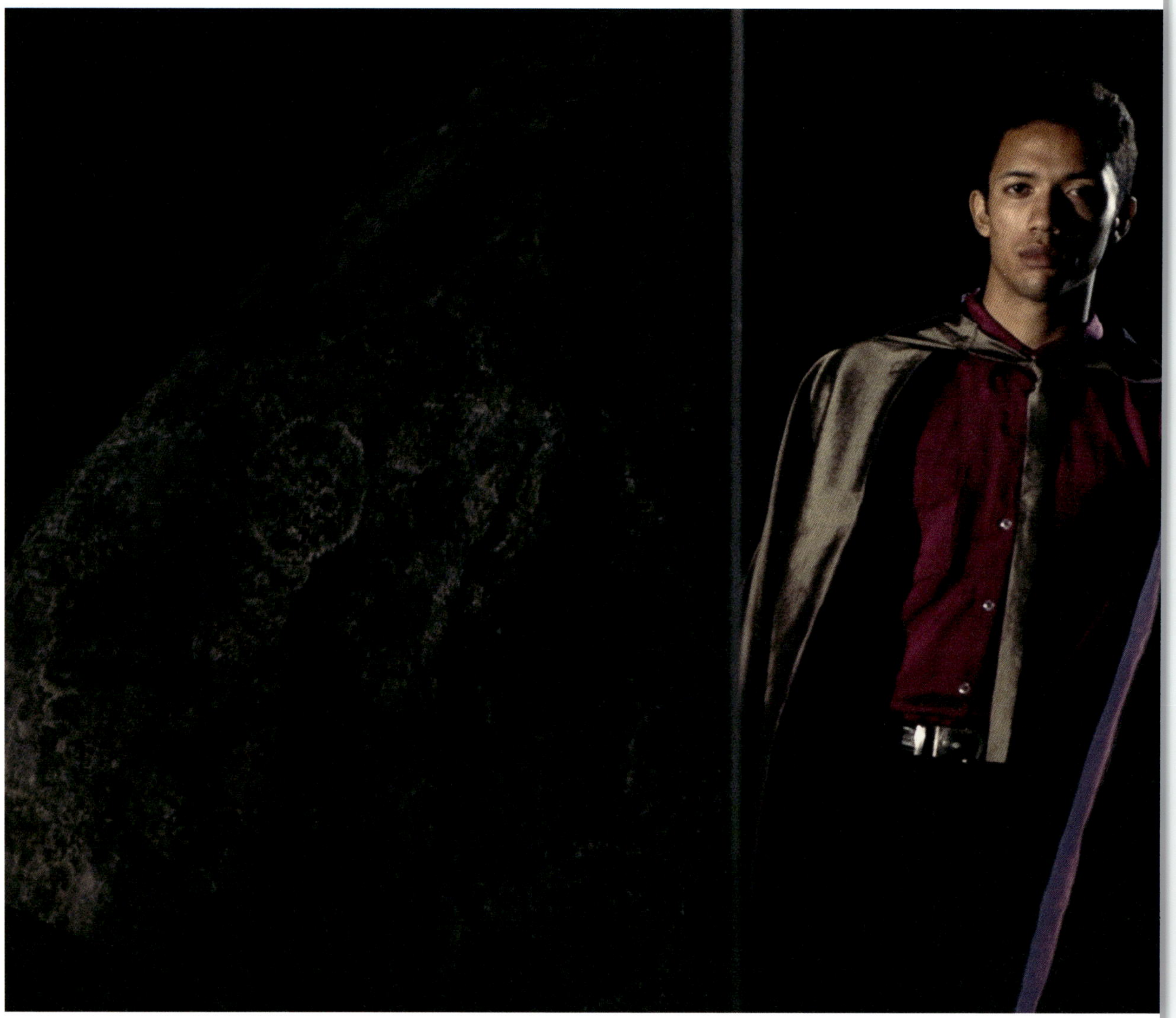

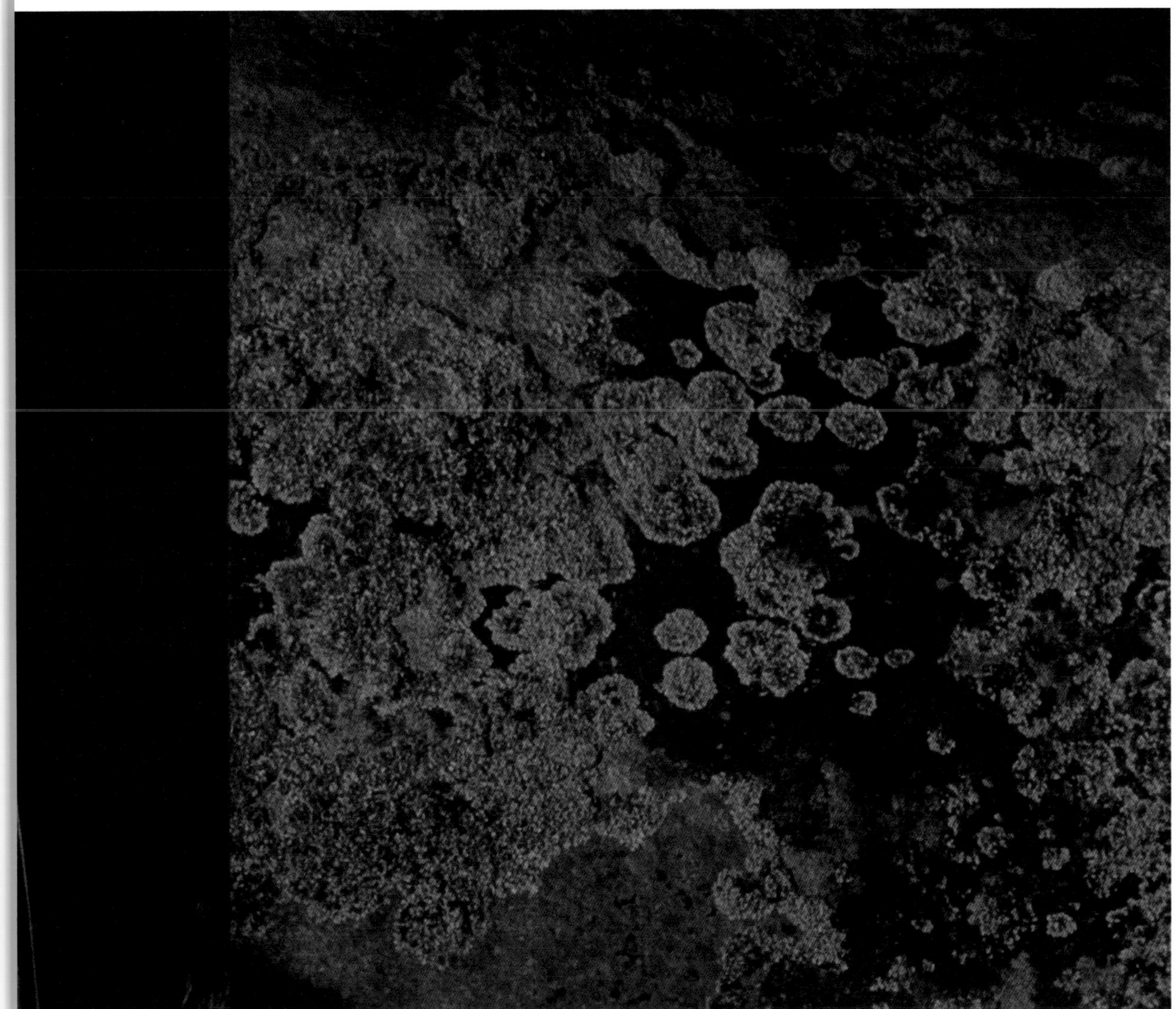

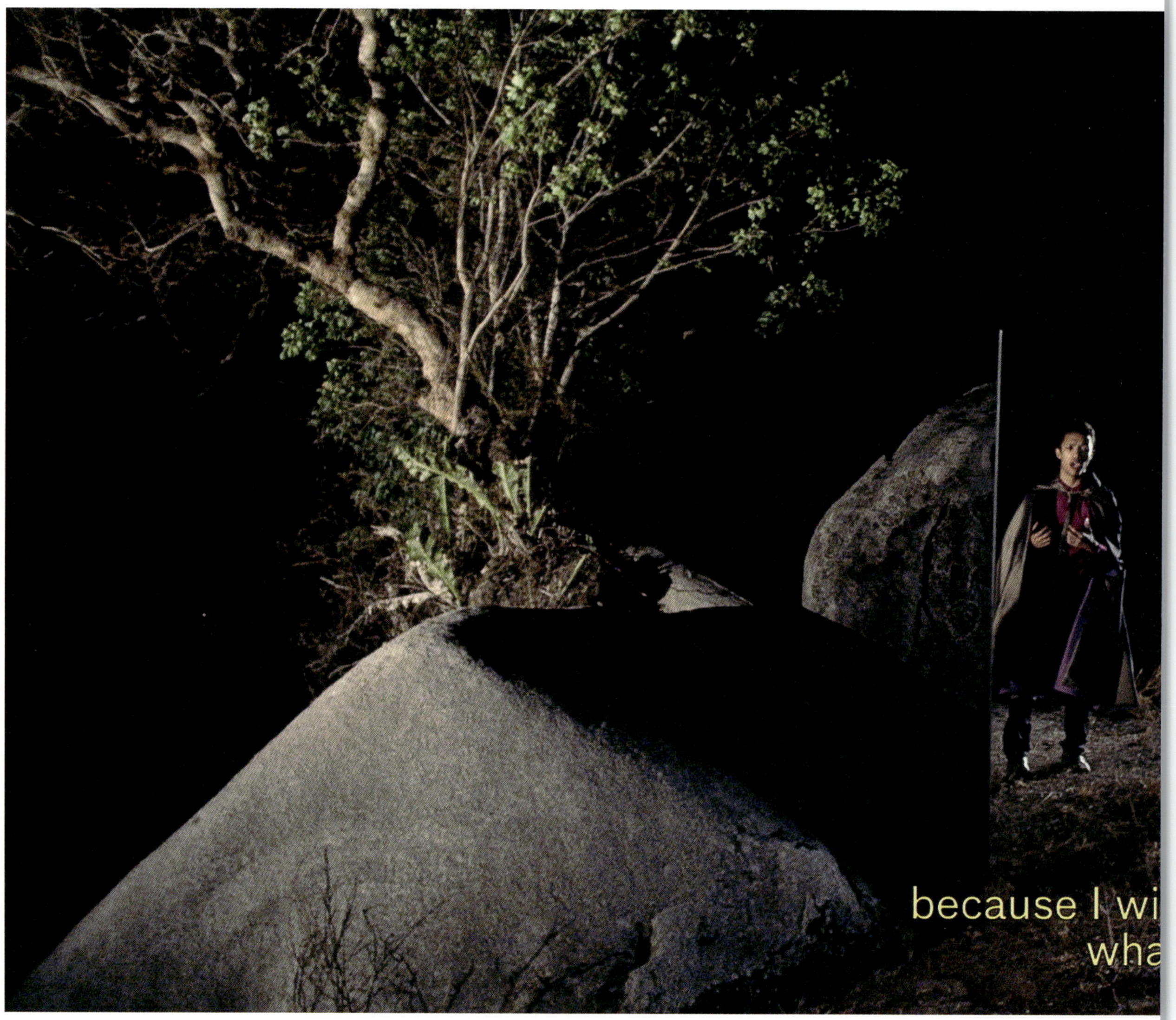
because I wi
wha

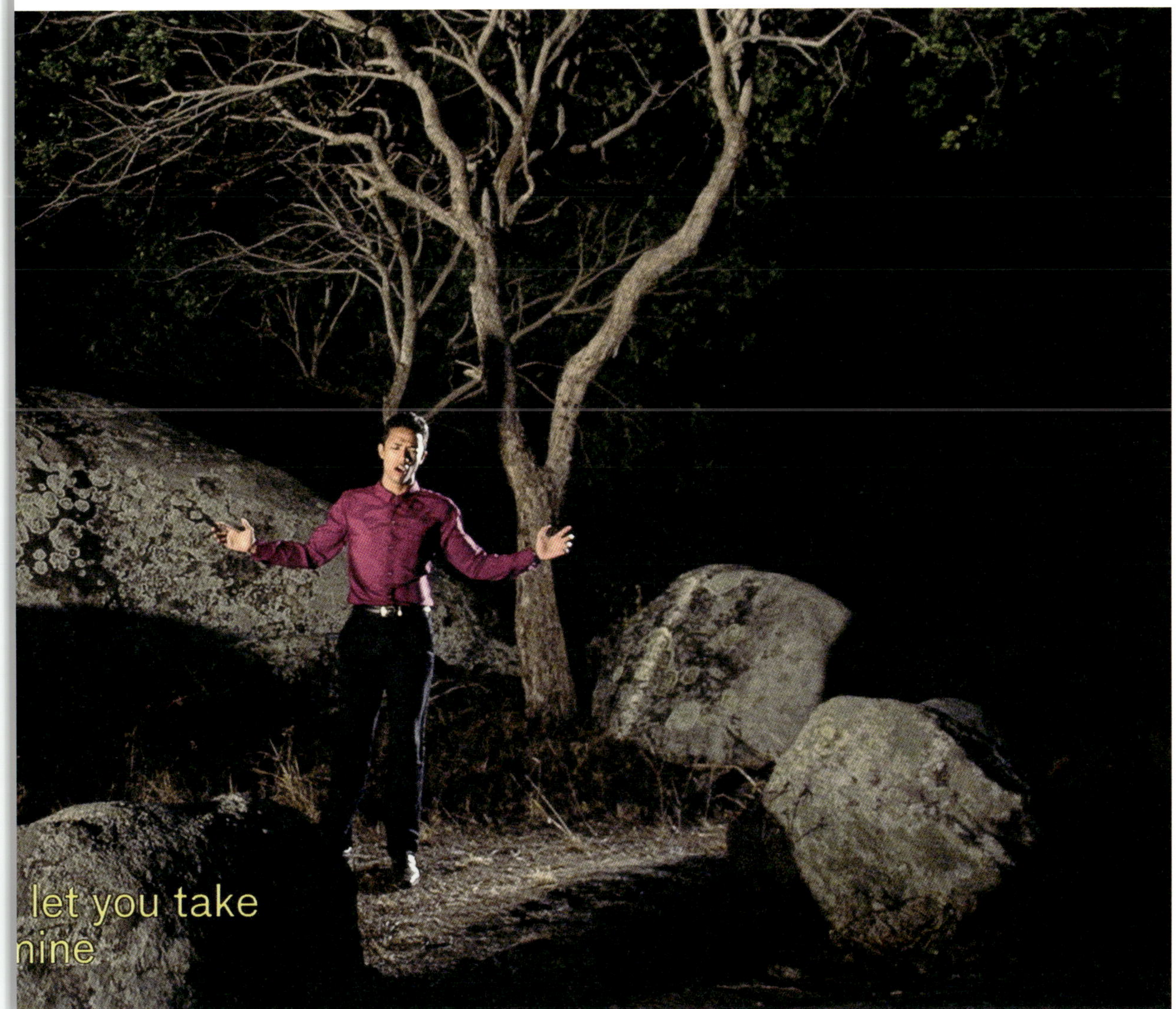
let you take
nine

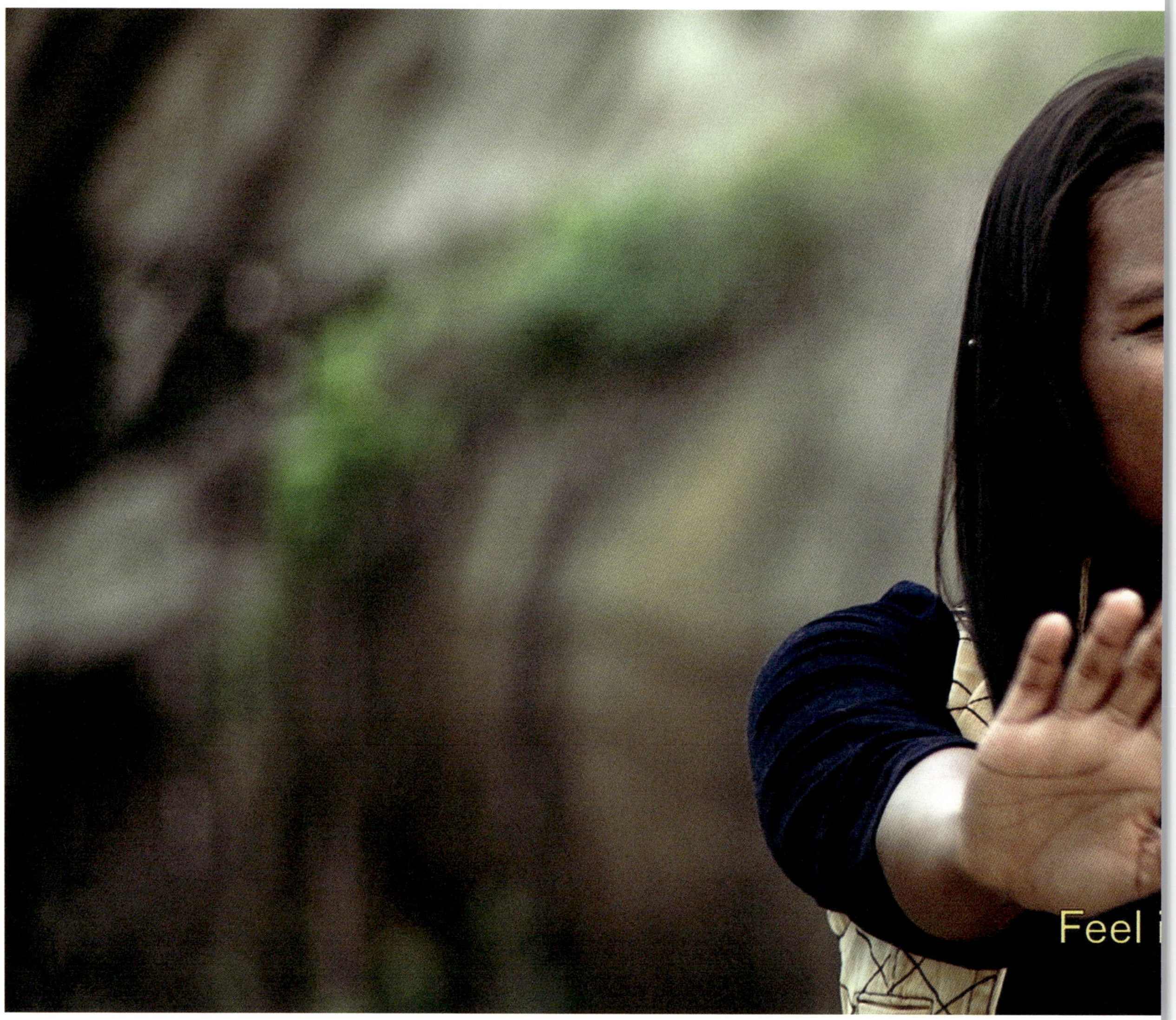
Feel i

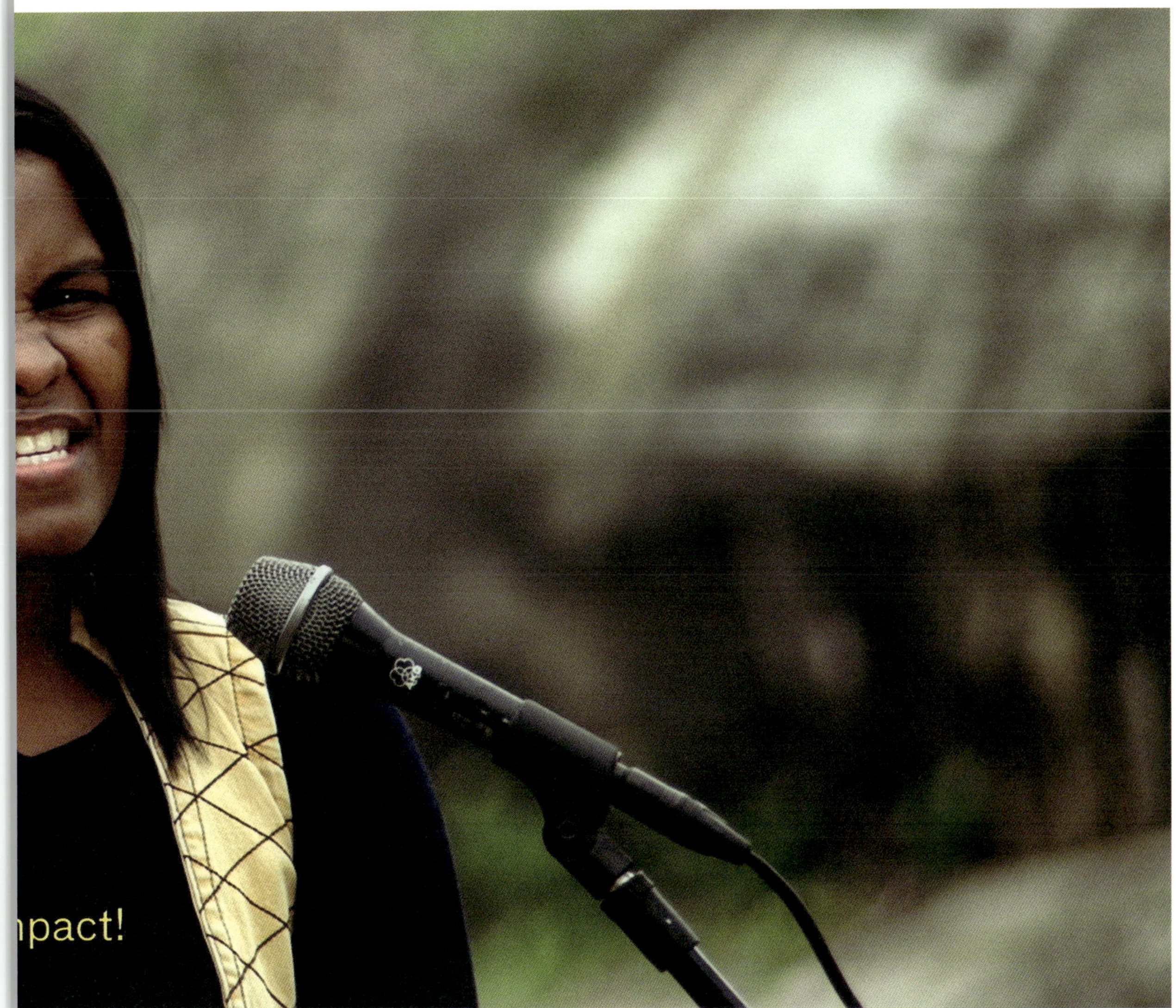
npact!

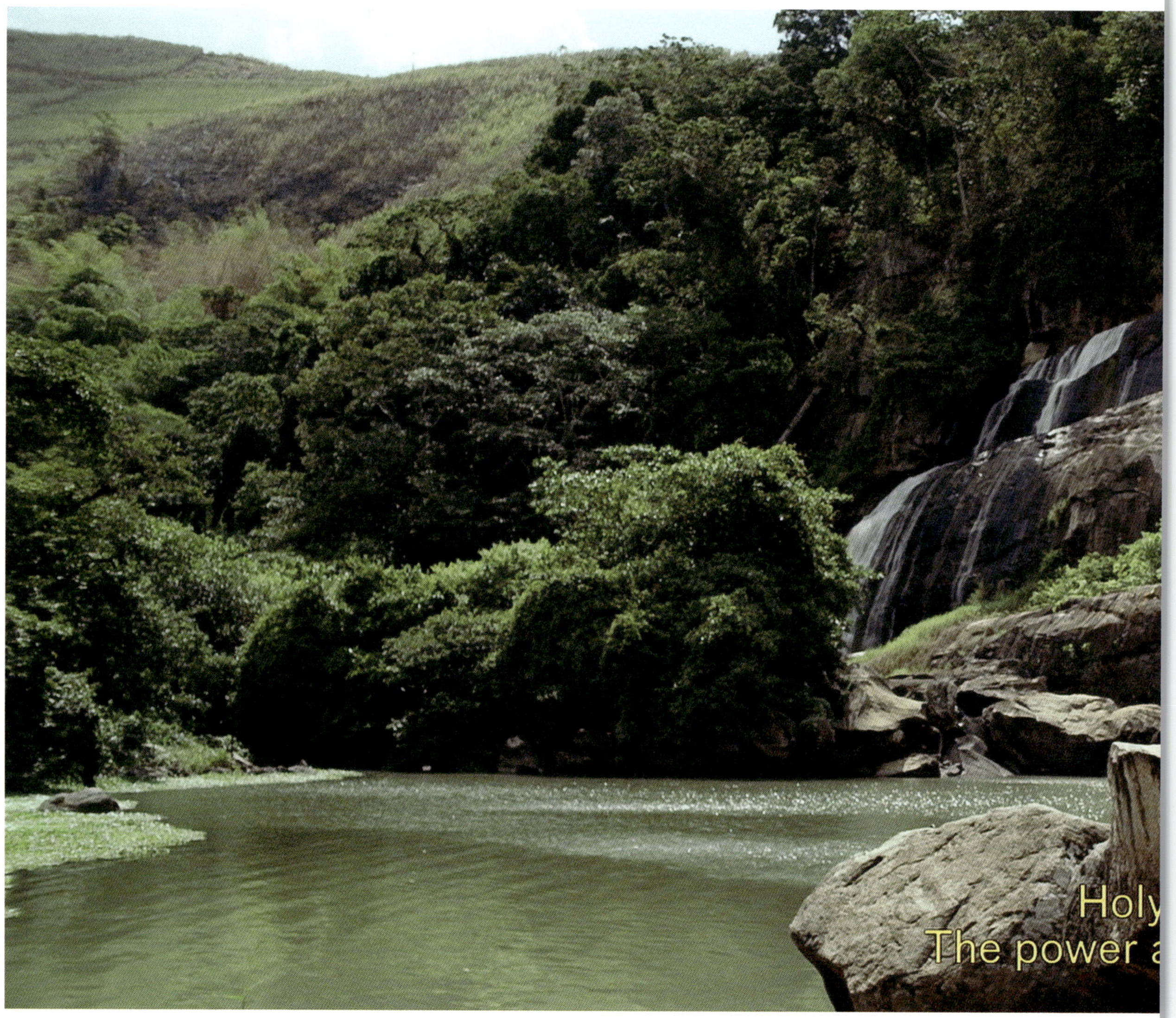
Holy
The power a

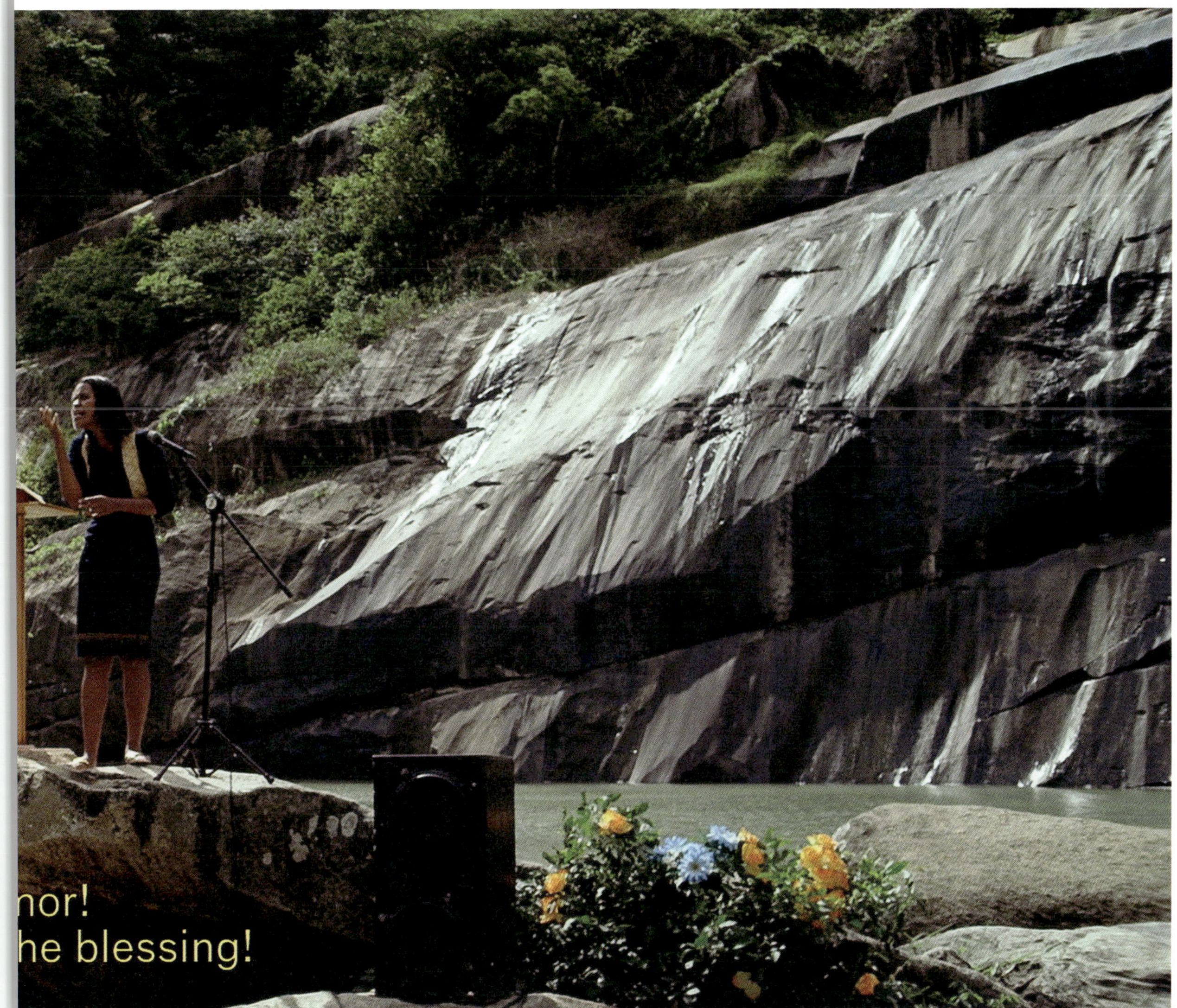
nor!
he blessing!

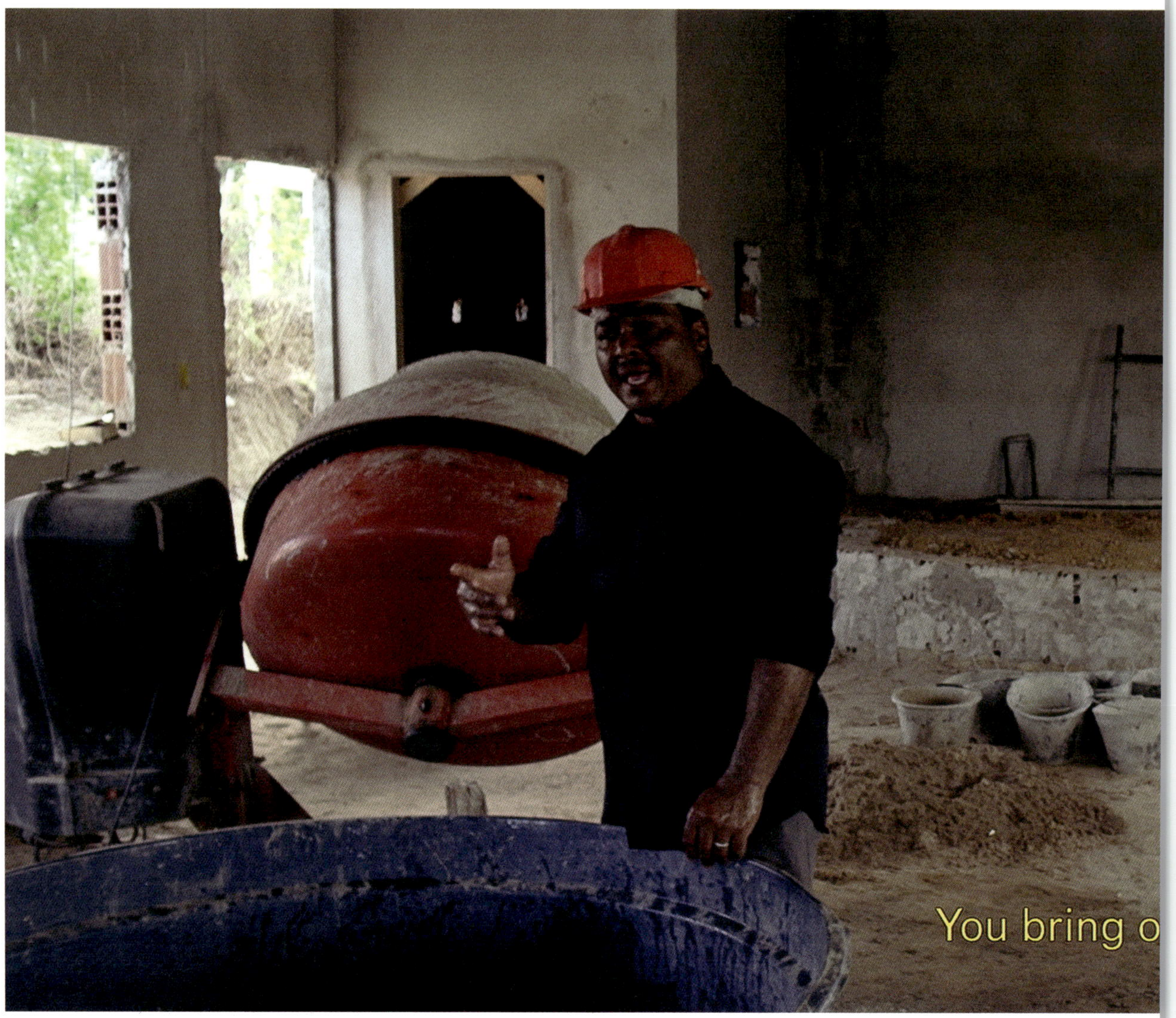
You bring o

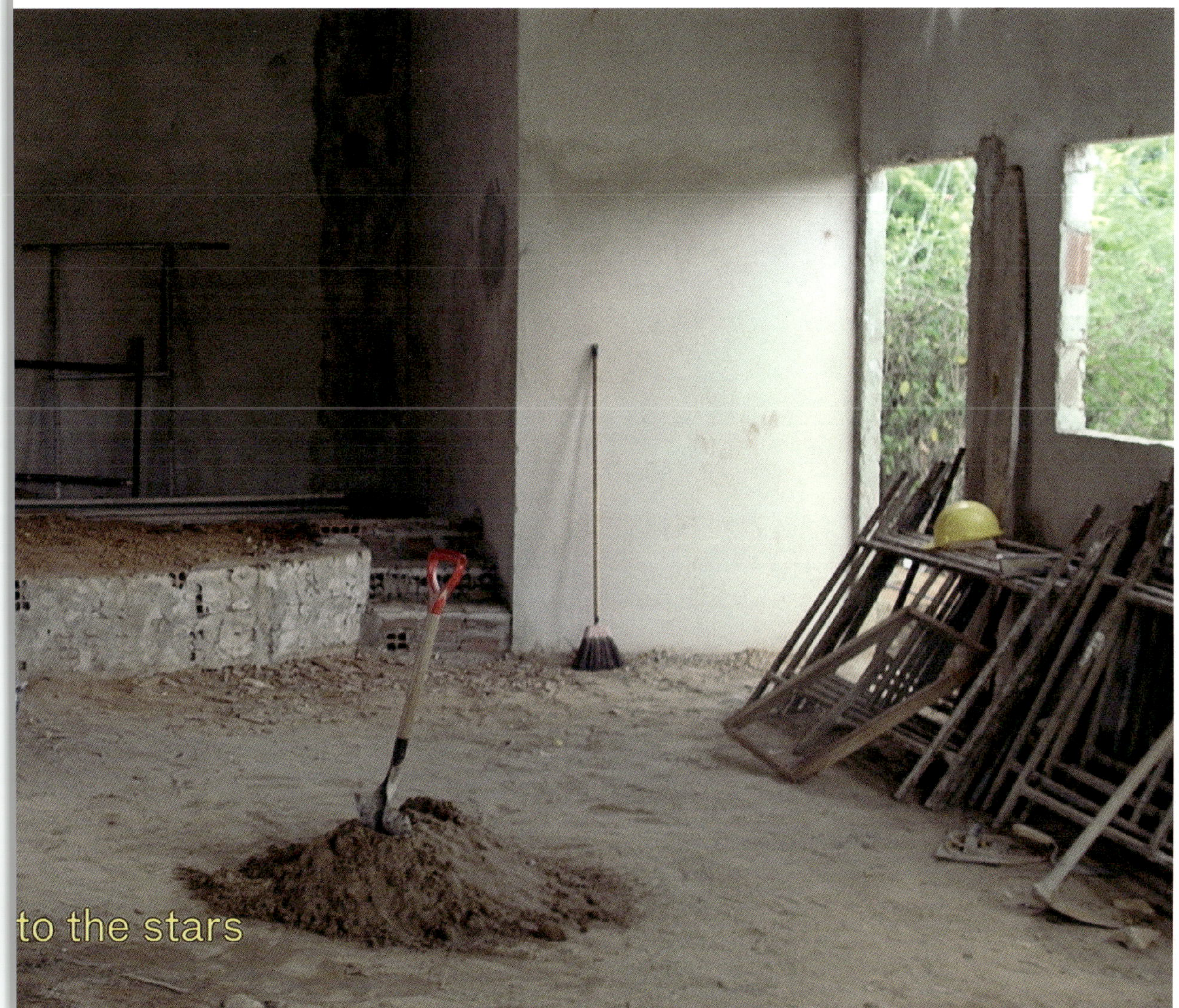
to the stars

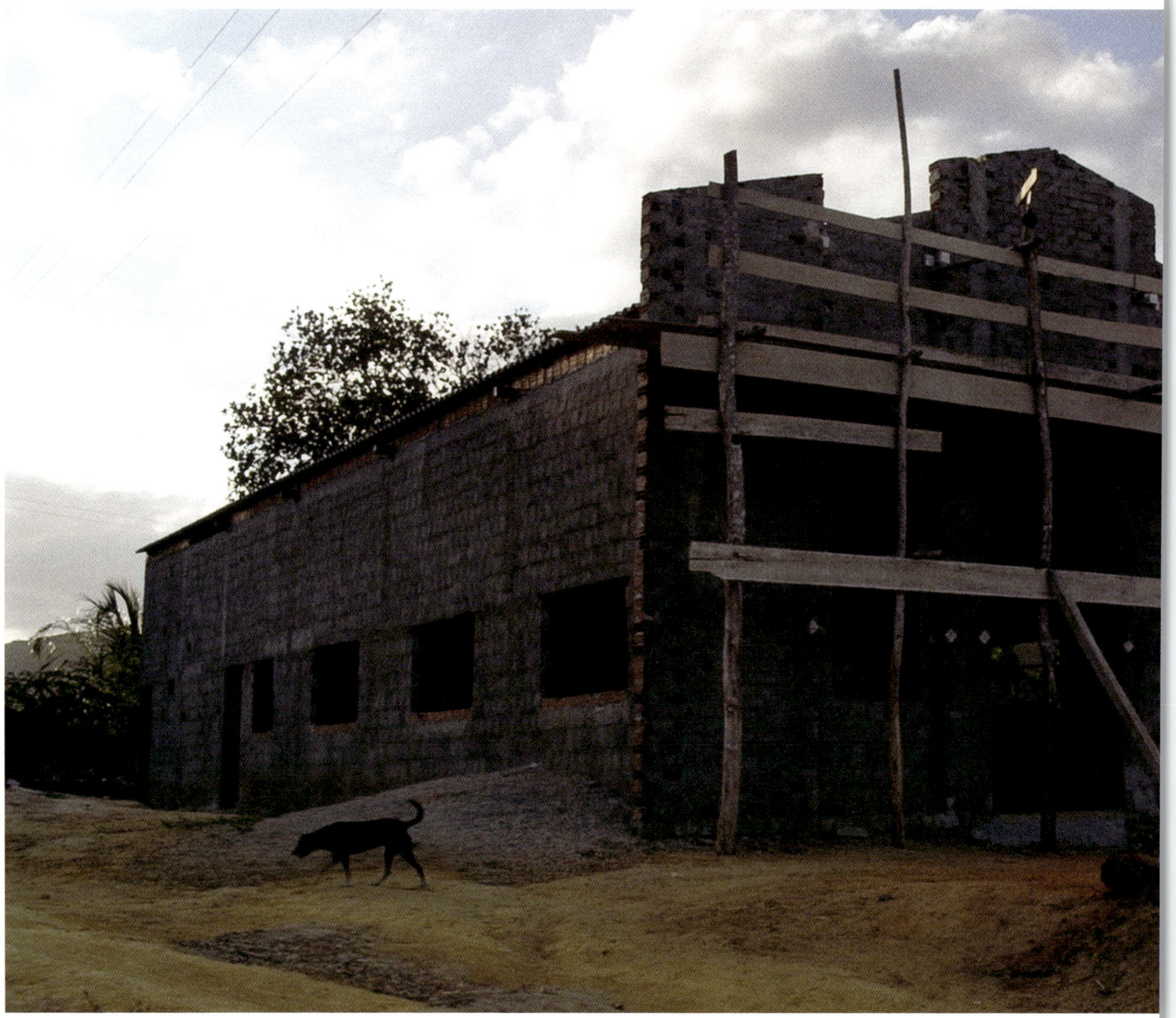

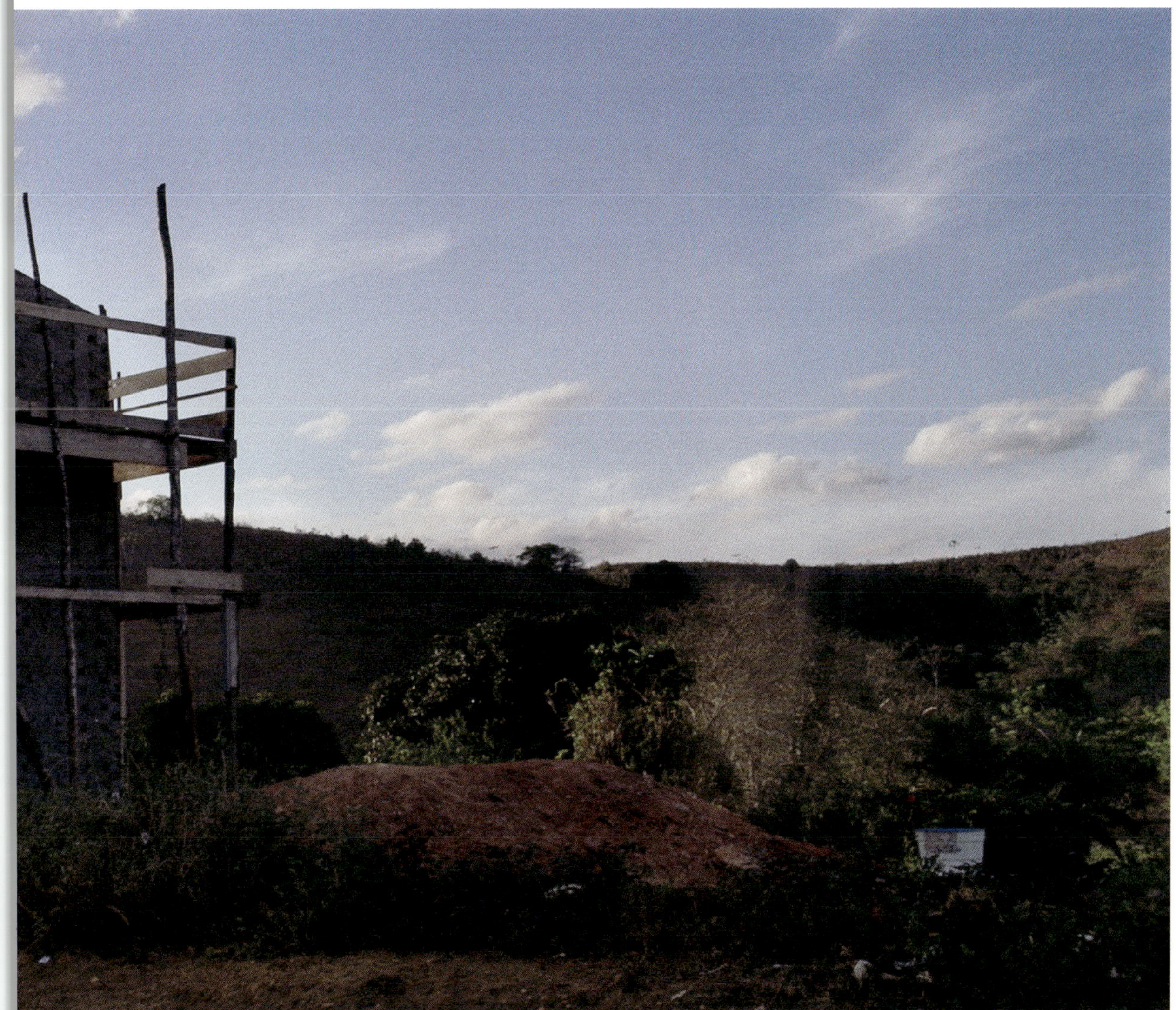

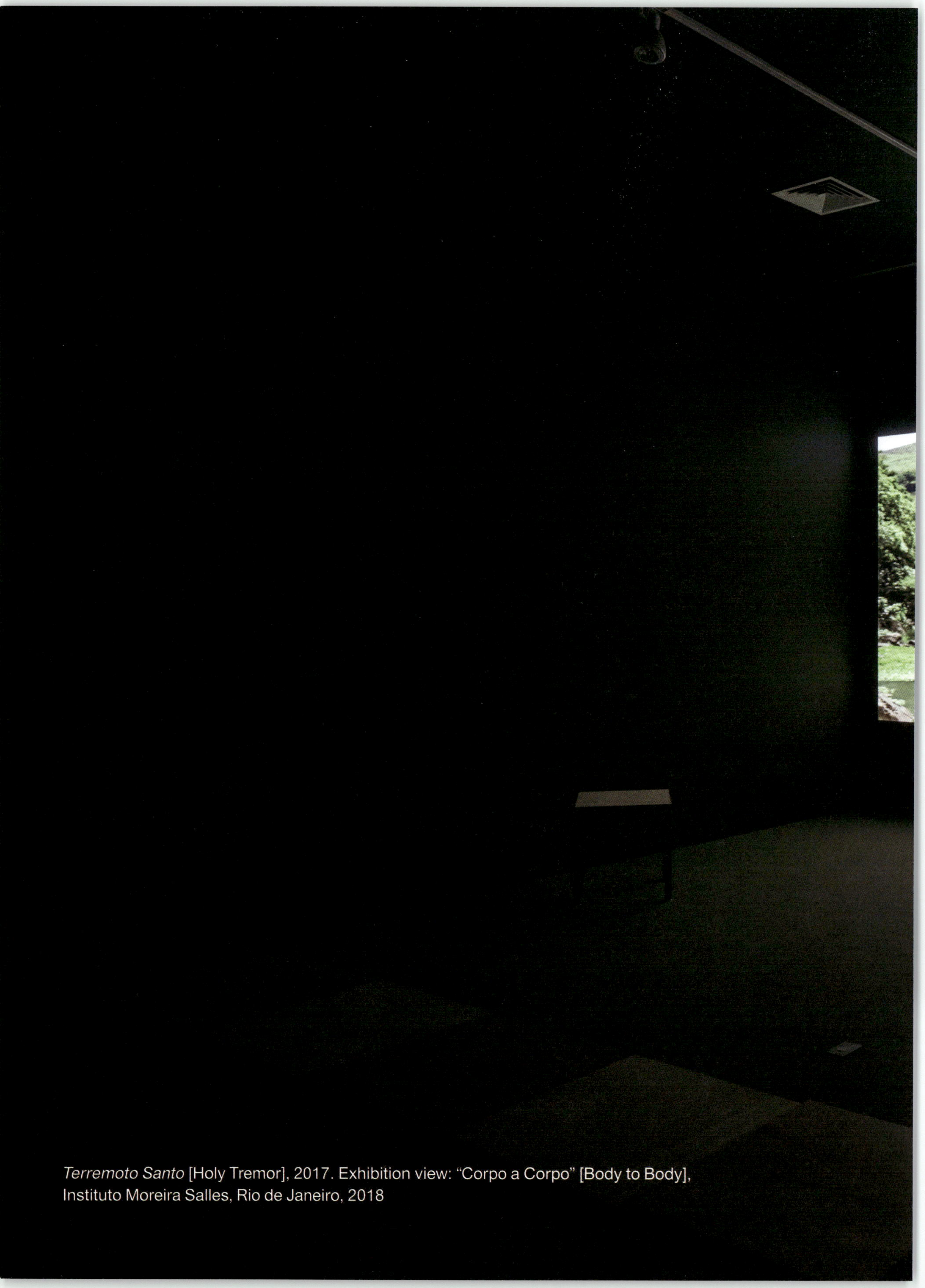

Terremoto Santo [Holy Tremor], 2017. Exhibition view: "Corpo a Corpo" [Body to Body], Instituto Moreira Salles, Rio de Janeiro, 2018

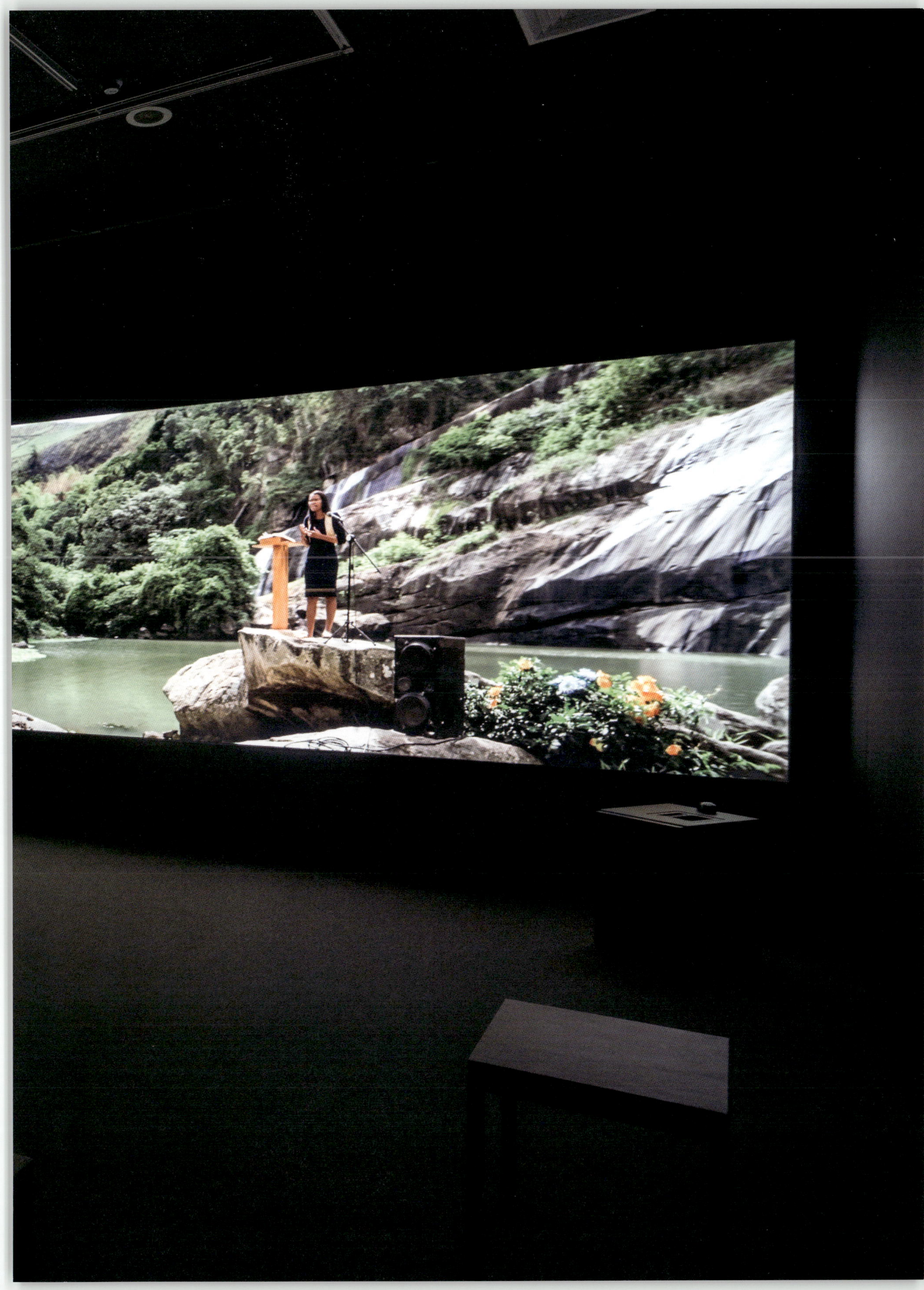

Swinguerra, 2019

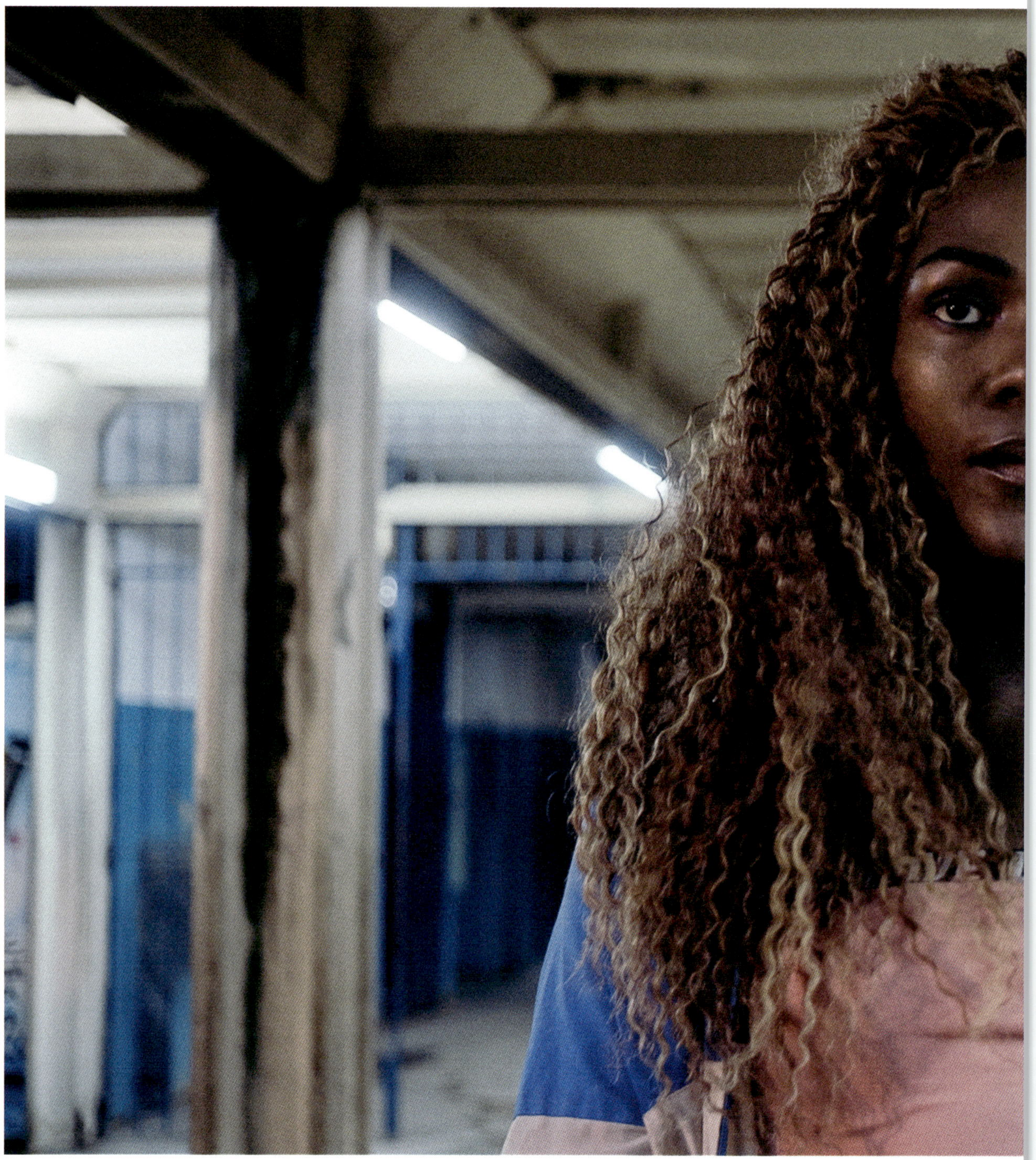

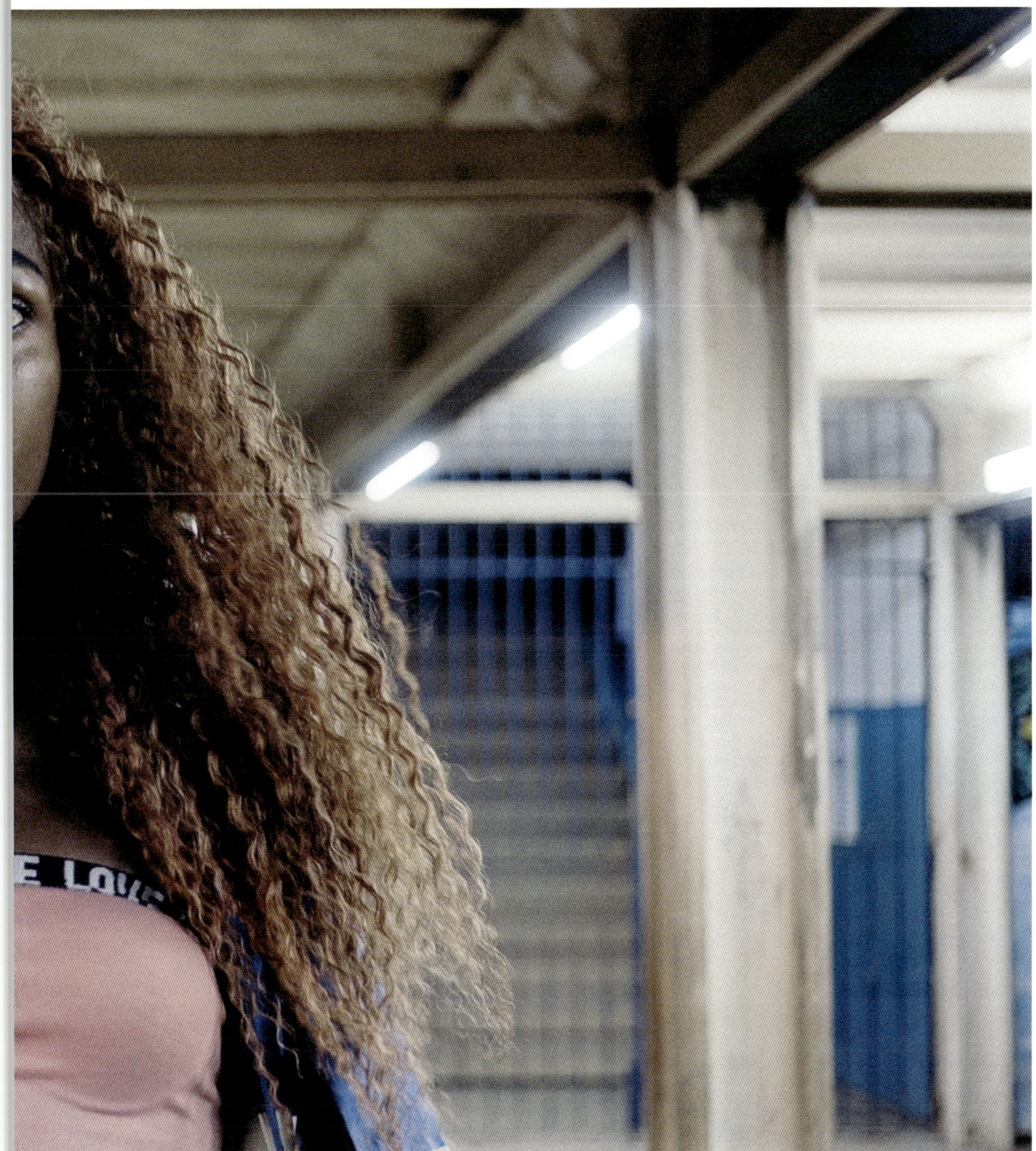

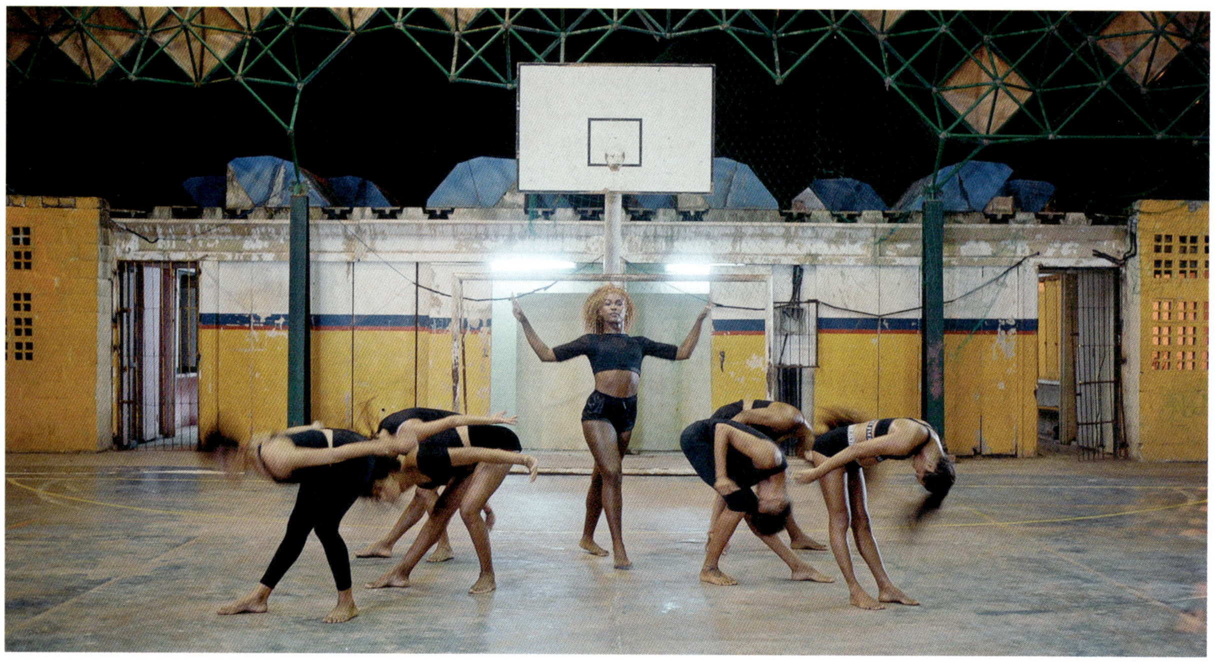

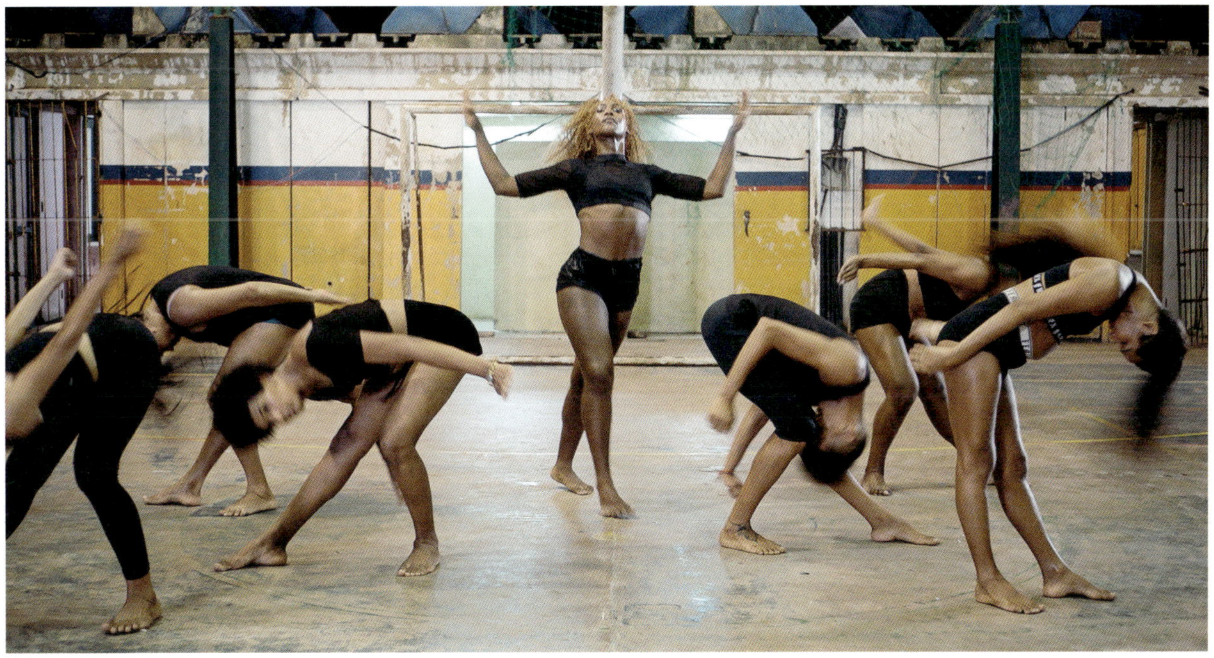

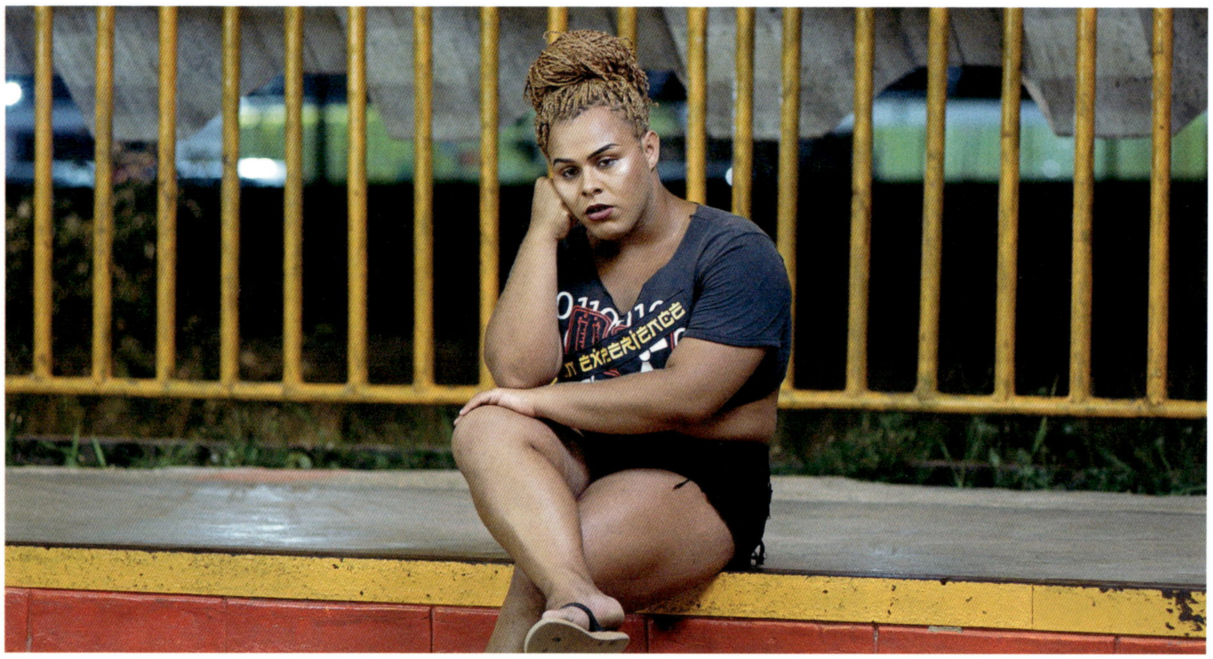

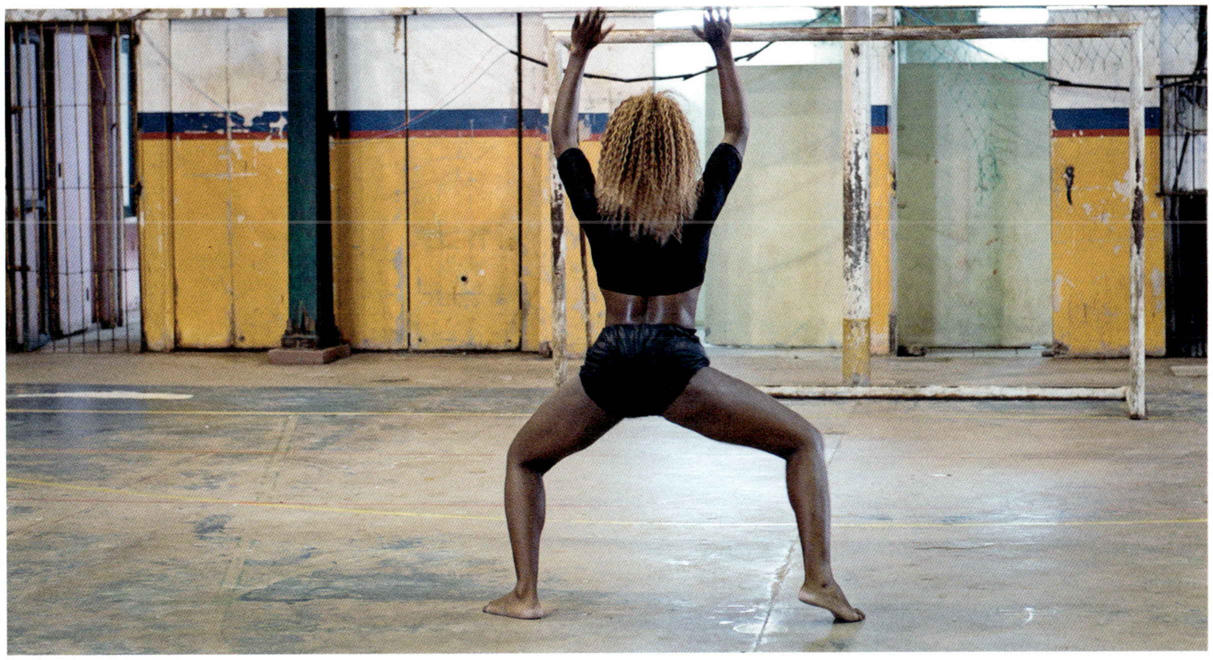

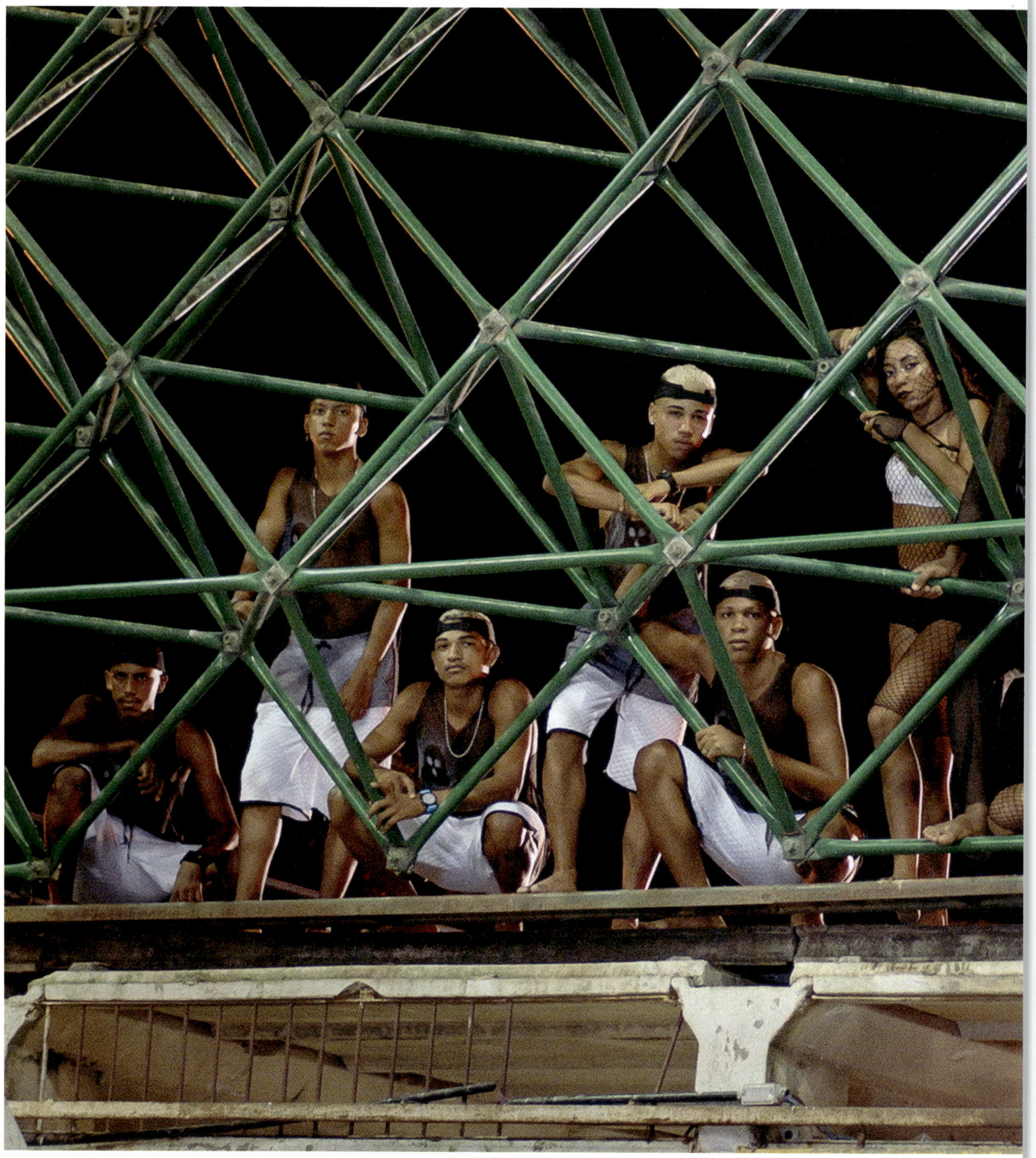

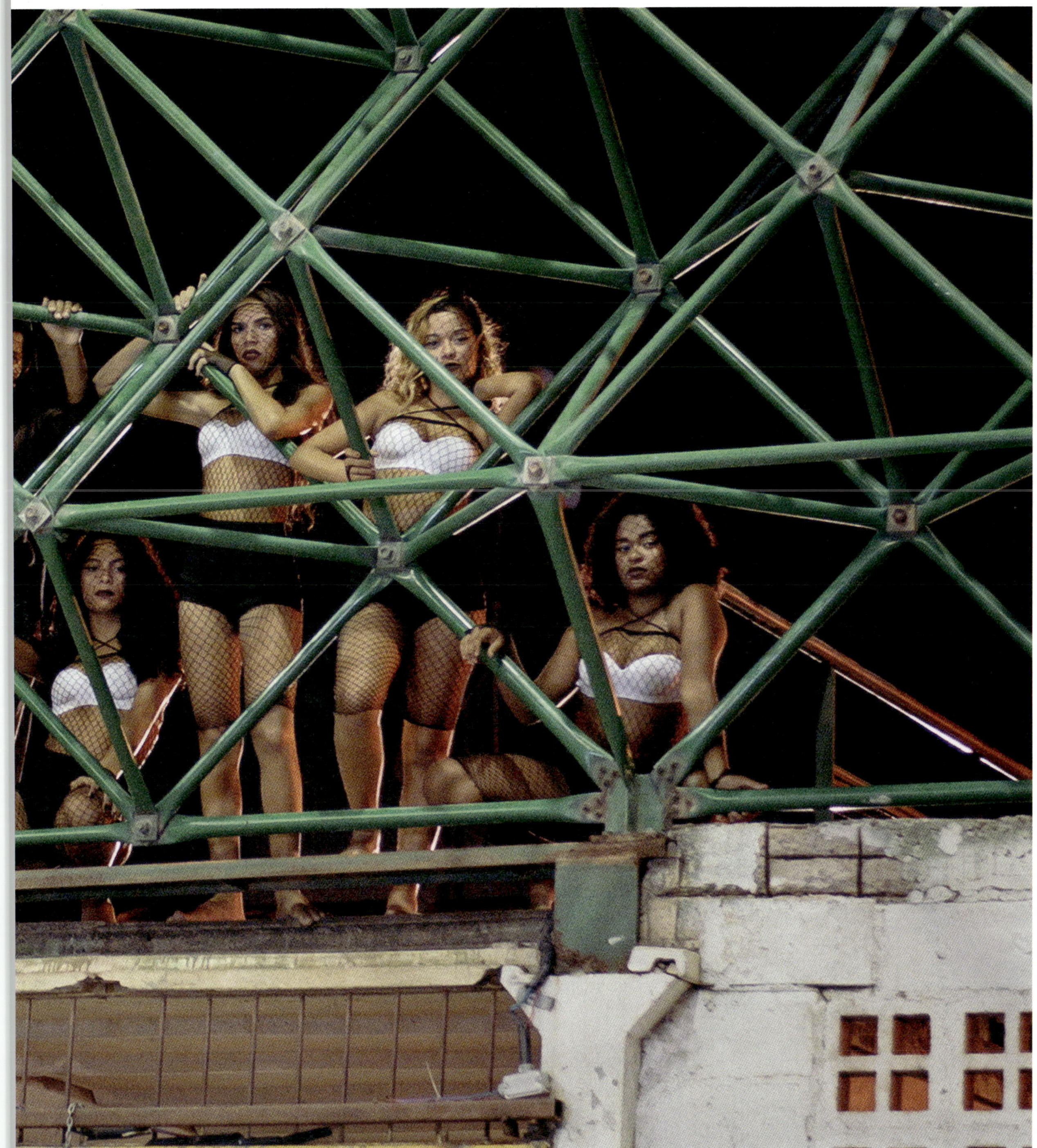

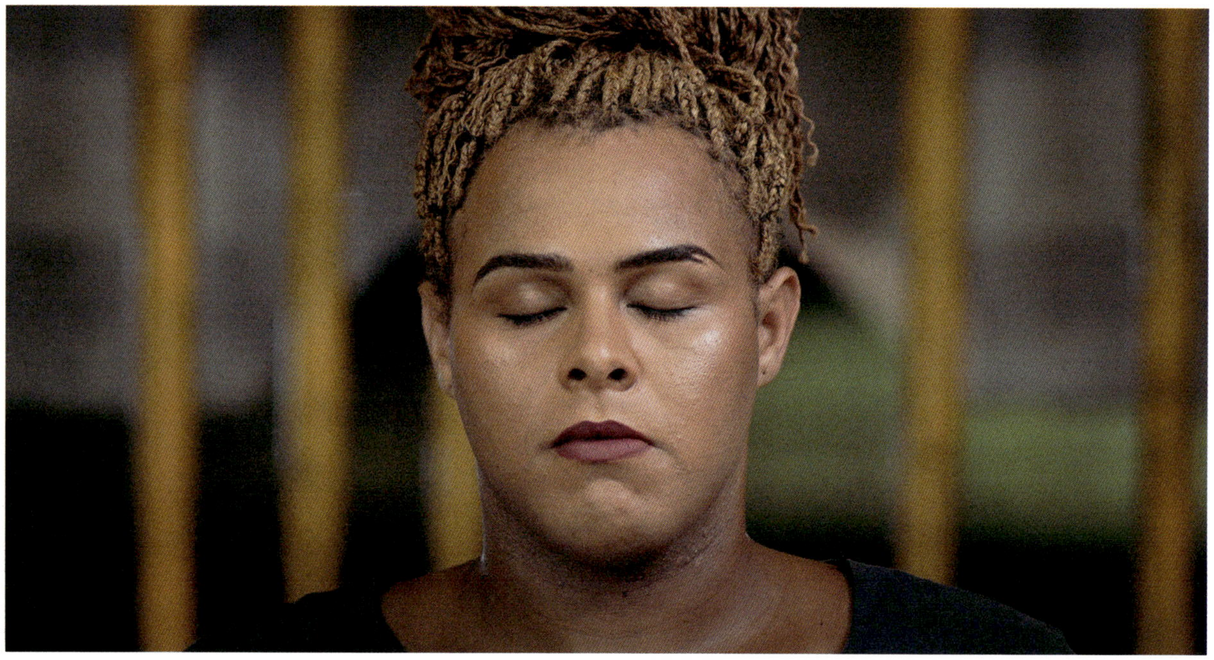

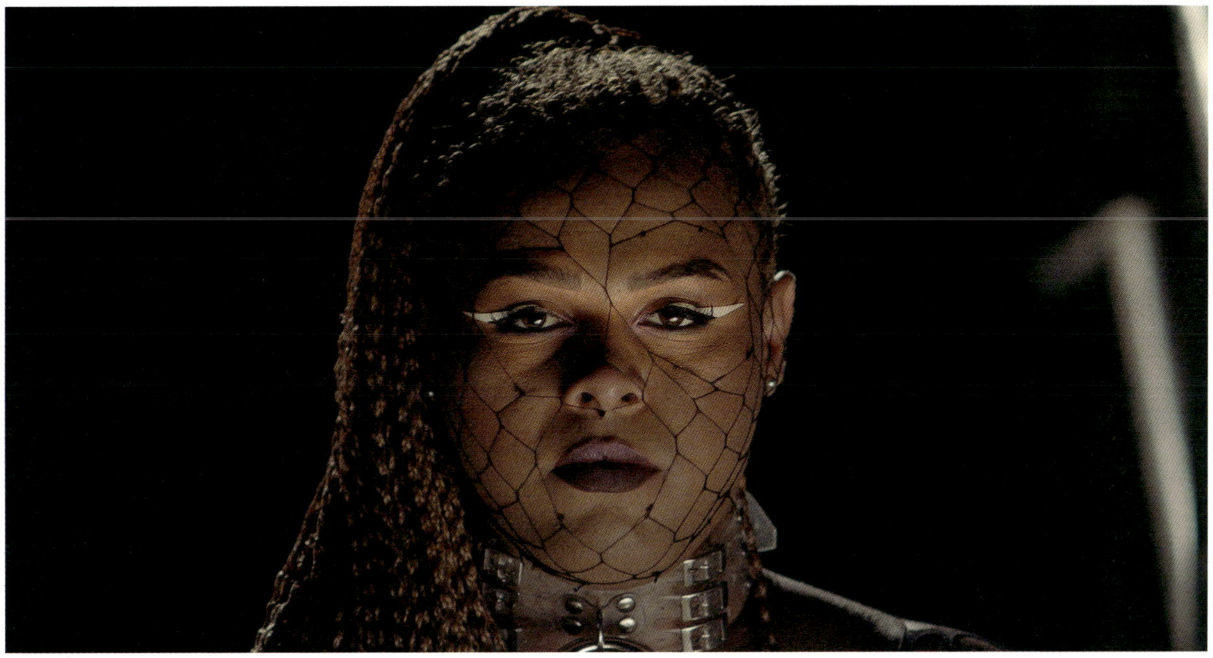

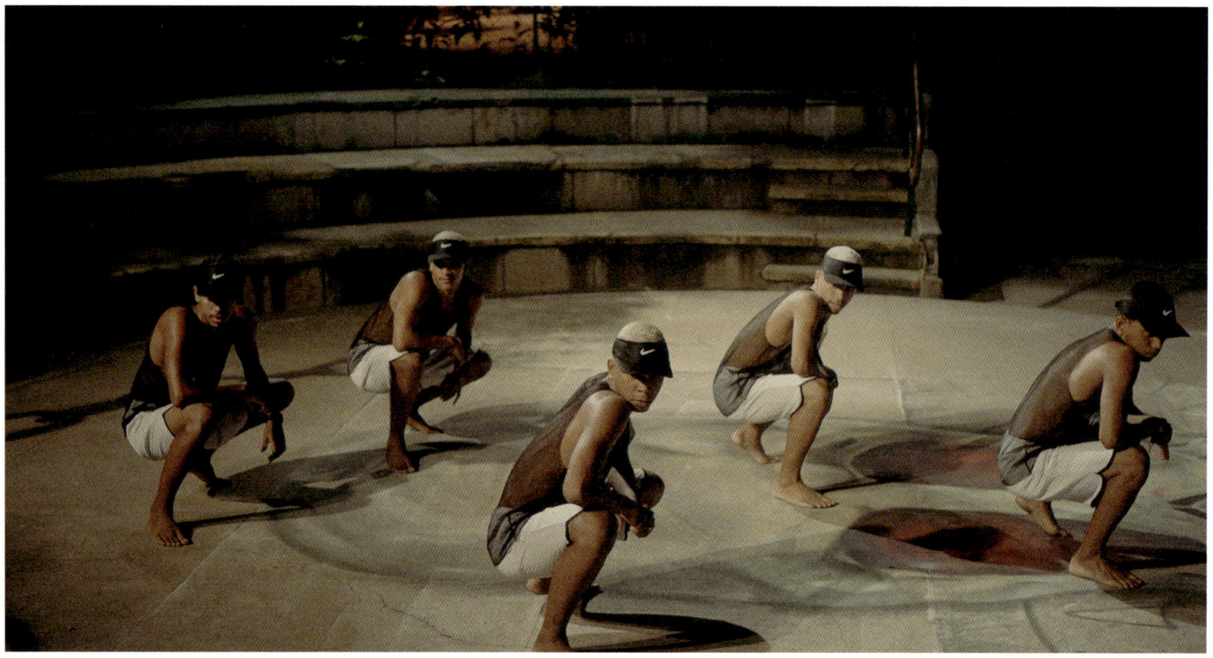

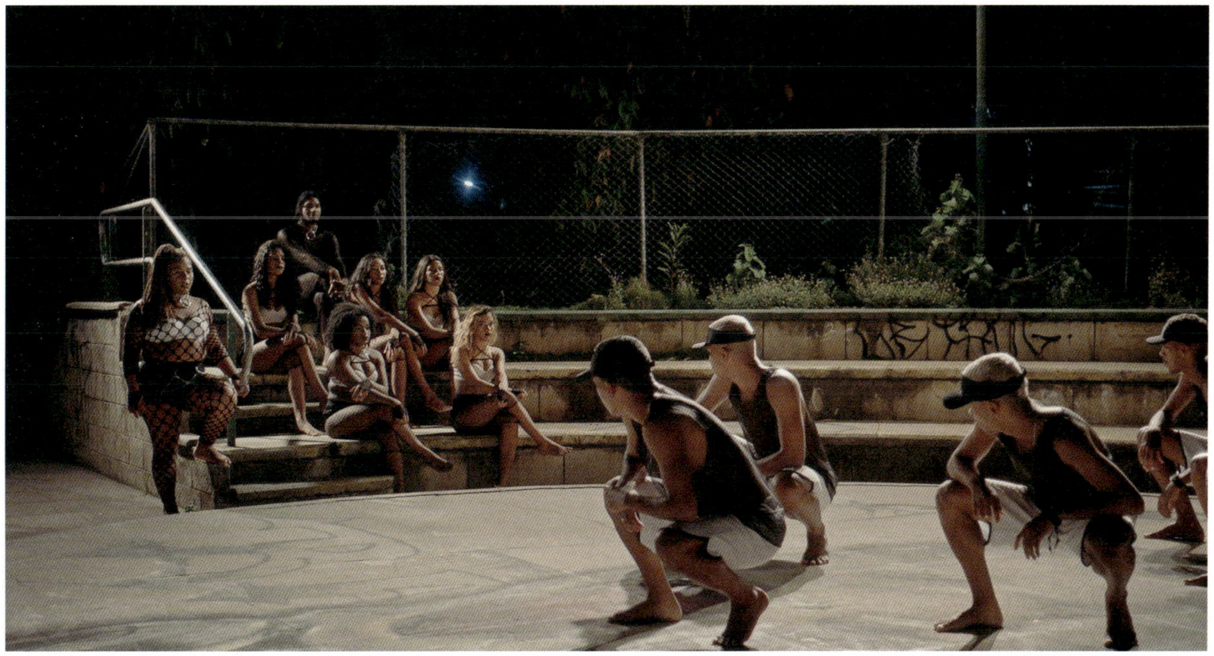

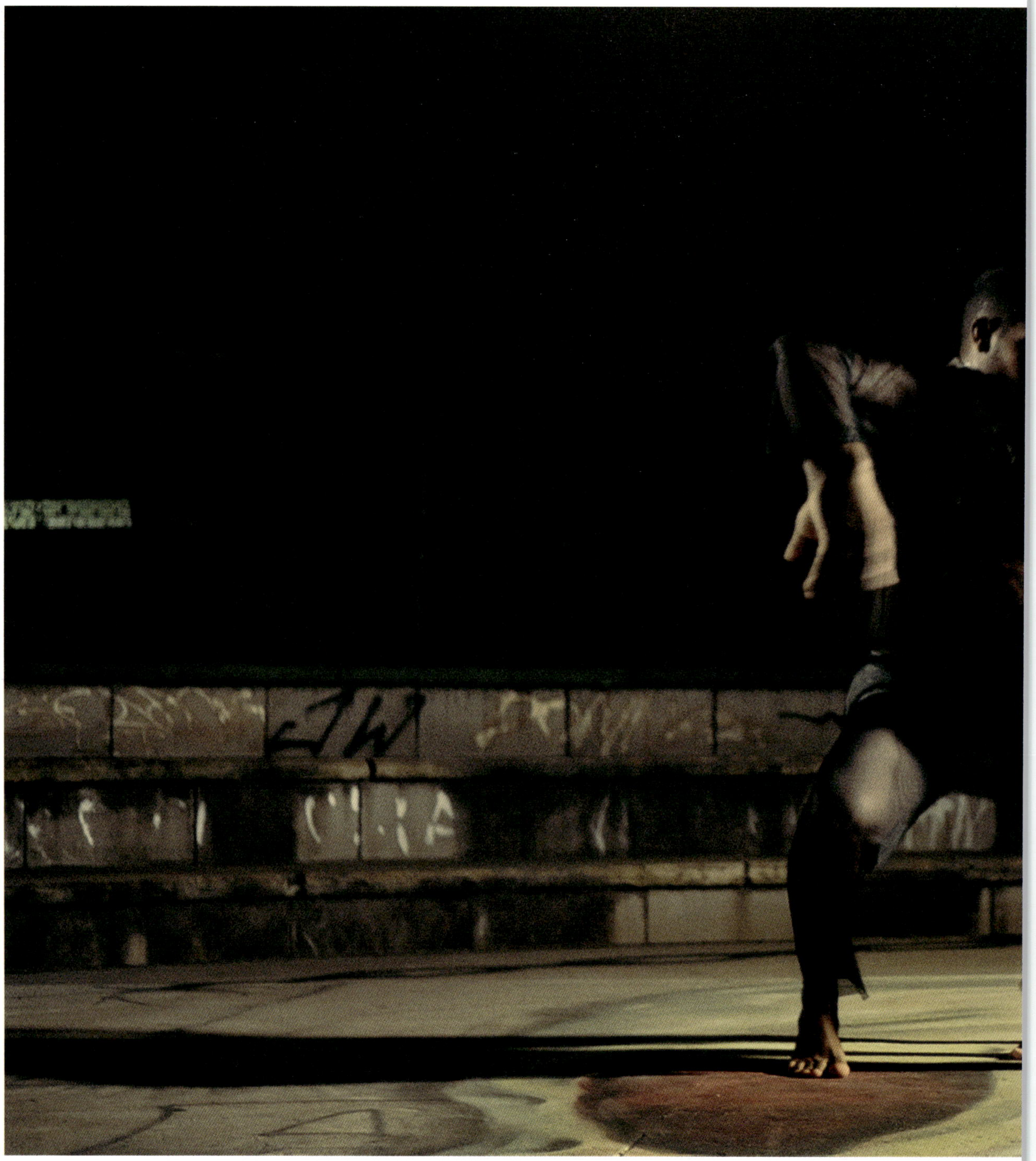

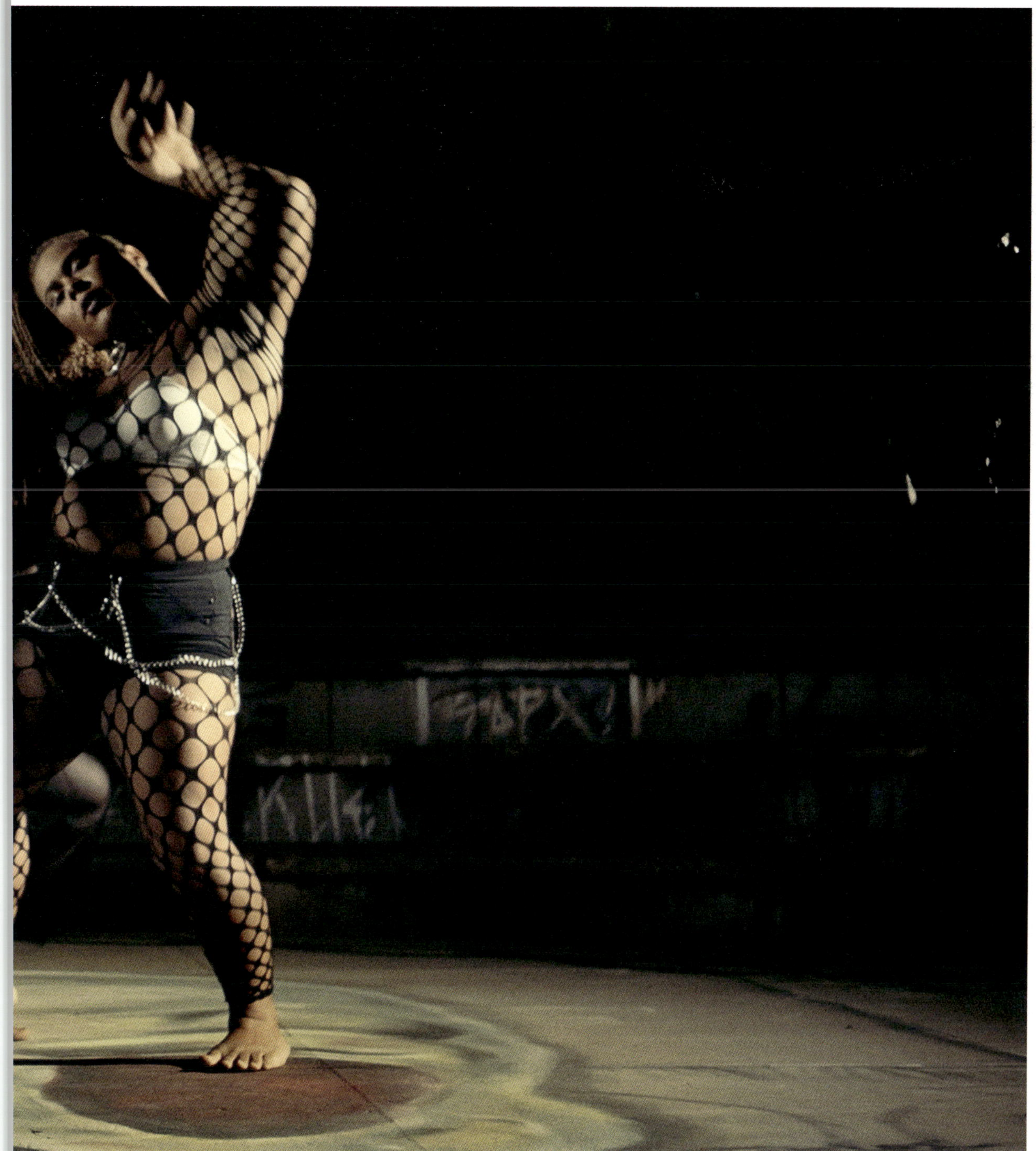

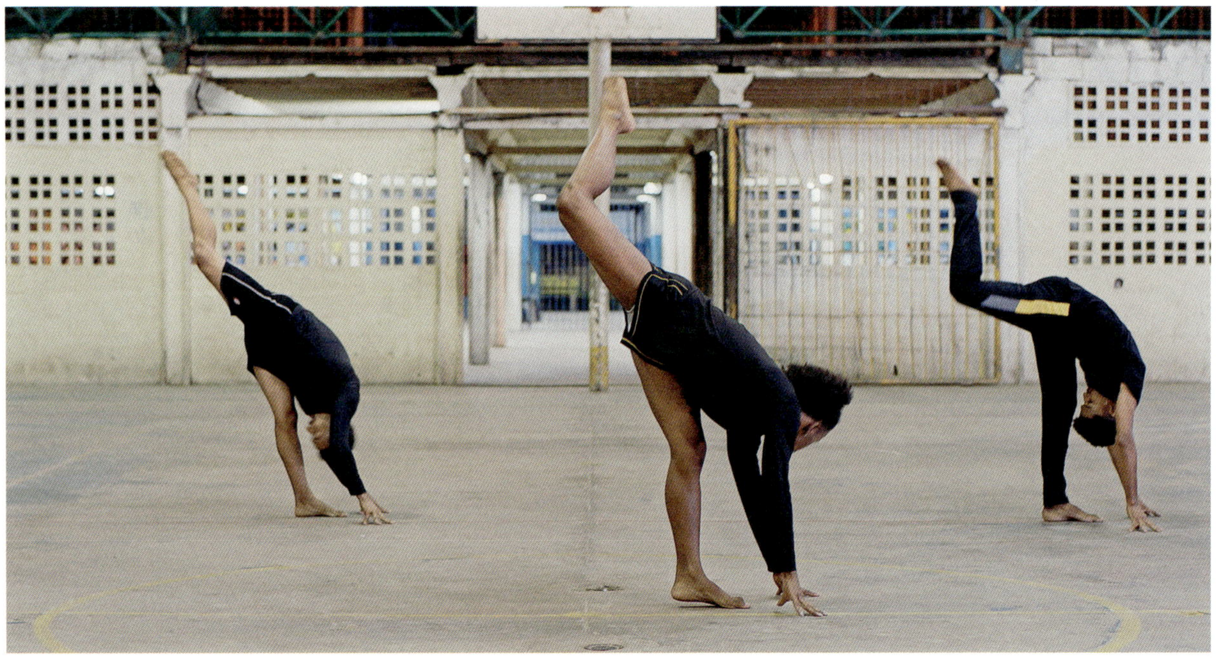

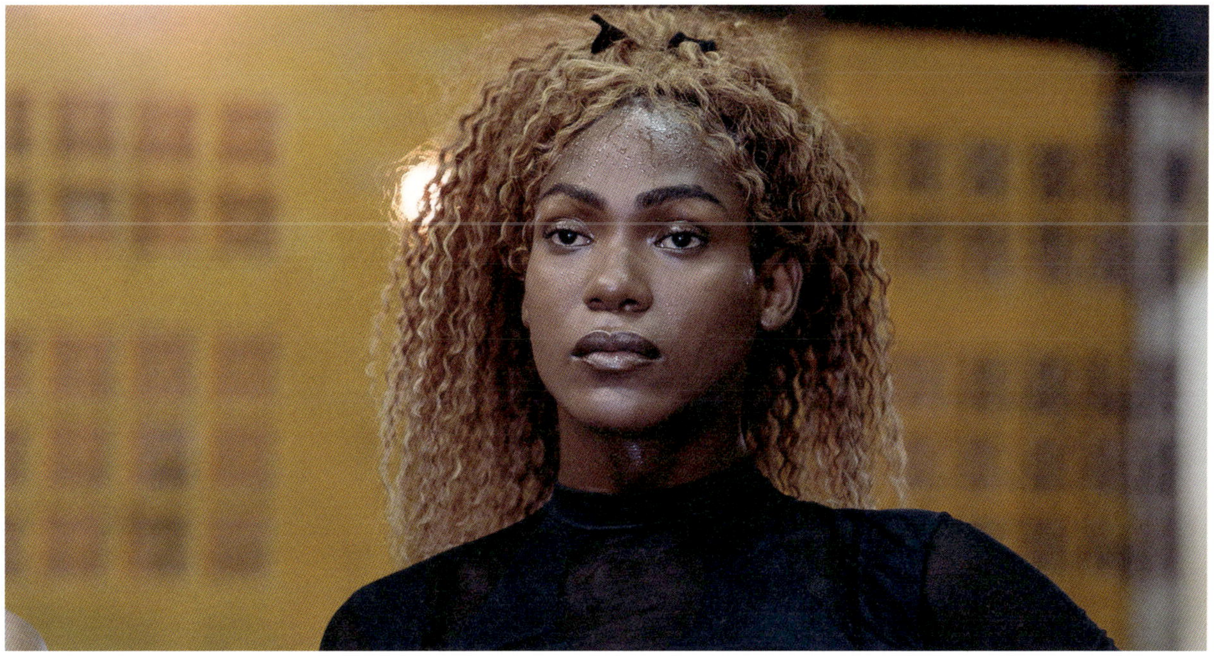

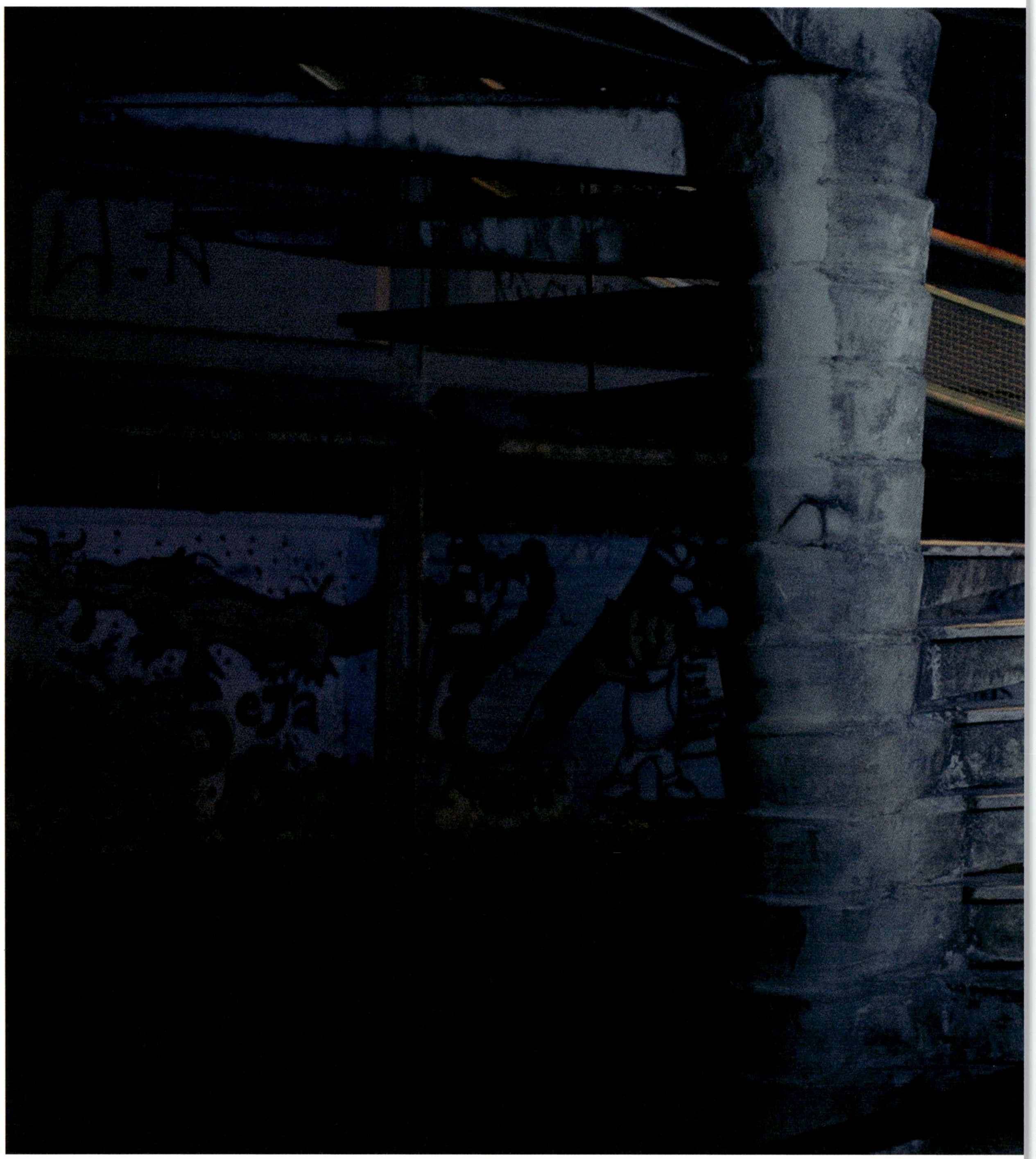

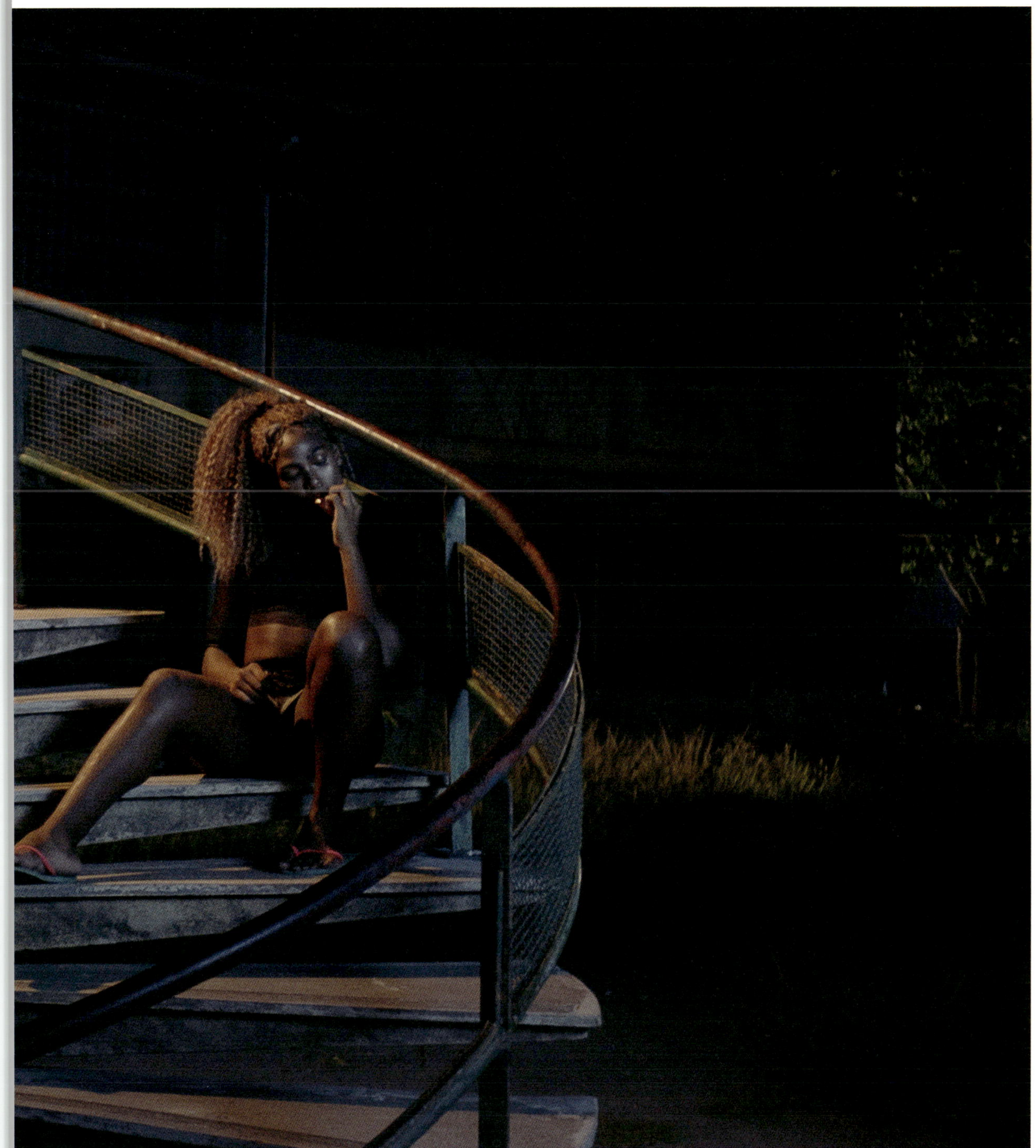

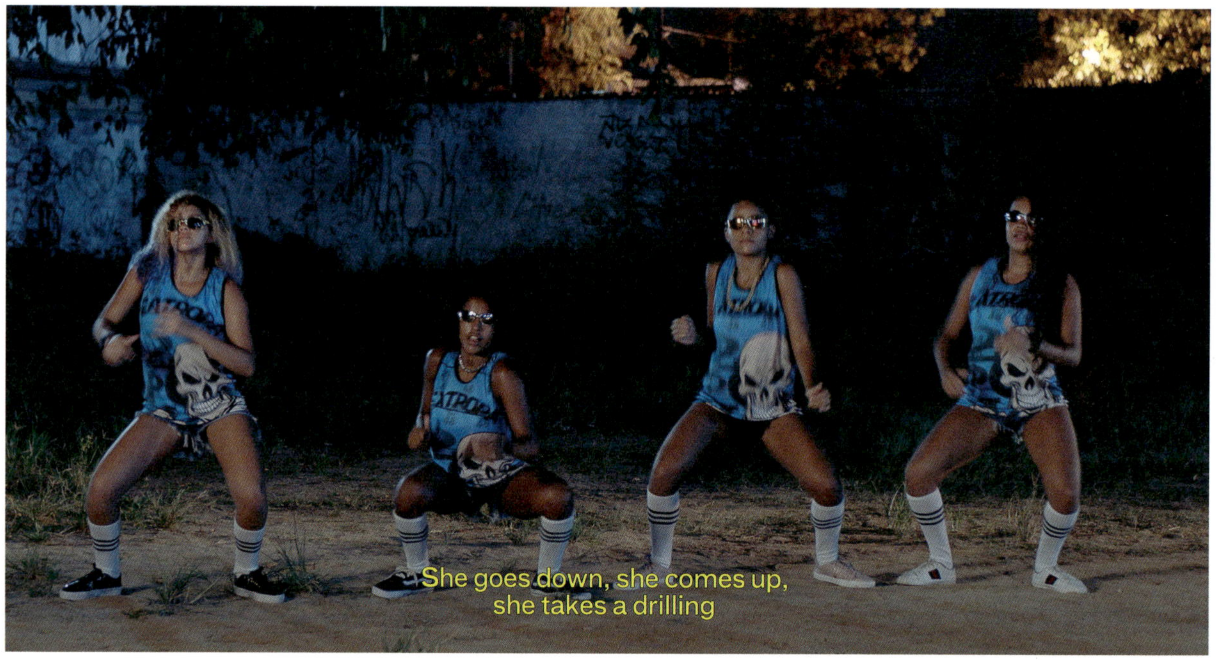
She goes down, she comes up,
she takes a drilling

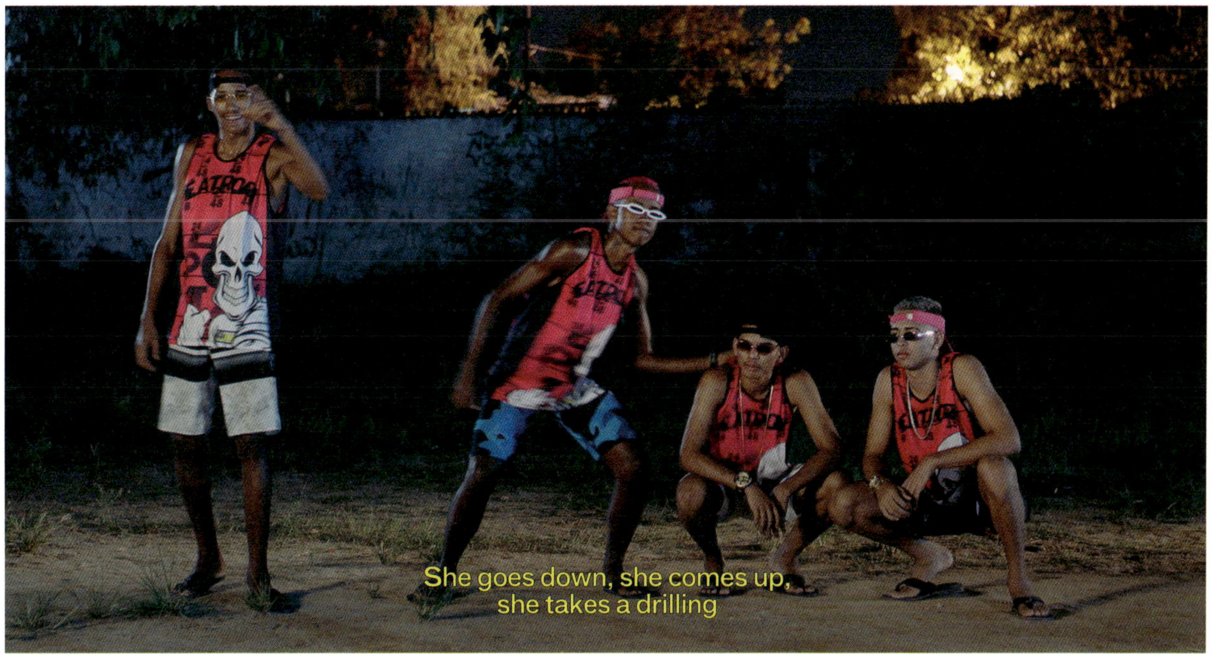
She goes down, she comes up,
she takes a drilling

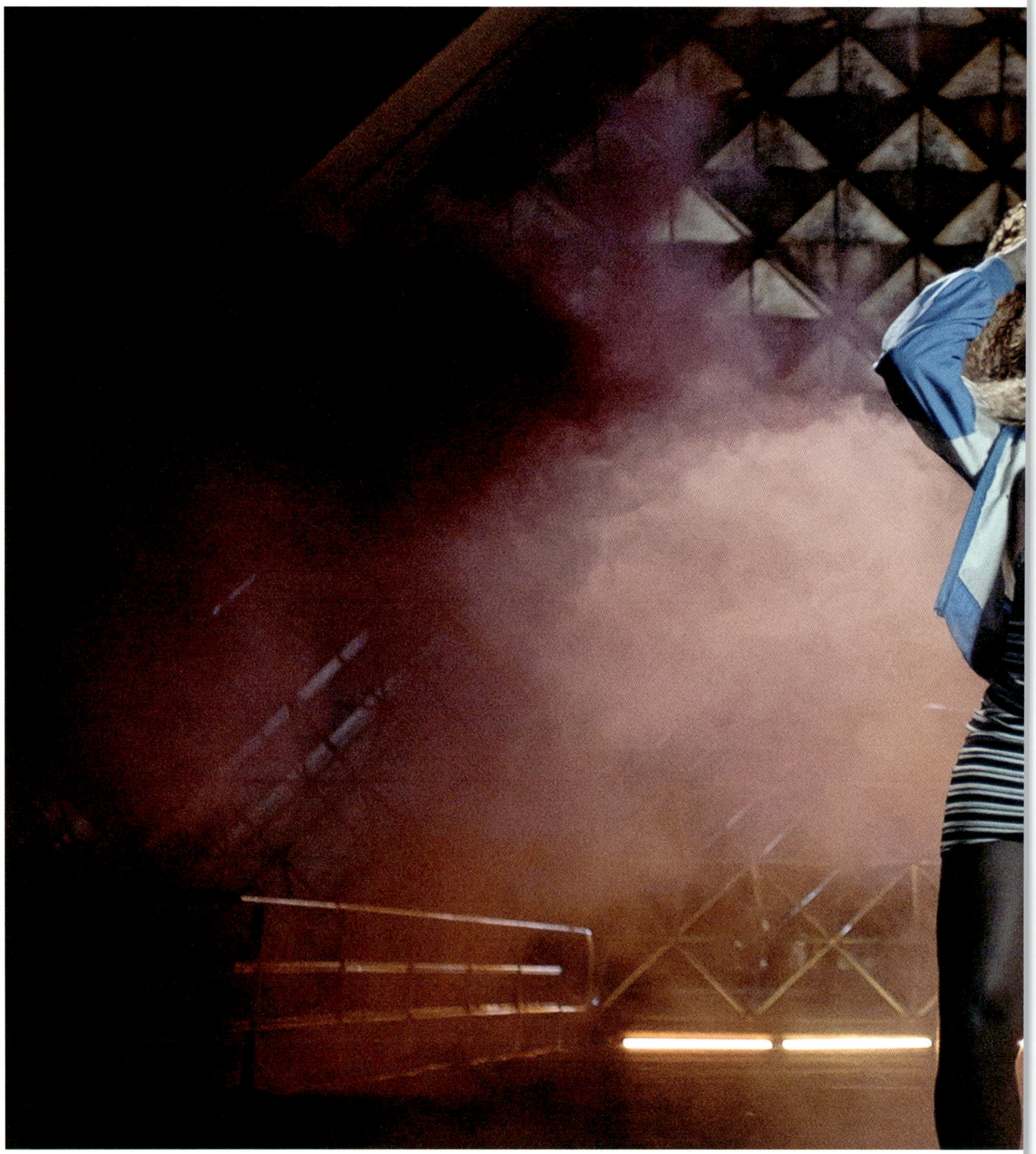

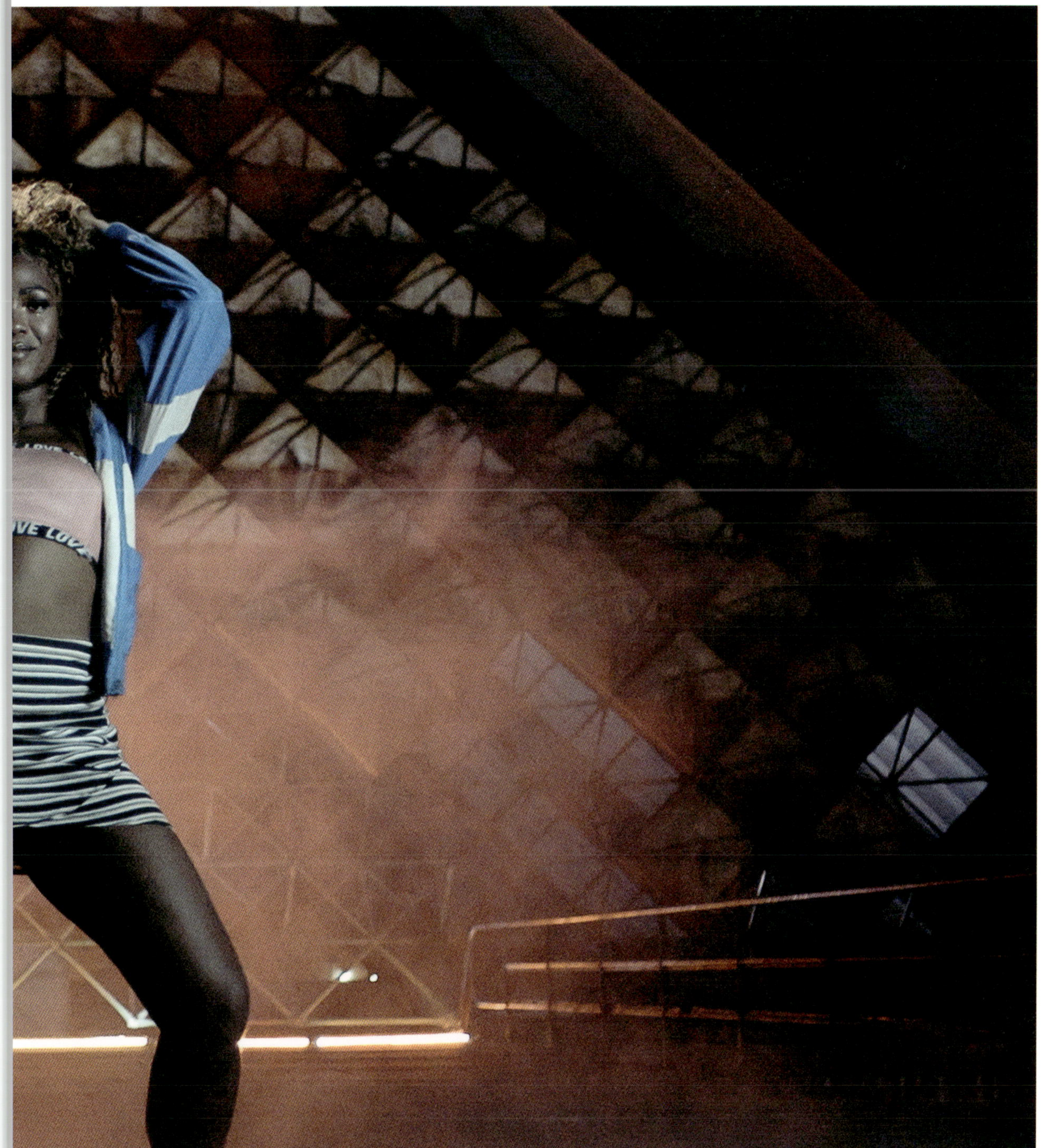

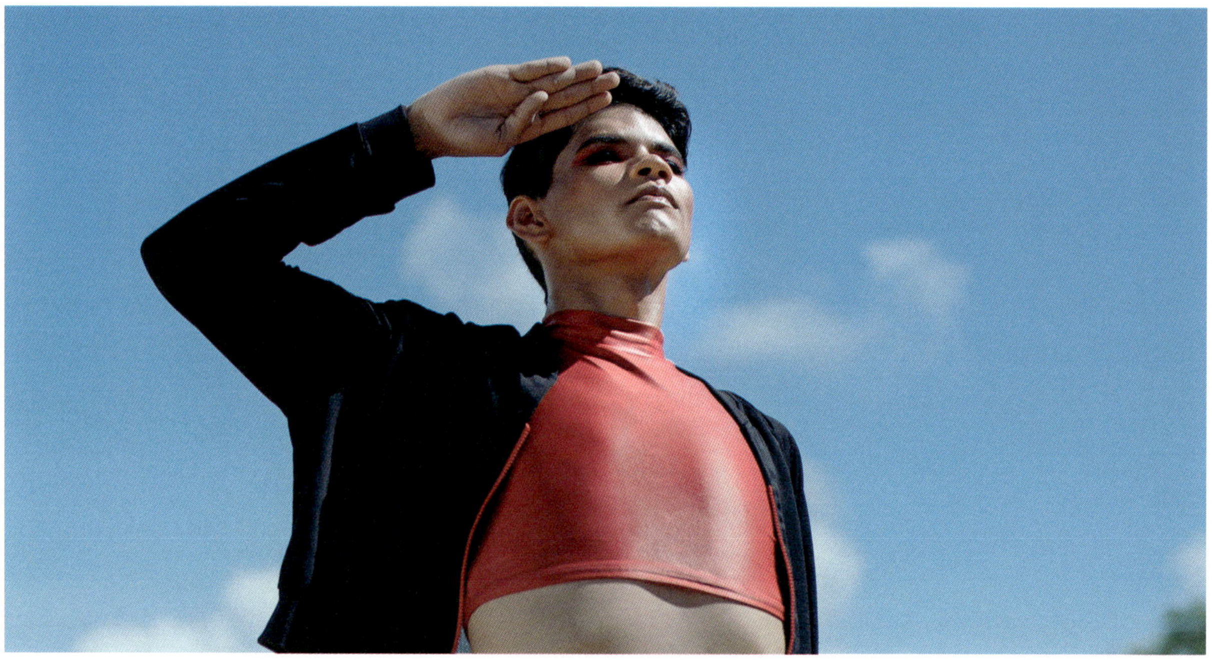

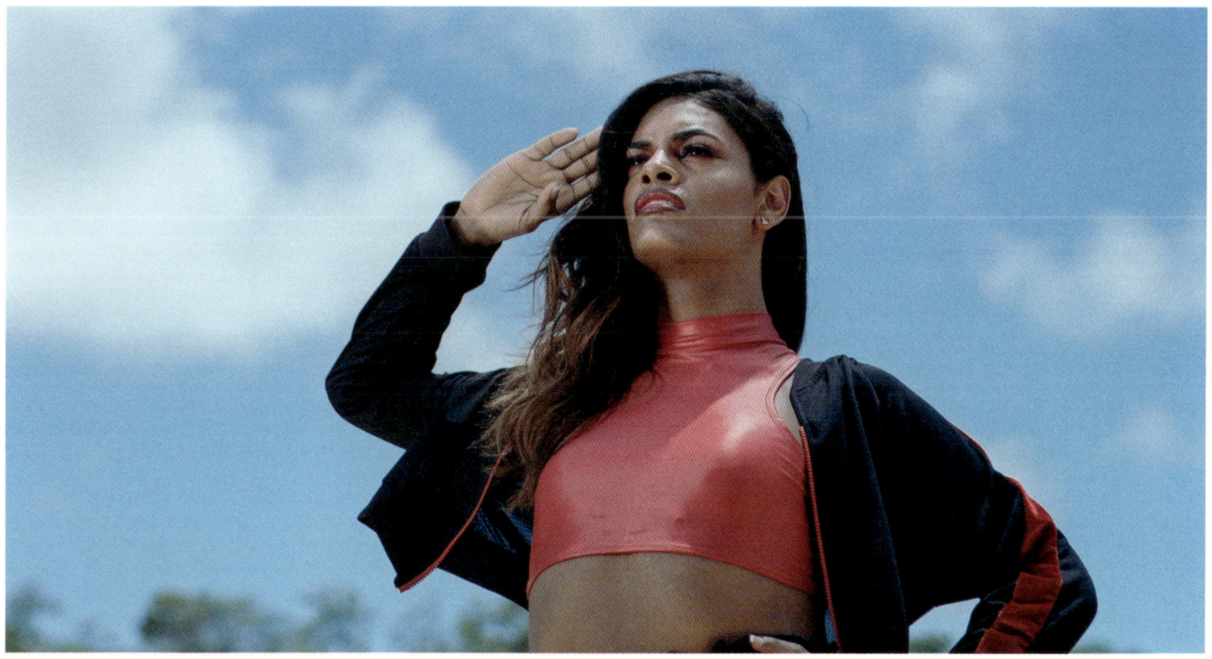

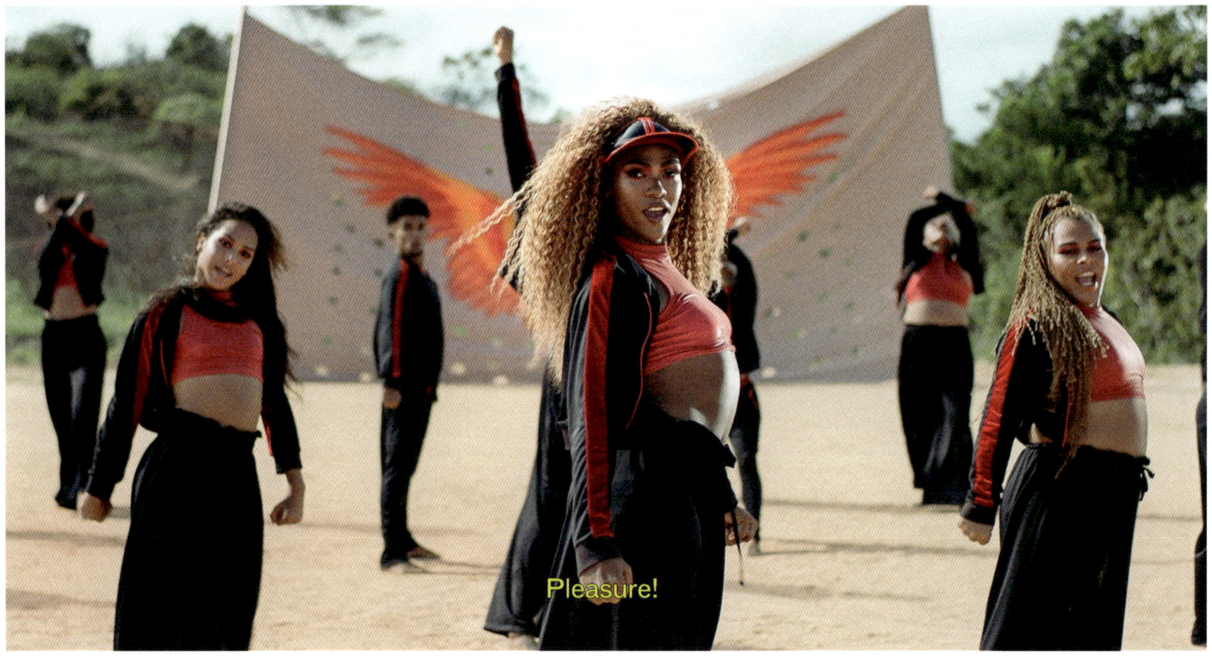
Pleasure!

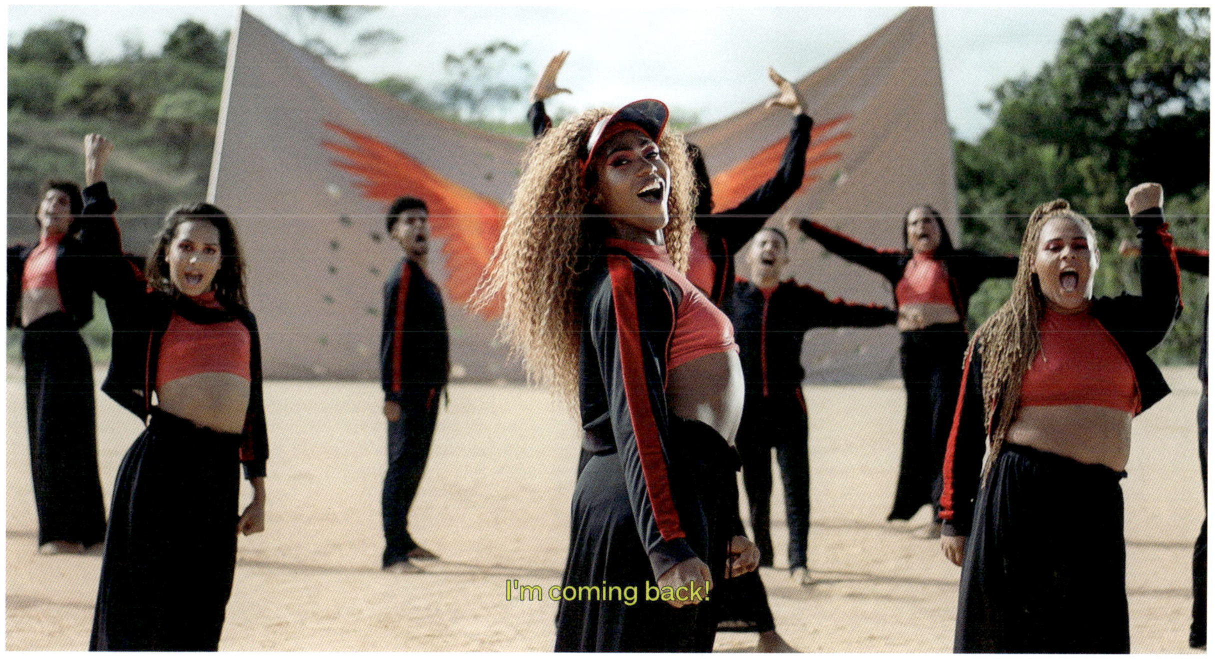
I'm coming back!

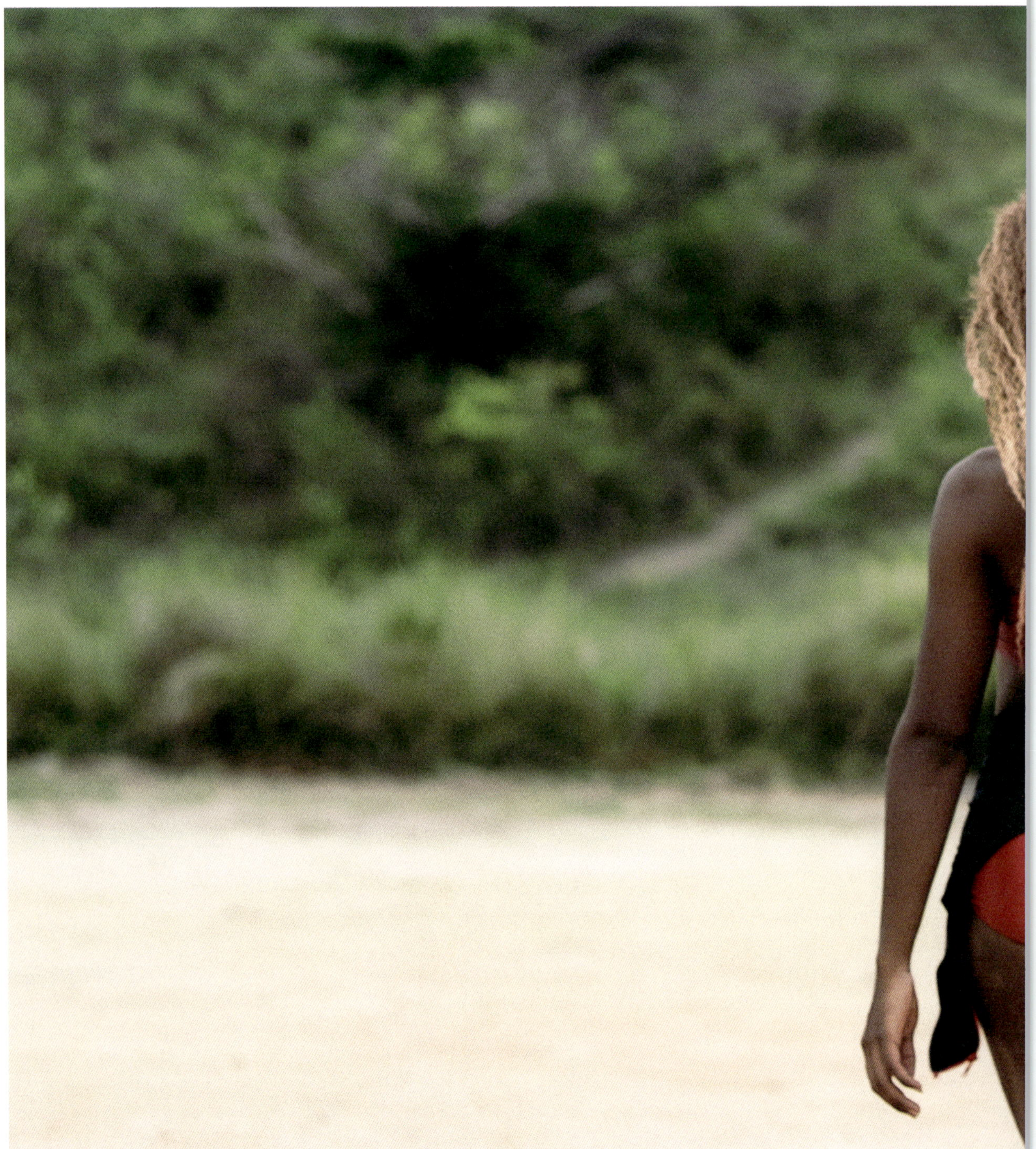

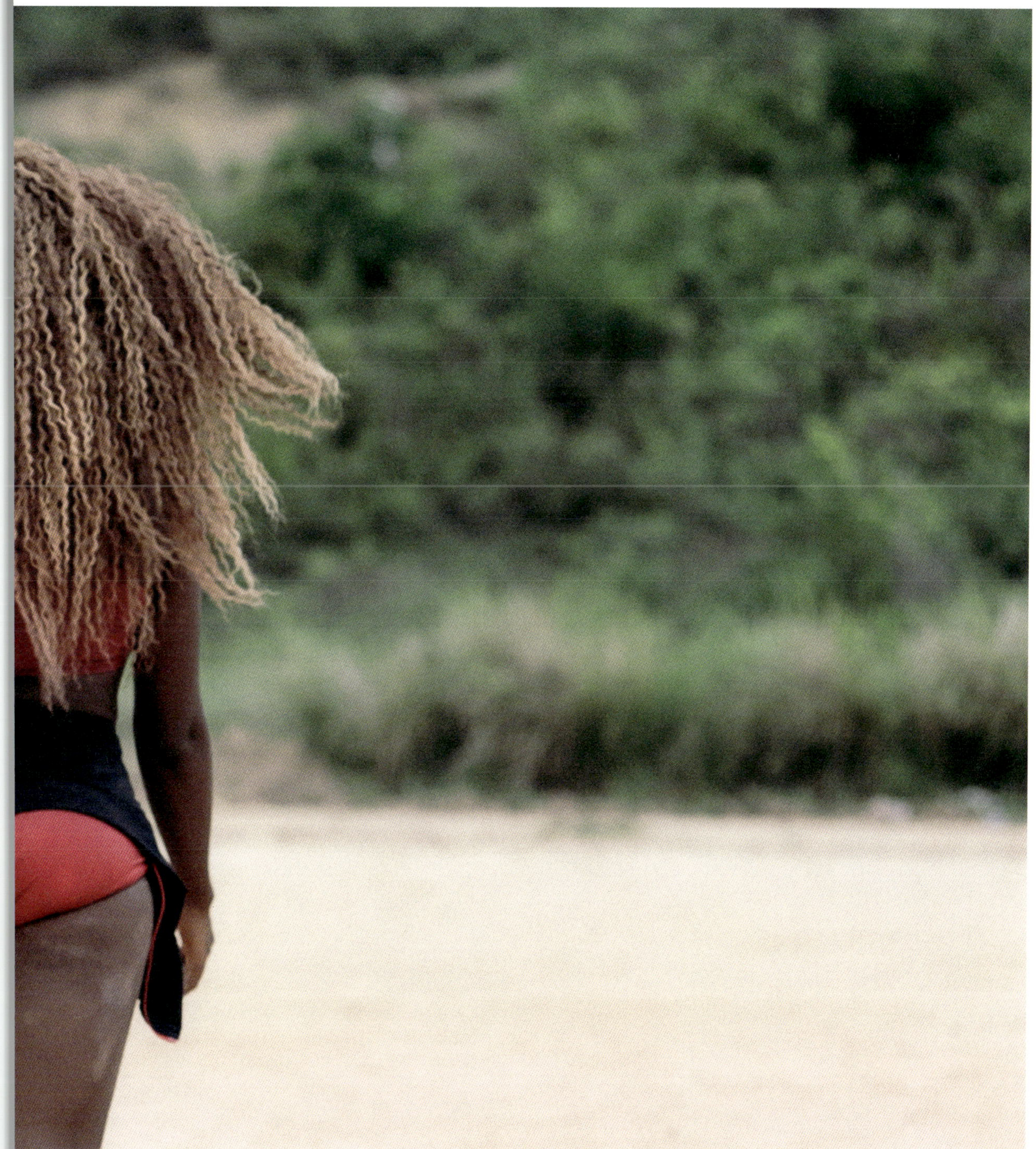

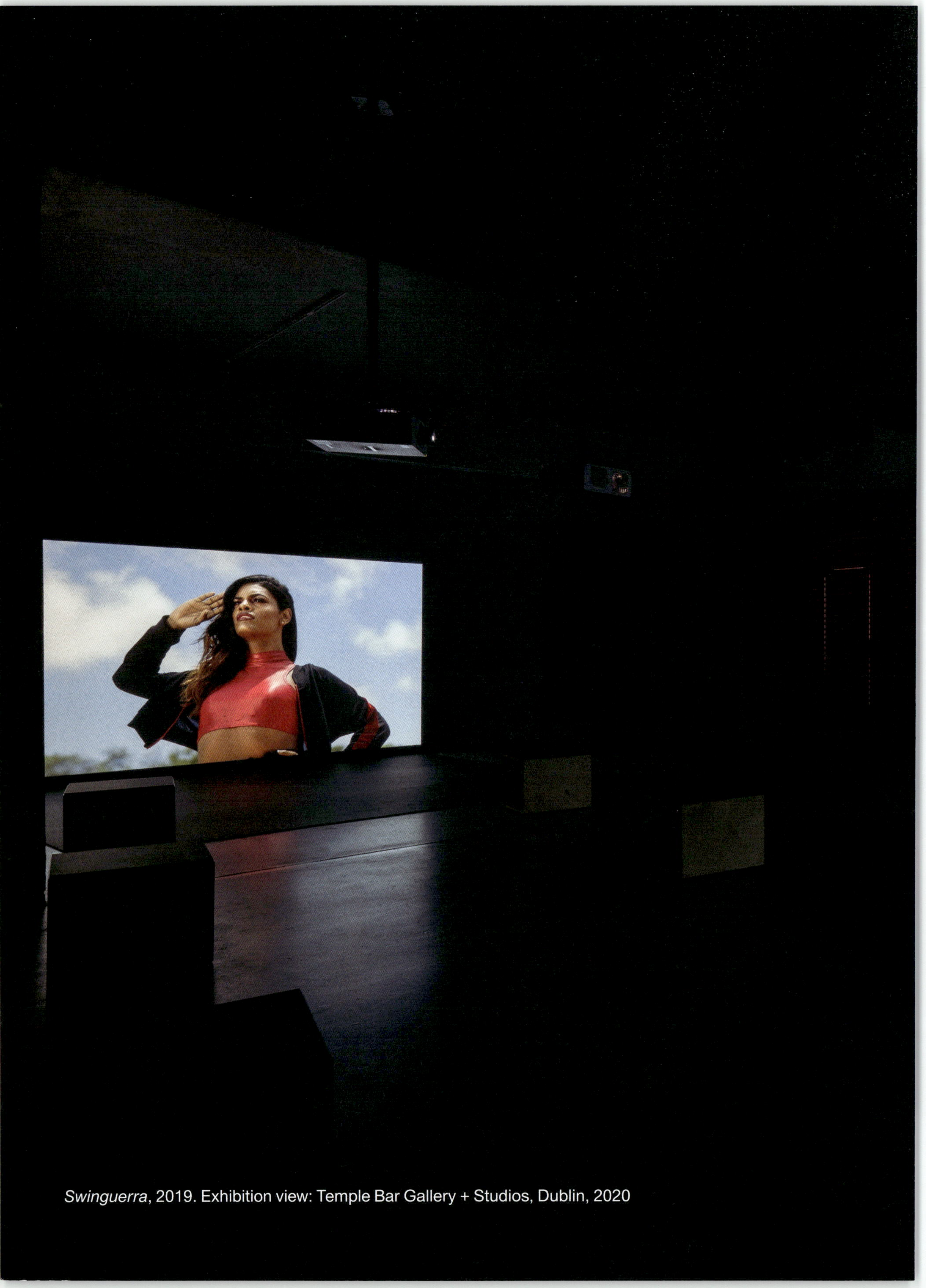

Swinguerra, 2019. Exhibition view: Temple Bar Gallery + Studios, Dublin, 2020

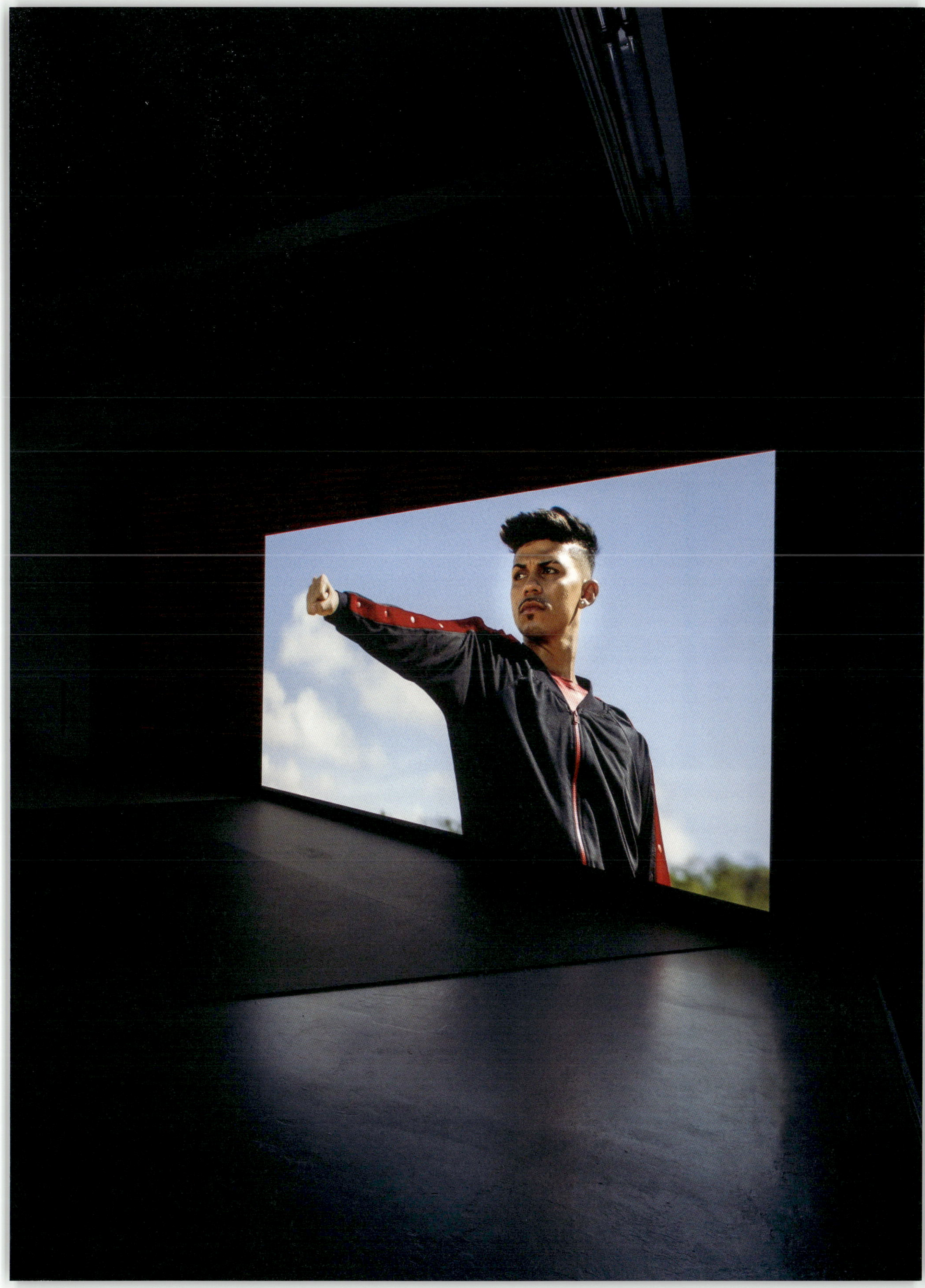

Fala da Terra
[Voice of the Land],
2022

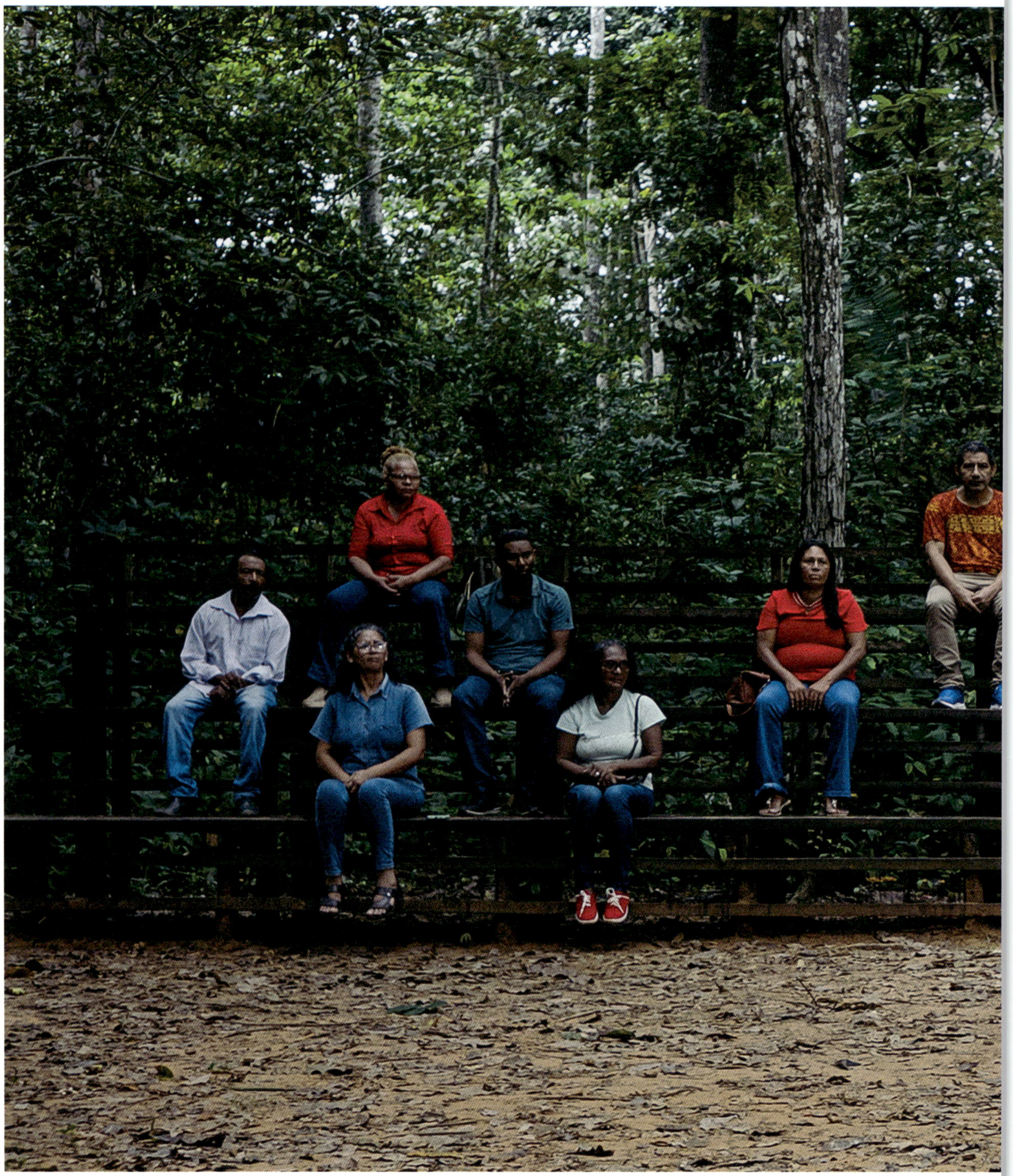

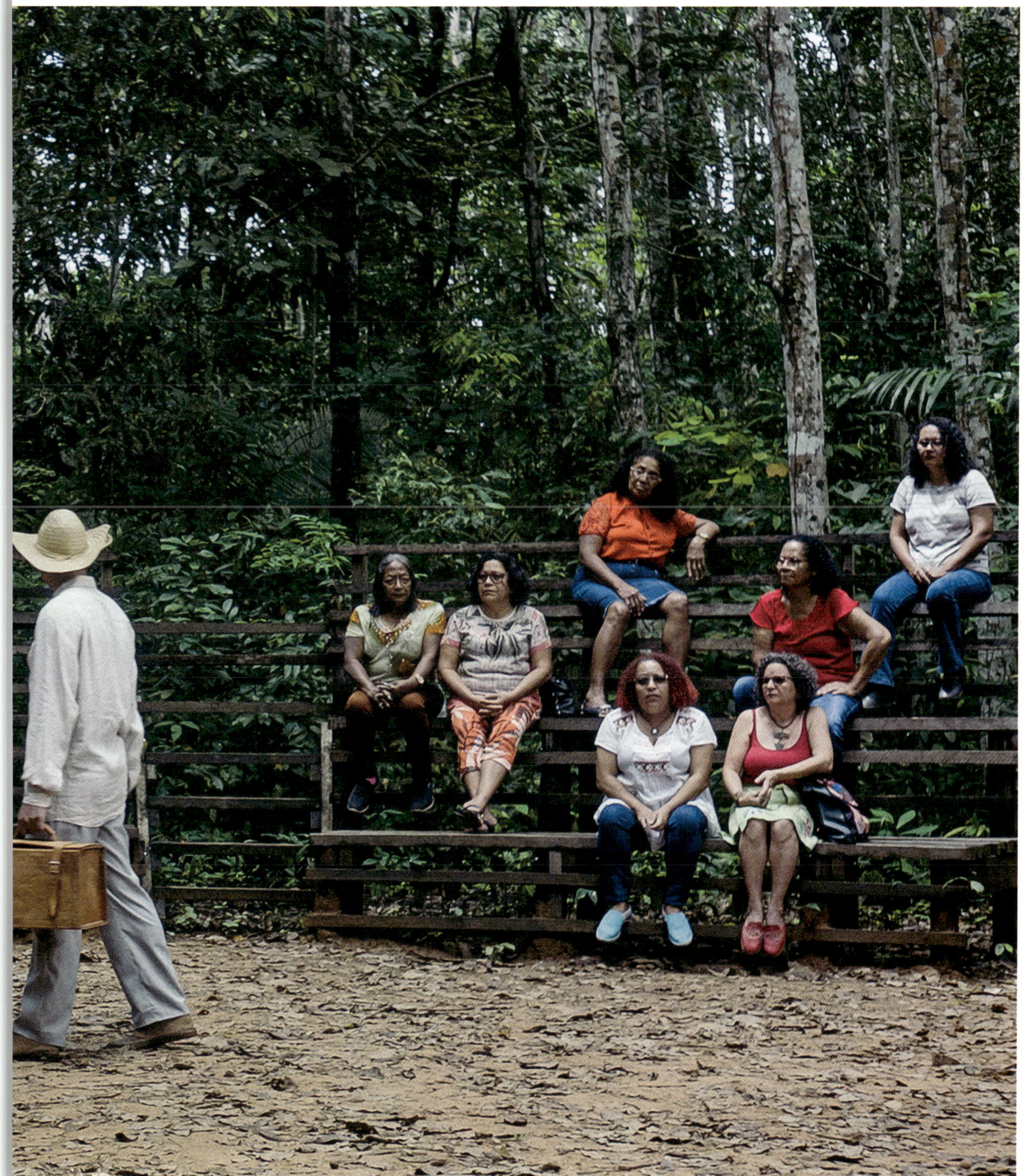

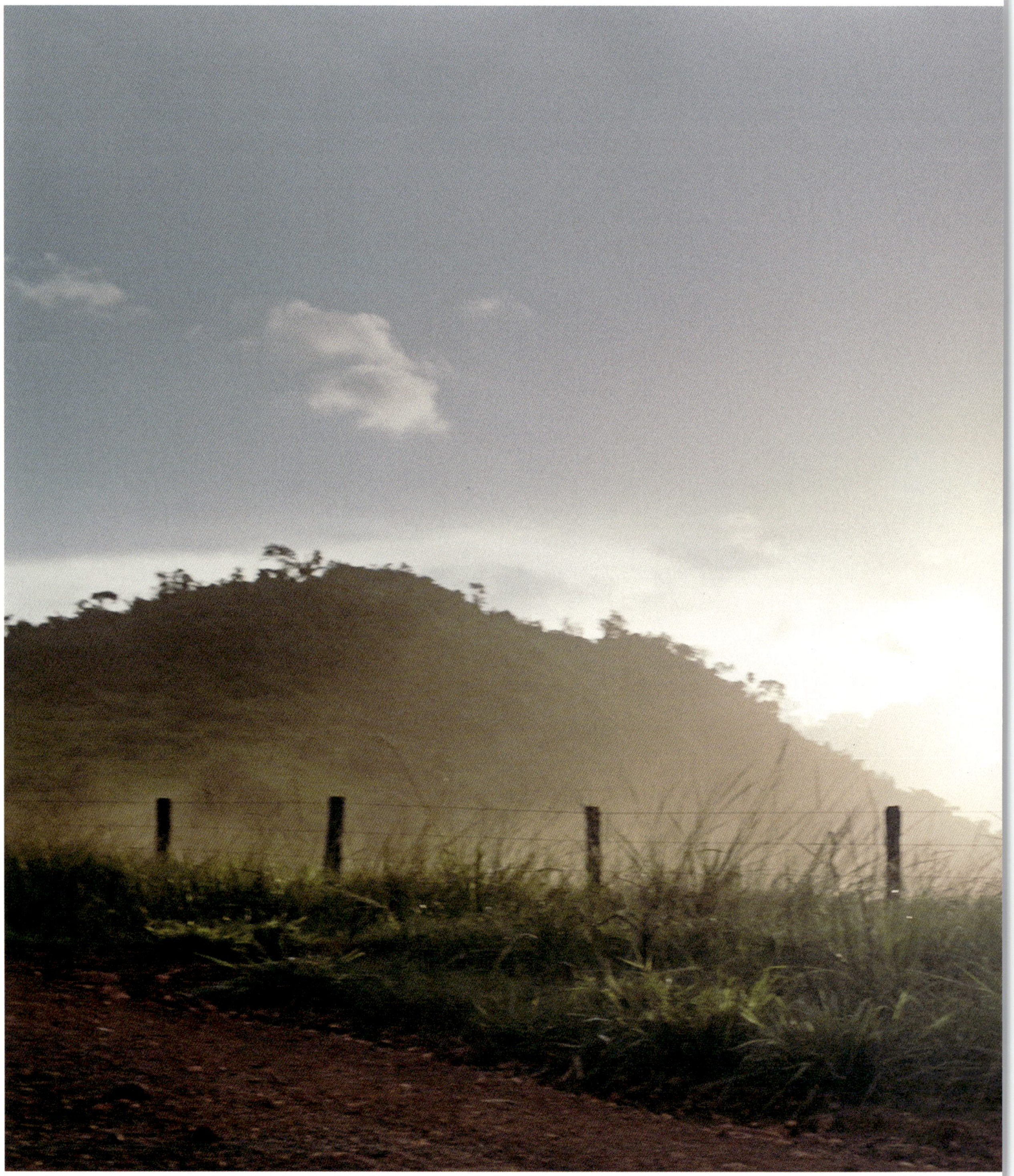

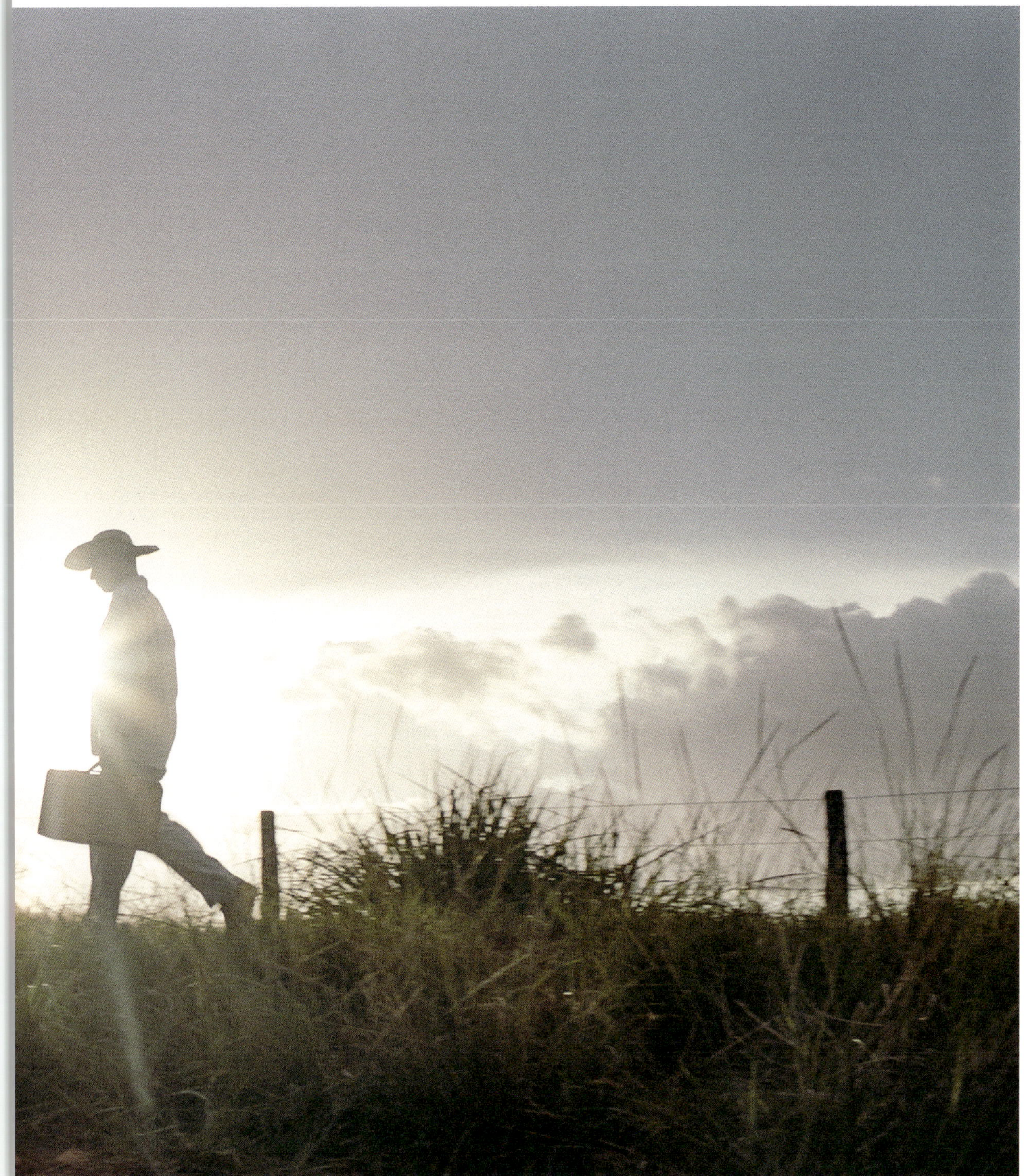

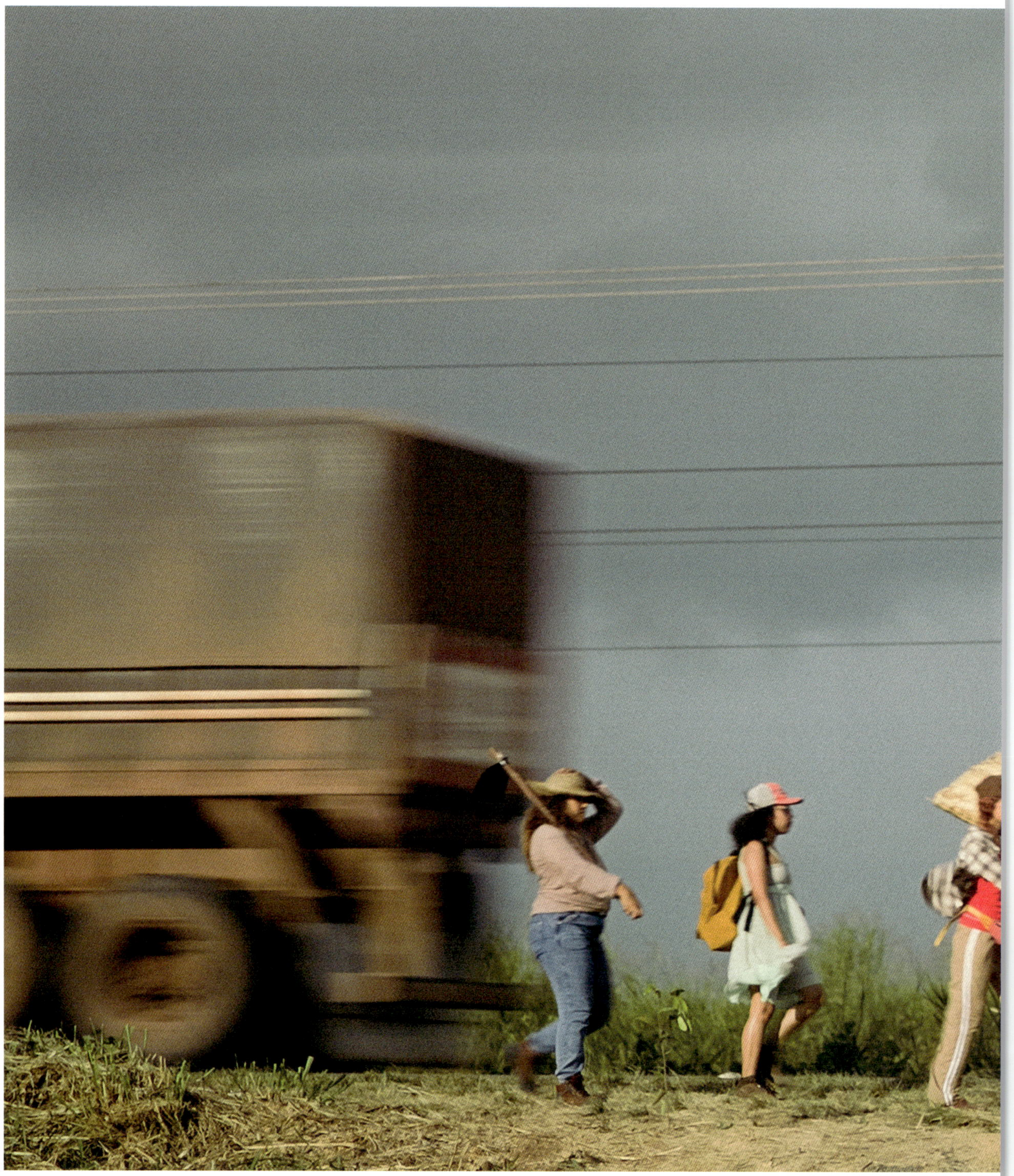

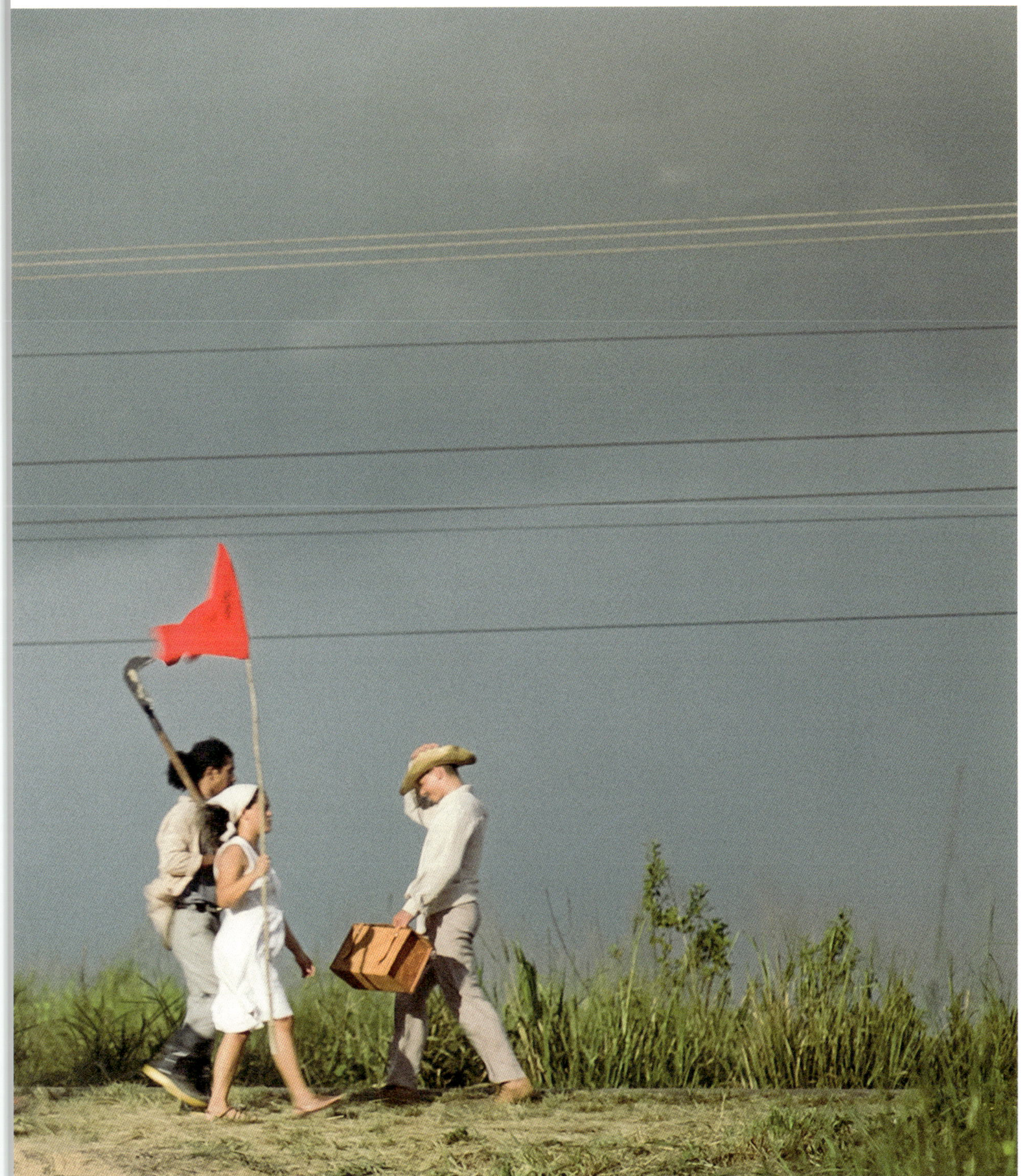

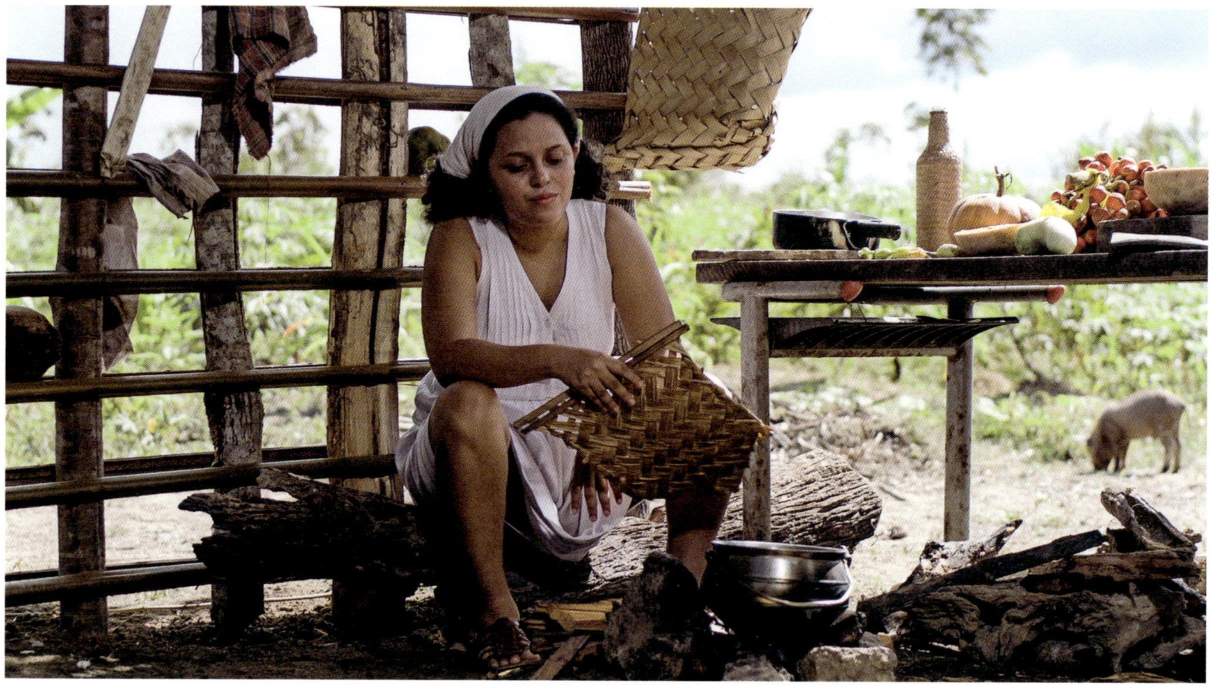

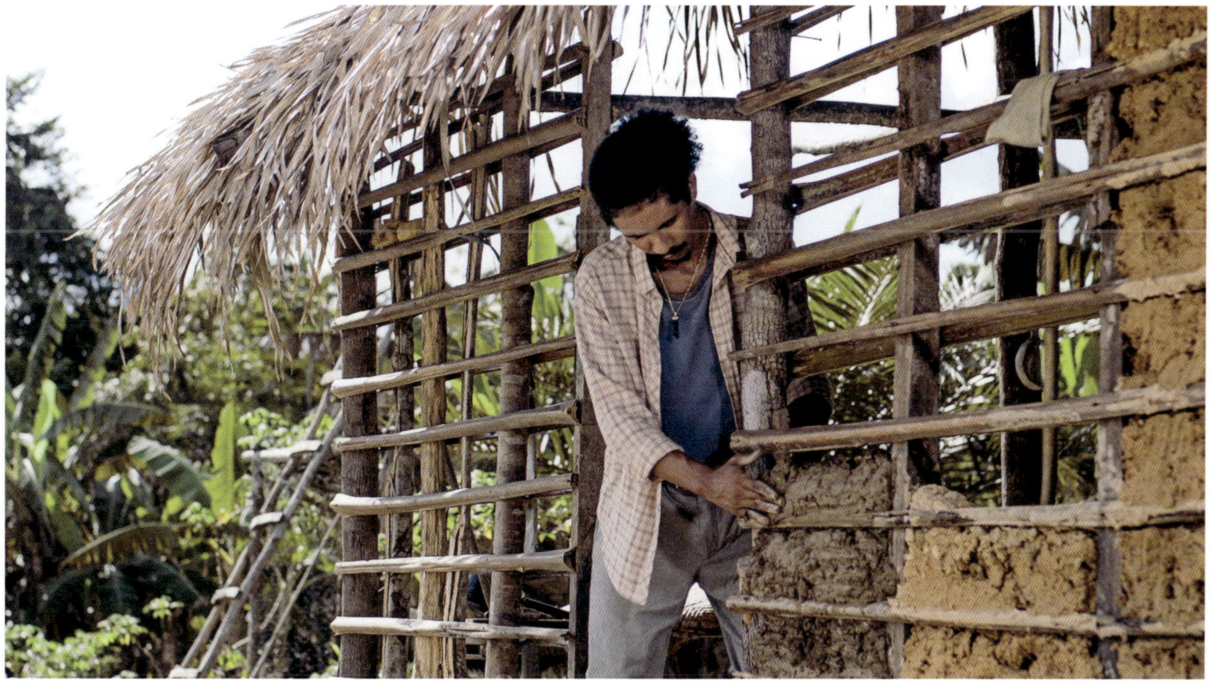

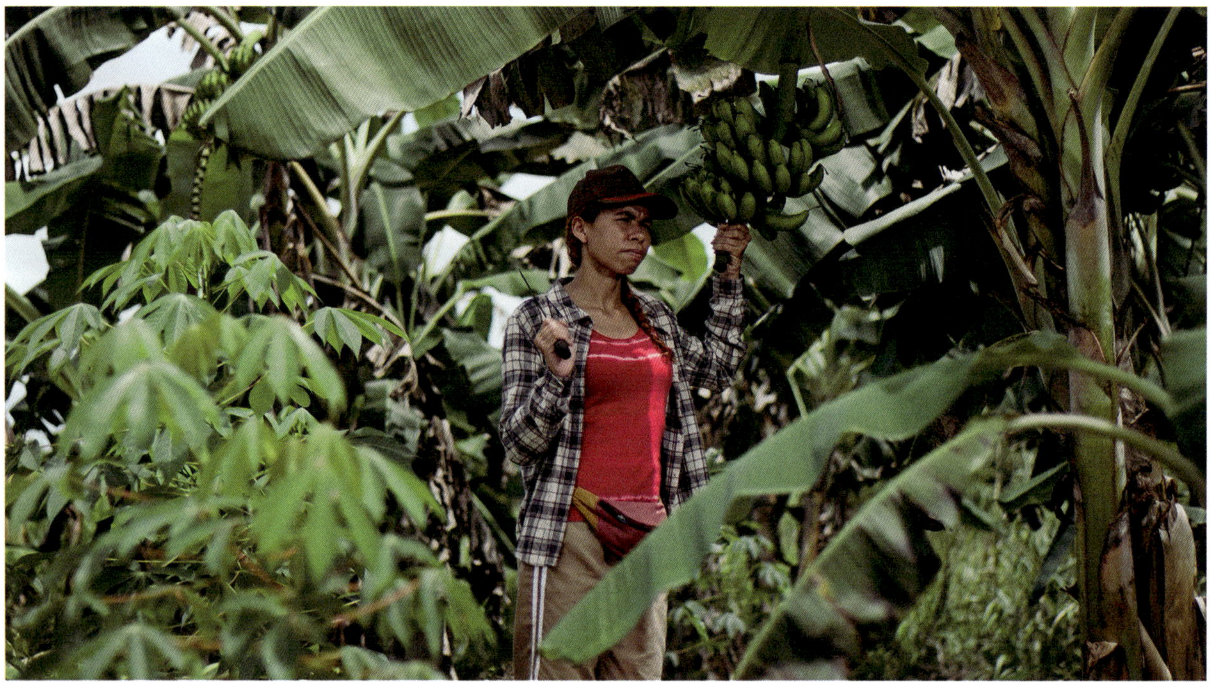

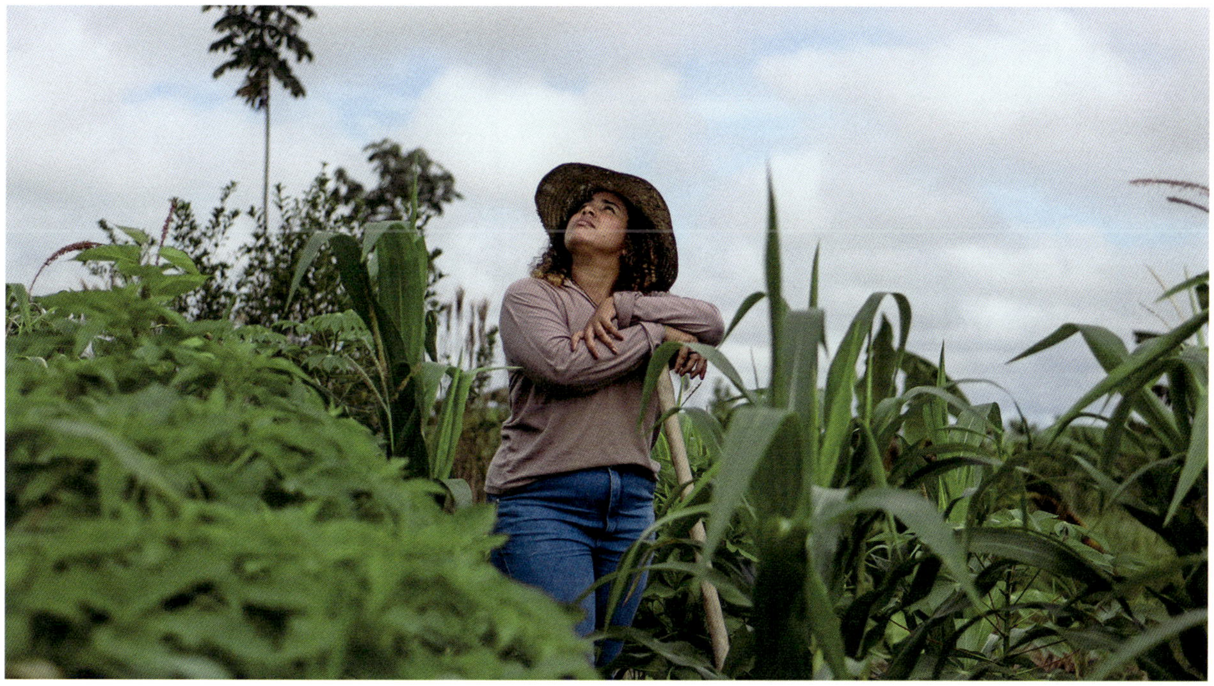

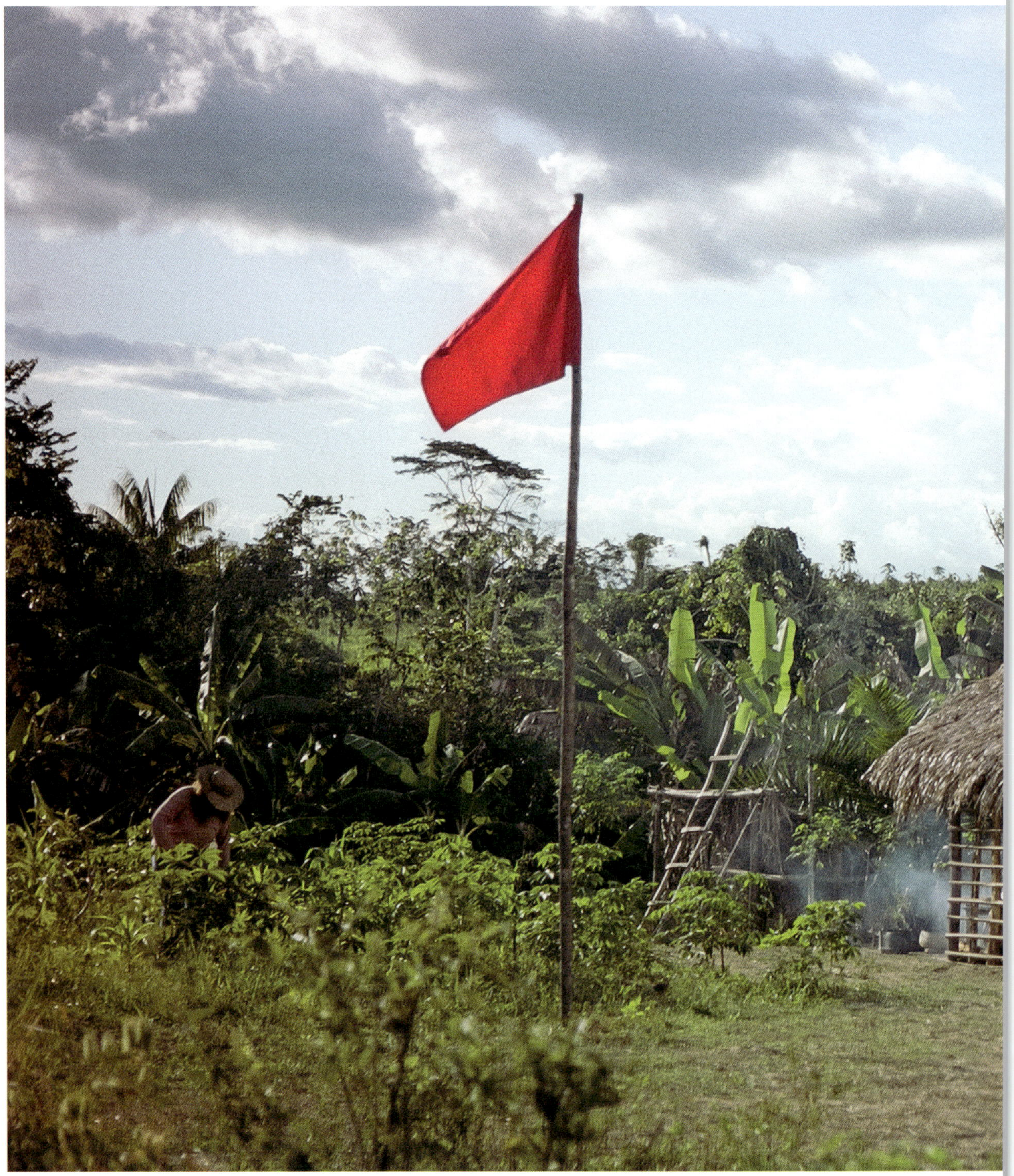

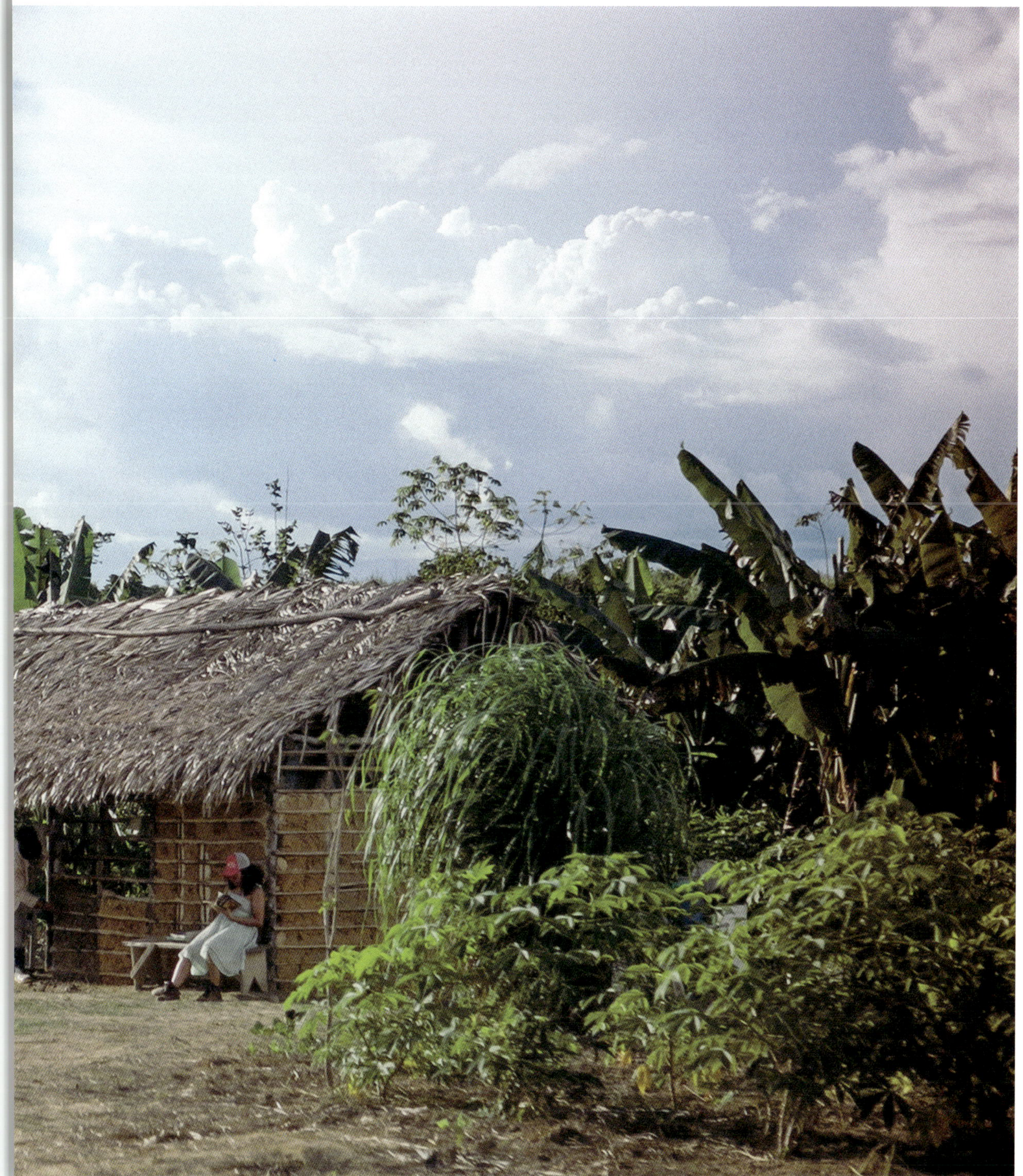

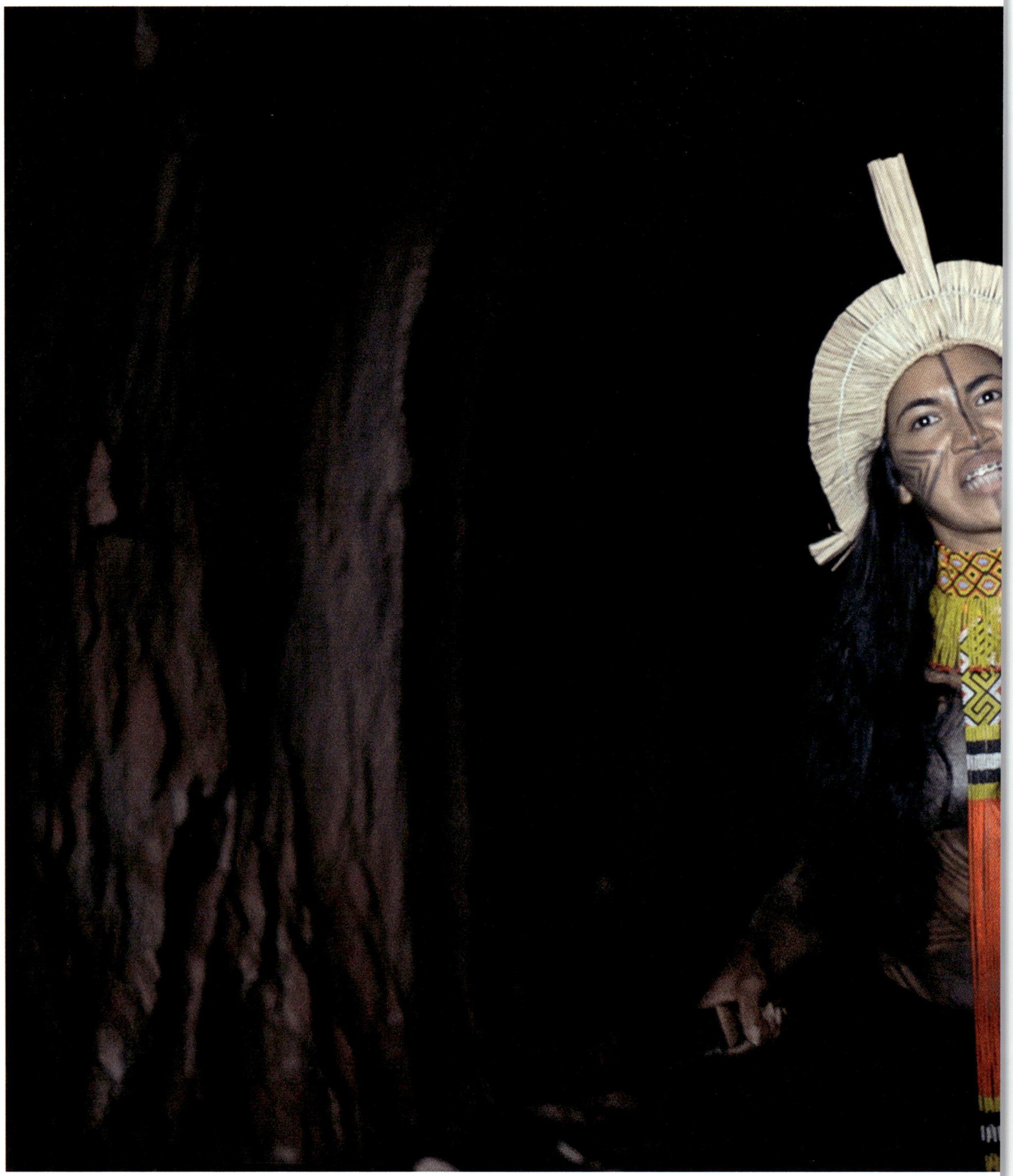

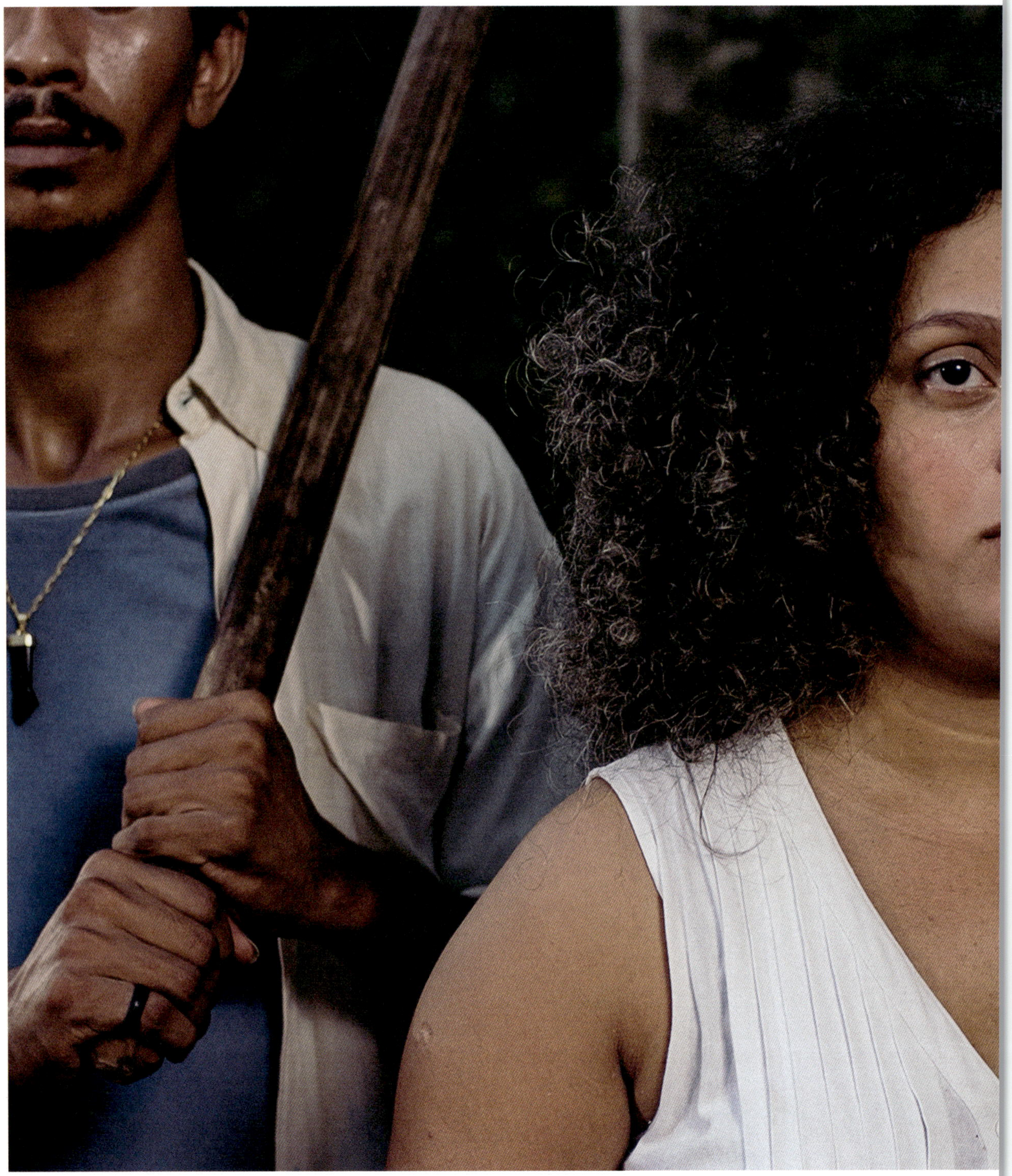

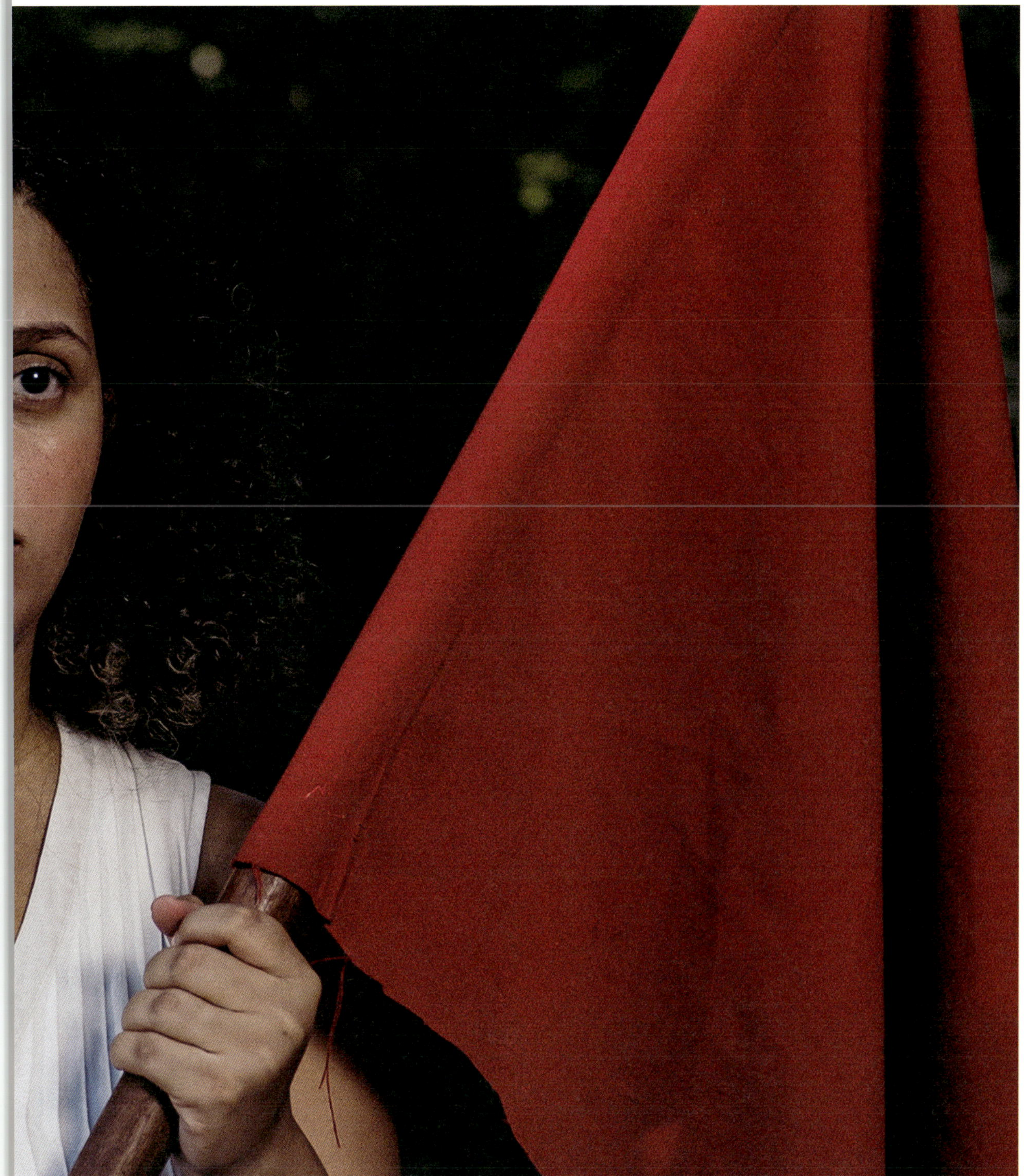

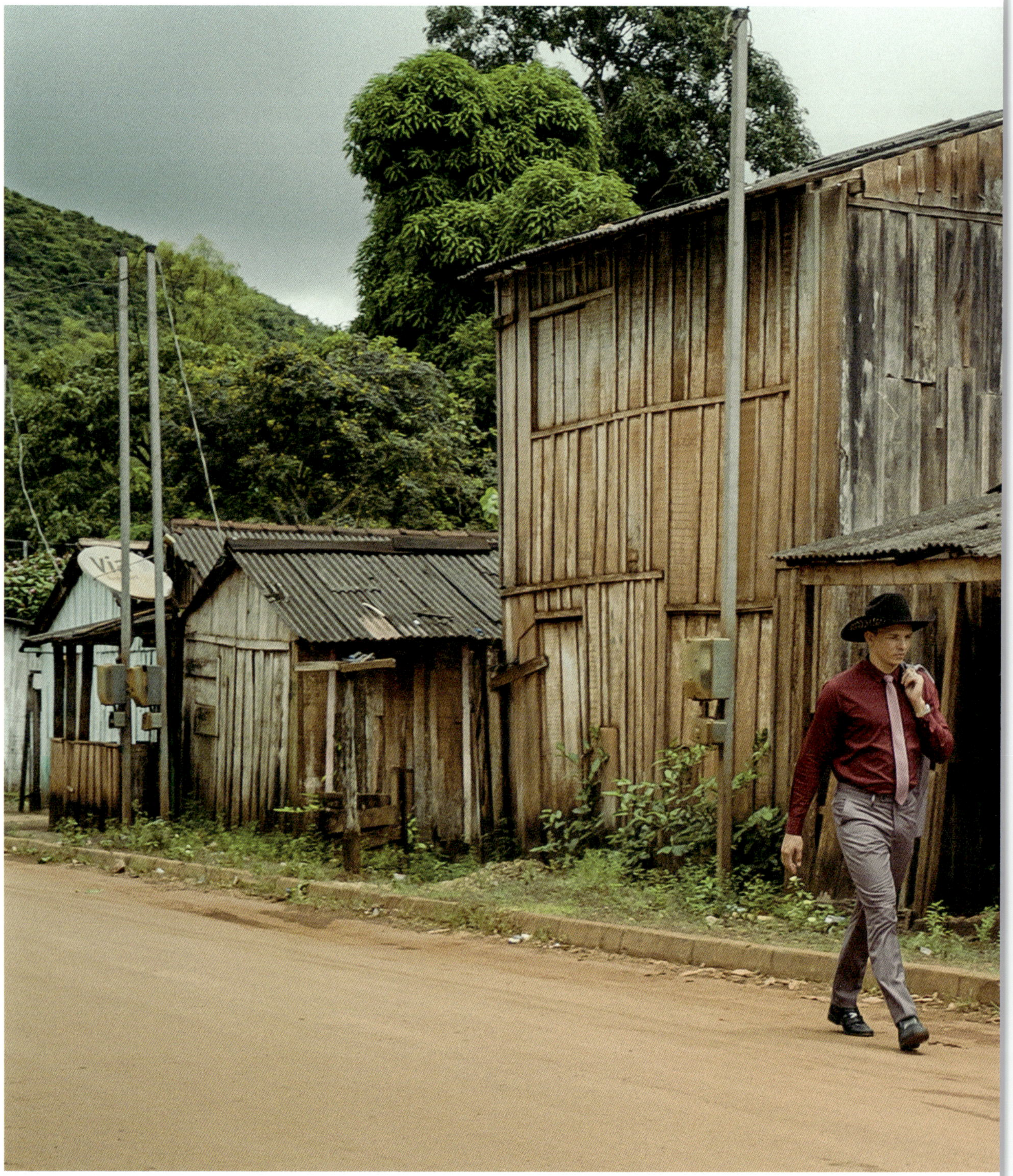

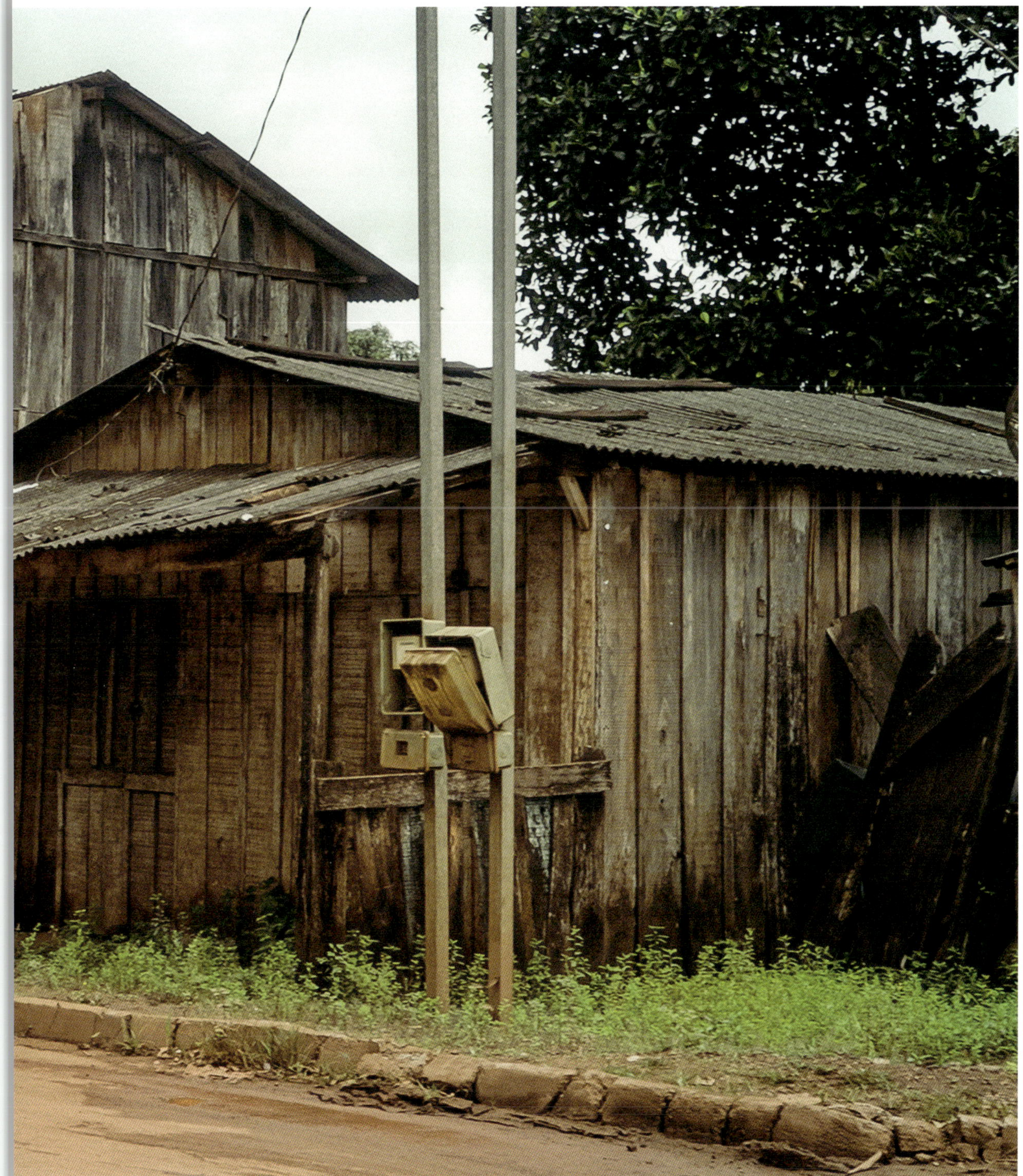

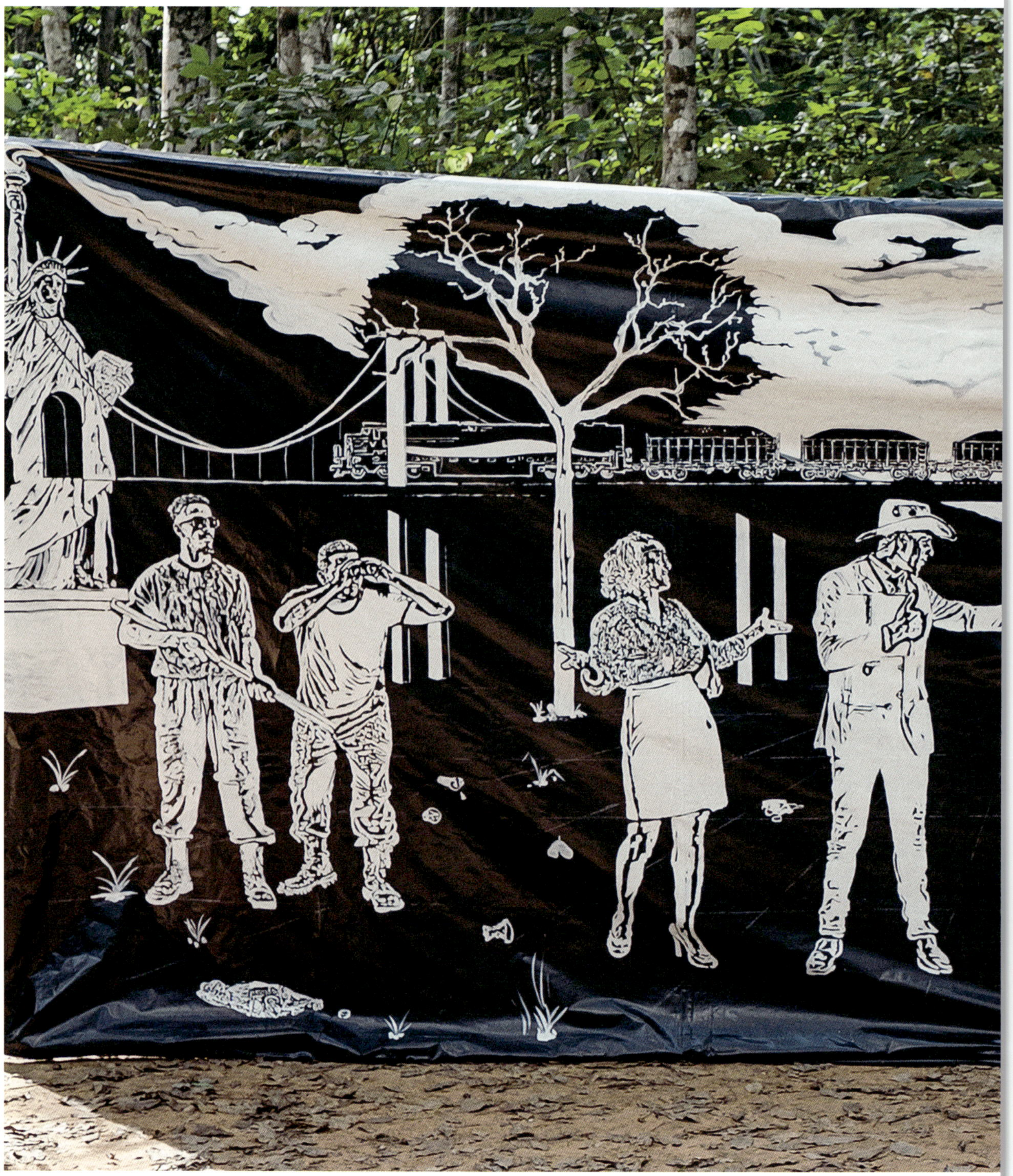

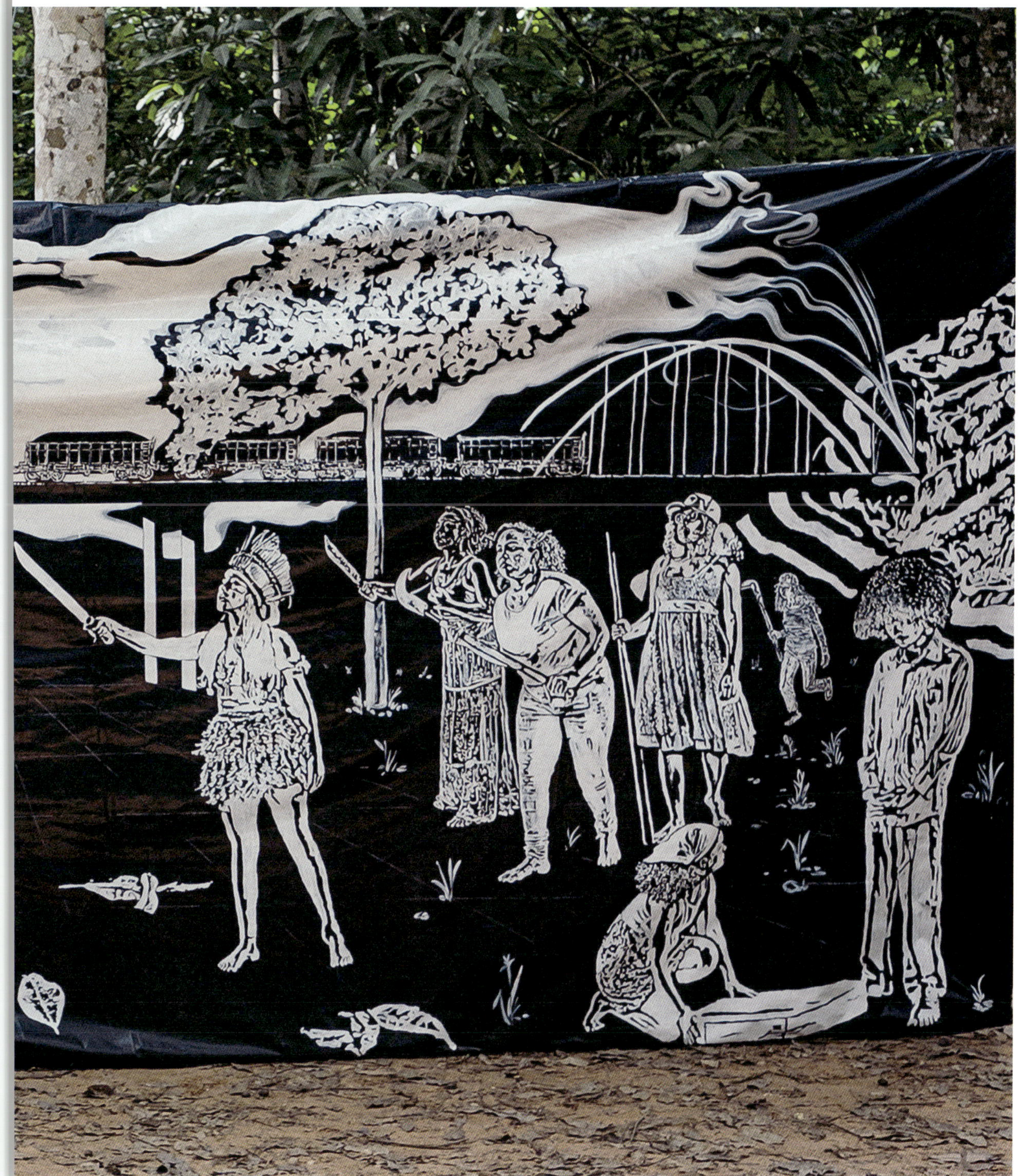

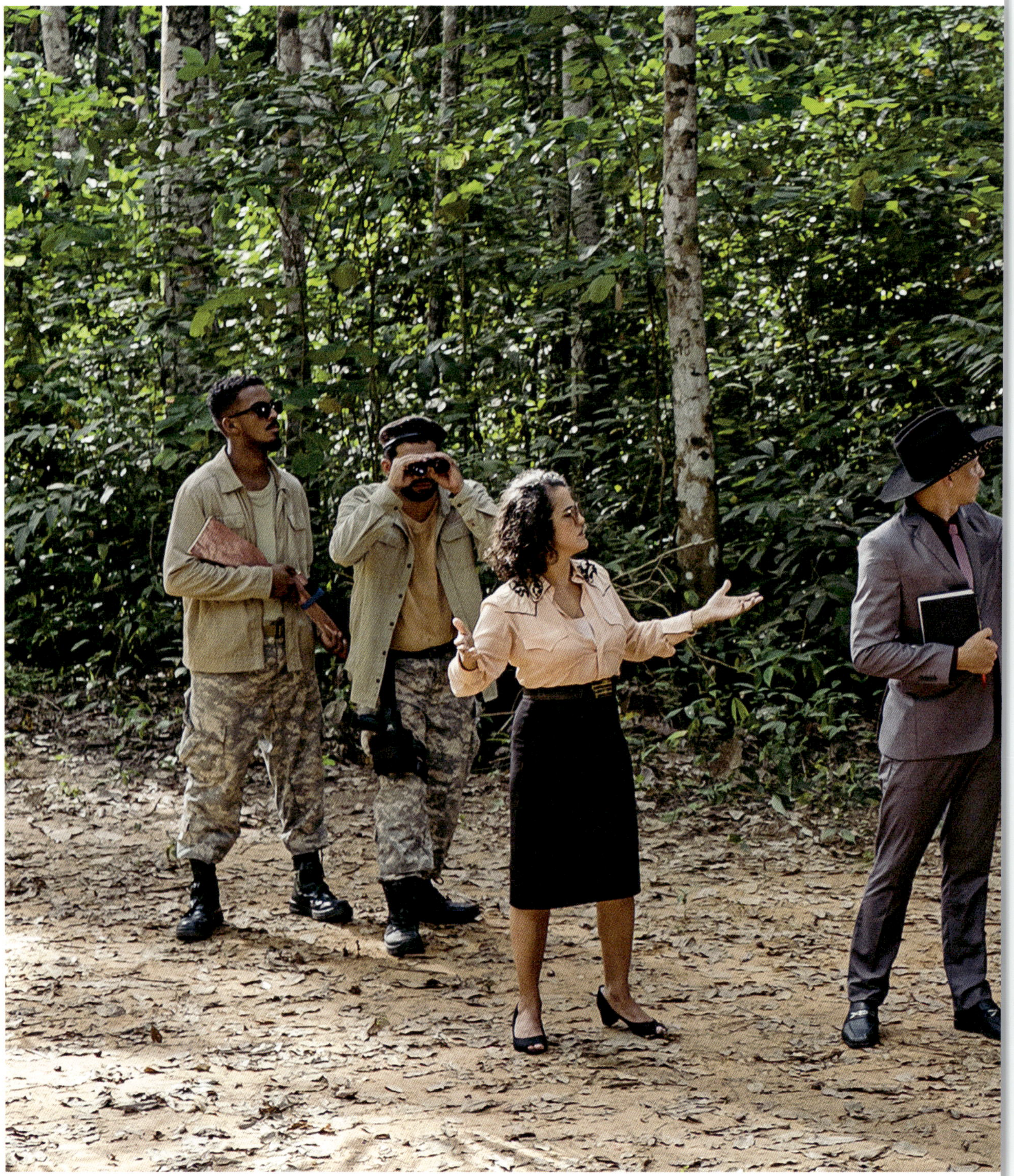

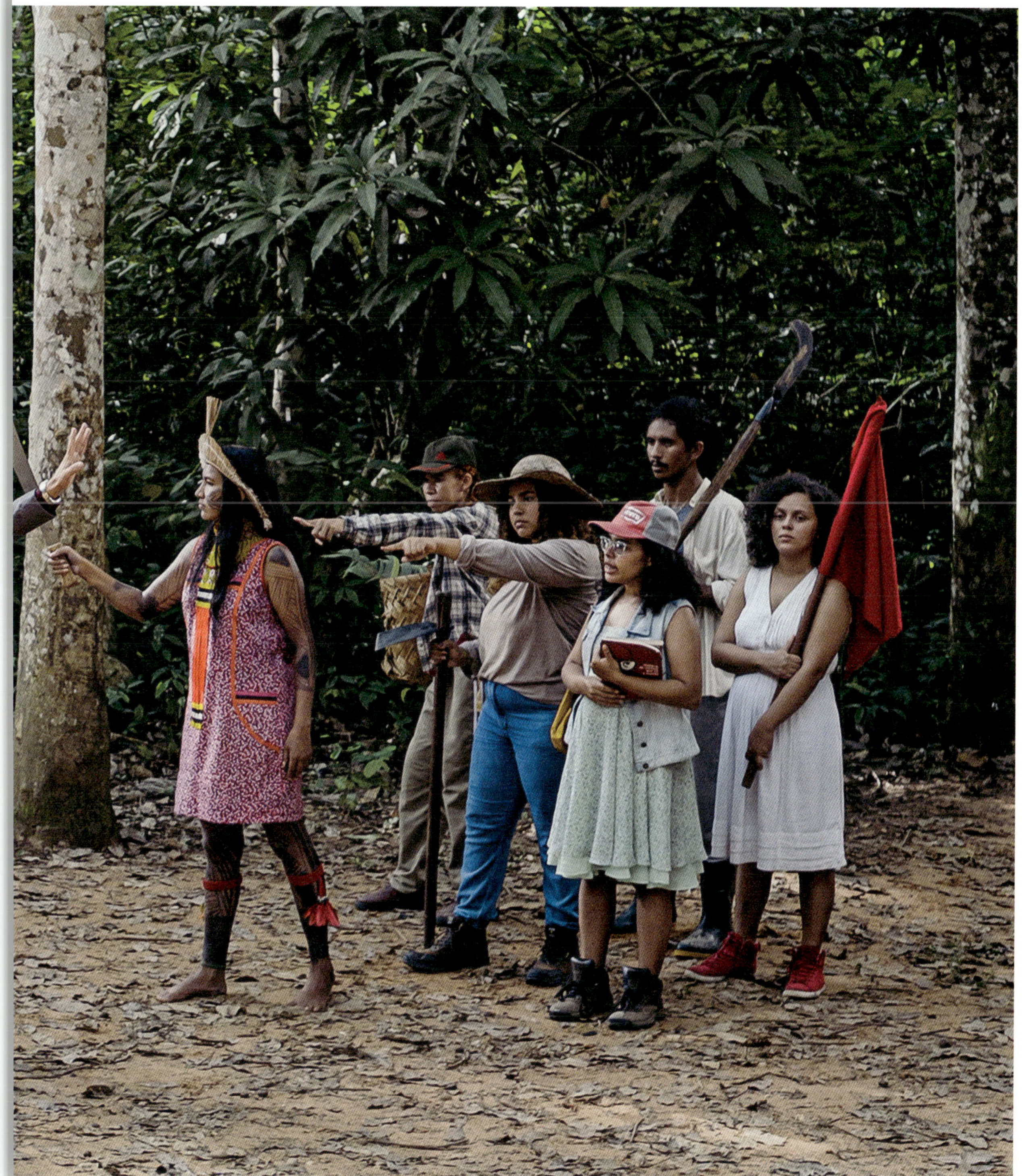

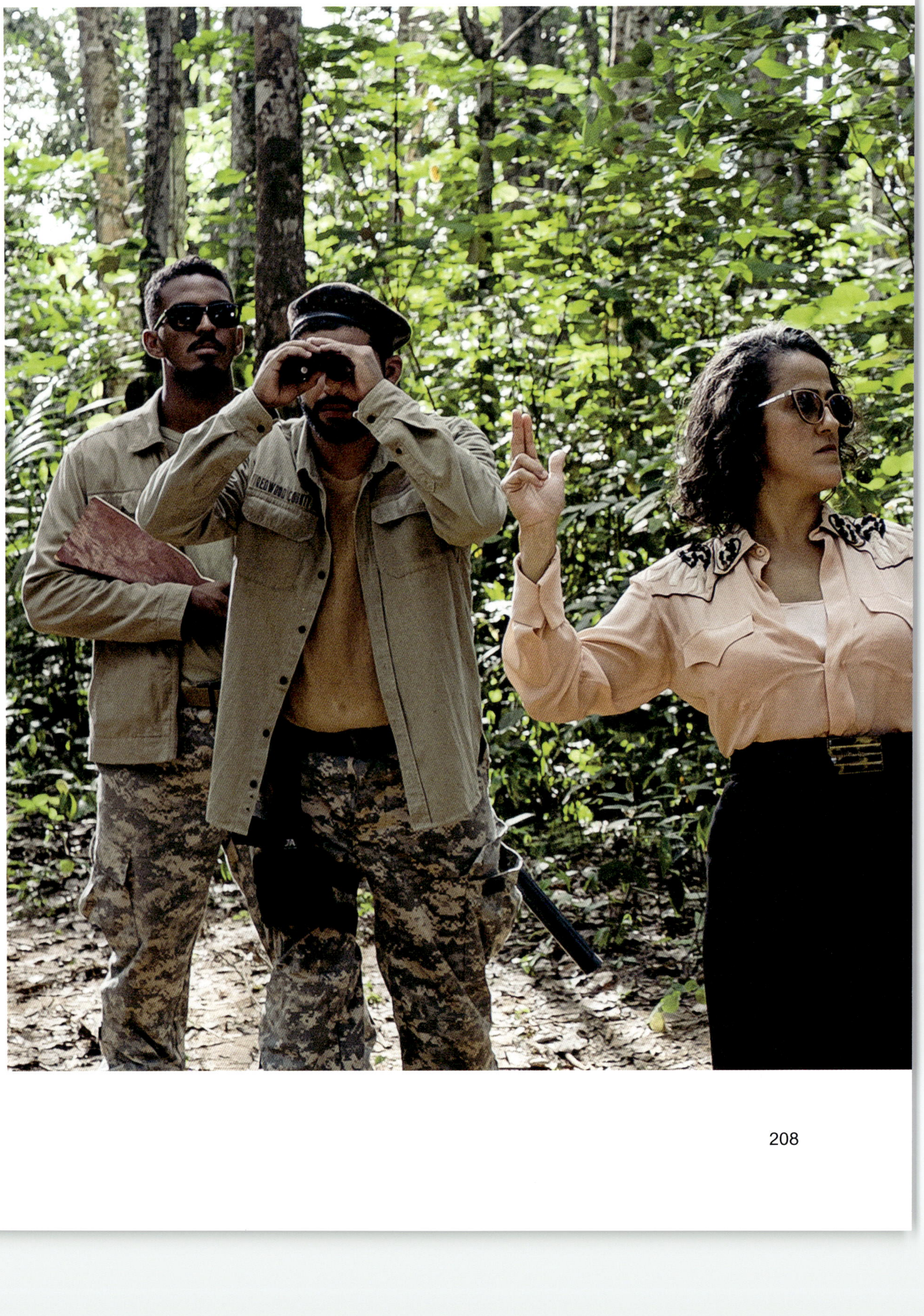

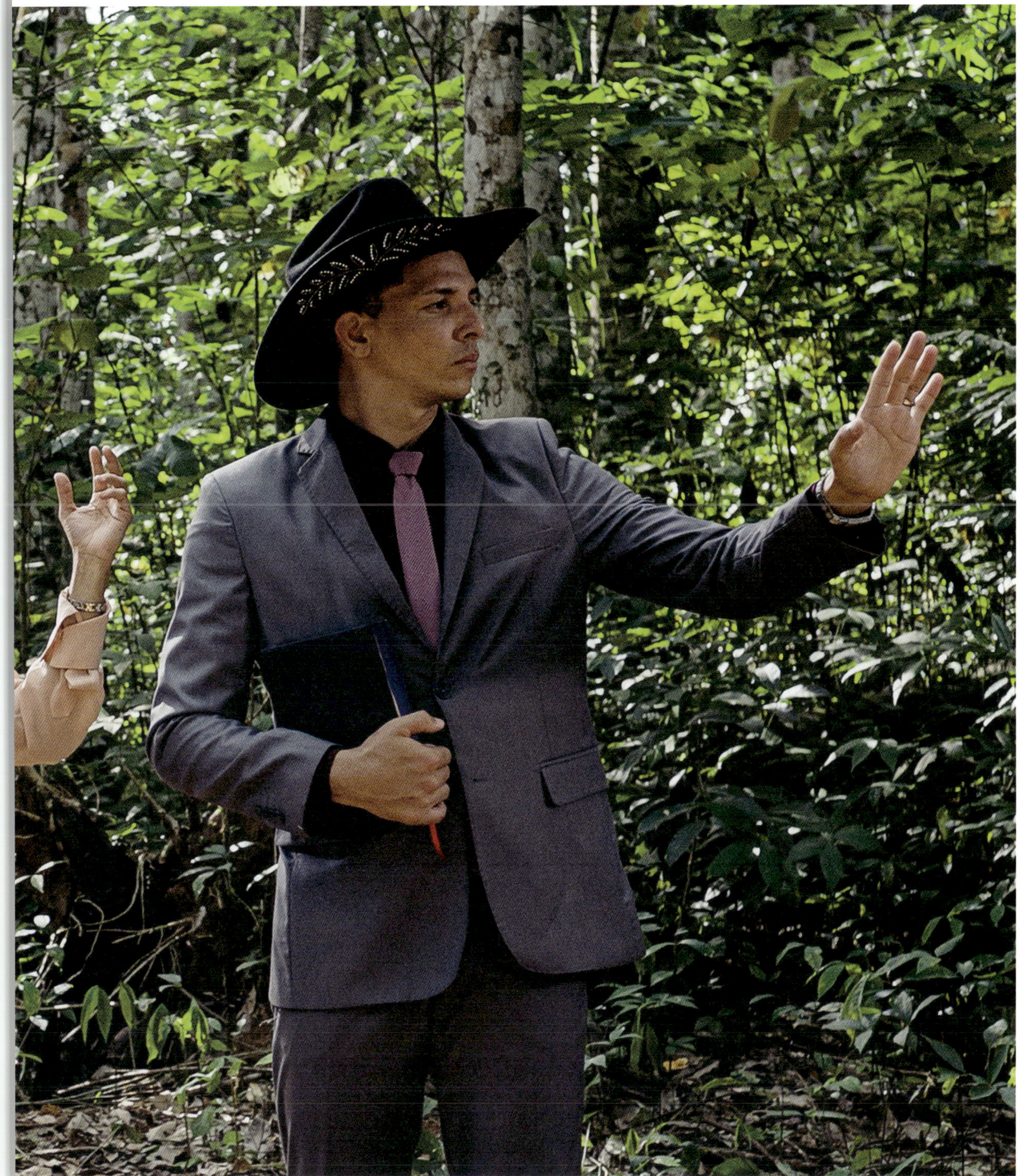

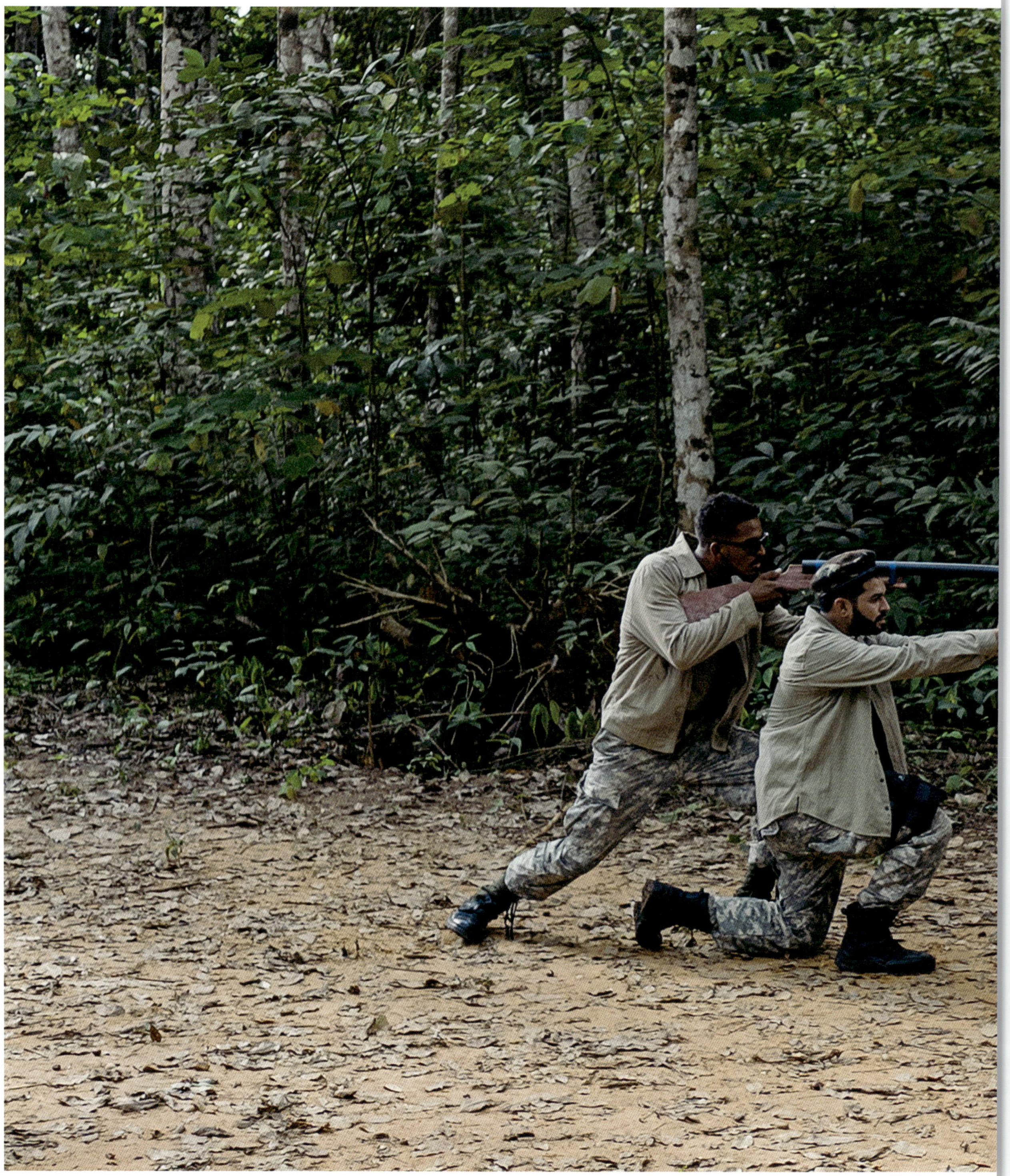

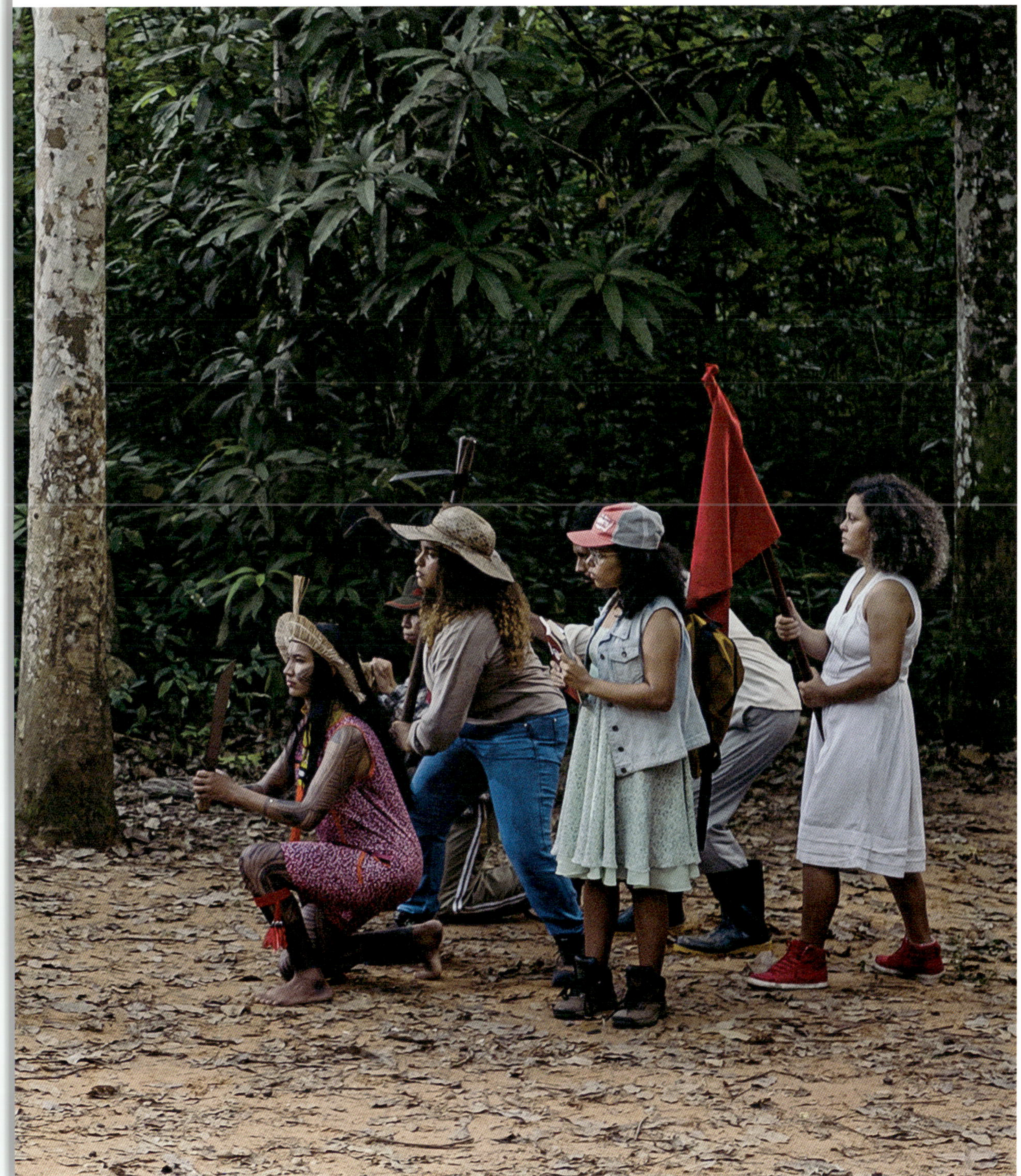

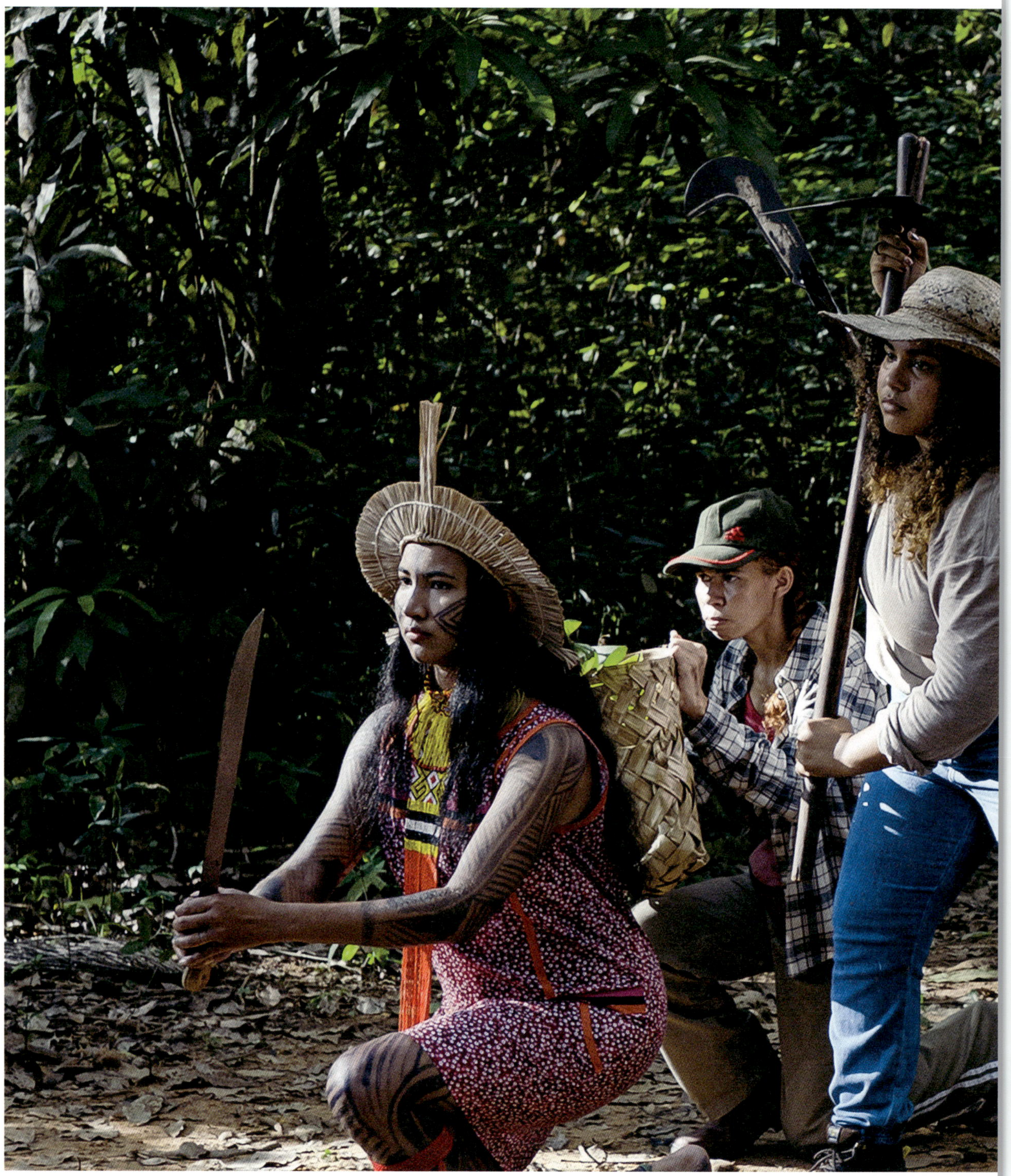

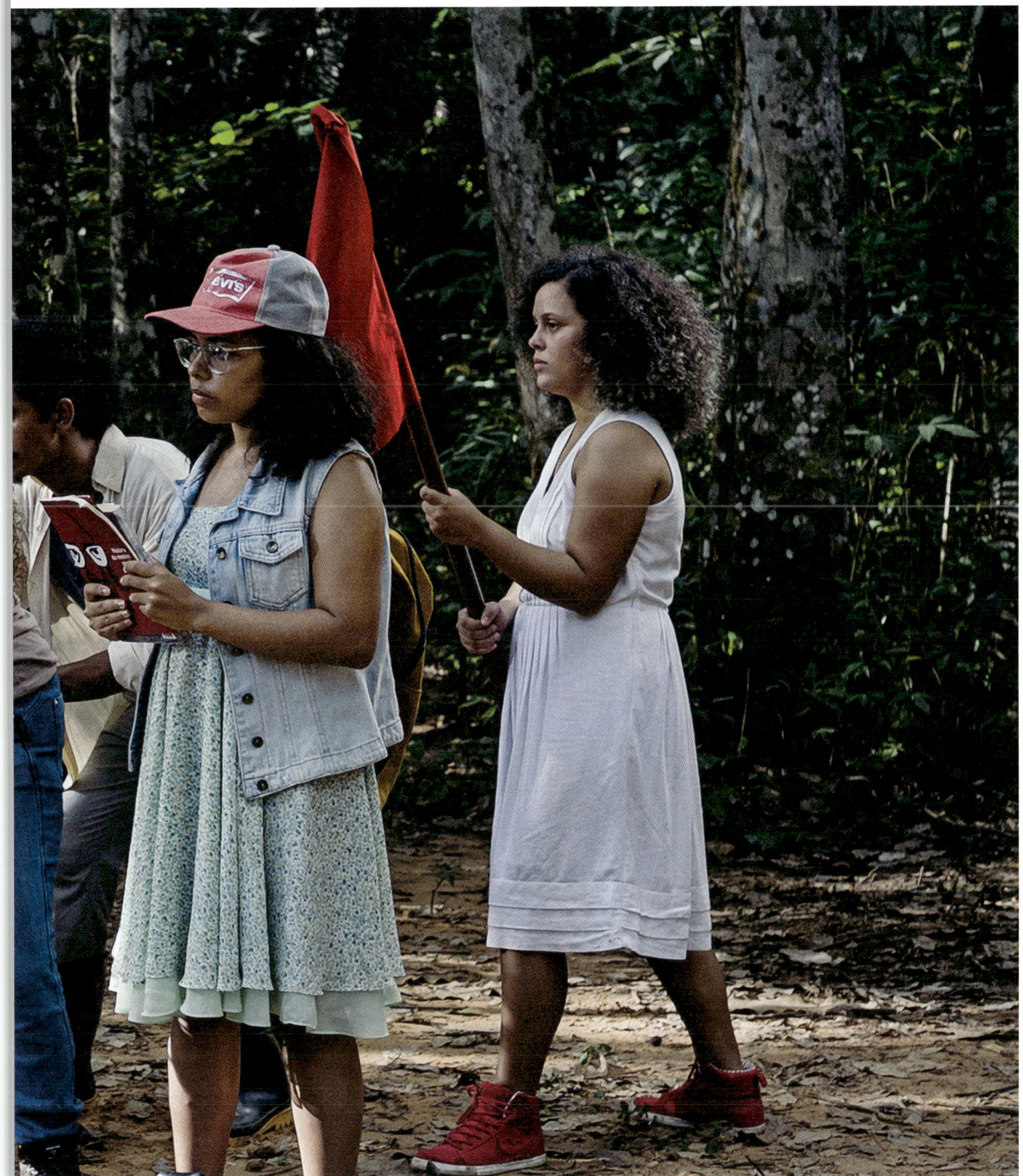

Film Credits

Faz Que Vai [Set to Go], 2015

2K HD video, color, 5.1 sound; 12 min
Courtesy the artists and Fortes D'Aloia & Gabriel, São Paulo/Rio de Janeiro

Cast
Ryan Neves, Edson Vogue, Bhrunno Henryque, Eduarda Lemos

Crew
Cinematographer: Pedro Sotero
Camera Assistant: Raphael Malta Clasen
Electricians: Alexandre Aranha, Fernando Marinho
Production Assistant: Bia Lima
Makeup Artists: Rodrigo Cavalcanti, Eva Venenosa
Editor: Eduardo Serrano
Colorist: Pablo Nóbrega
Sound: Cícero Batom, Wellington Jamaica, Waltinho d'Souza—Orquestra Popular da Bomba do Hemetério
Recording and Mixing: Jeferson Japa
Shot in Recife, Pernambuco, Brazil
Produced in Brazil

Estás Vendo Coisas [You Are Seeing Things], 2016

4K HD video, color, 5.1 sound; 16 min
Courtesy the artists and Fortes D'Aloia & Gabriel, São Paulo/Rio de Janeiro

Cast
MC Porck, Dayana Paixão
Leydson Dedesso, Alan Kassio, Jurema Fox, Neguin do Charme, DJ Jadson, Italo Monteiro Singleds Cass, MC Meta Safadão, Dany Bala, Allany Carvalho, Joás Junior, Lucas Santos, Fernando Pato, Victor Ronã

Crew
Cinematographer: Pedro Sotero
Assistant Director: Jerônimo Lemos
Camera Assistant: Raphael Malta Clasen
Sound Recordists: Phelipe Joannes, Sálua Oliveira
Electricians: Alexandre Aranha, Fernando Marinho
Executive Producers: Carol Vergolino, Daiana Dultra (Alumia)
Production Assistant: Lara Mafra
Editor: Rodrigo Carneiro
Colorist: Frederico Benevides
Original Soundtrack: Dany Bala, Tiquinho Lira (Studio Grife)
Sound Mixing and Mastering: Daniel Turini, Fernando Henna (Confraria de Sons & Charutos)
Transcription, Translation, and Subtitles: Esdras Bezerra
Supported by: Fundo de Incentivo à Cultura do Estado de Pernambuco (Funcultura), The Arts Council of Ireland, Fundação Bienal de São Paulo, Dubcolor, Portomídia
Shot in Recife, Pernambuco, Brazil
Produced in Brazil

Terremoto Santo [Holy Tremor], 2017

2K HD video, color, 5.1 sound; 19 min
Courtesy the artists and Fortes D'Aloia & Gabriel, São Paulo/Rio de Janeiro

Cast
Ana Cléa Gomes, Luiz Fernando Gomes, Alyne Azevedo, Tanya Marques, Ozeias Souza, Caique Alves, Jeiziane Maria, Felipe Moura, Joalysson Anderson, Tacy Silva, Berg Simplício

Crew
Executive Producer: Cecília da Fonte
Assistant Director: Jerônimo Lemos
Cinematographer: Pedro Sotero
First Camera Assistant: Maíra Iabrudi
Second Camera Assistant: Roberto Jaffier
Set Producer: João Lucas
Gaffer: Carlinhos Tareco
Light Assistant: Alexandre Aranha
Art Directors: Benjamin de Burca, Dani Vilela
Costume Designer: Rita Azevedo
Editor: Eduardo Serrano
Sound Recordist: Guga Rocha
Music Production: Naaliel Nascimento (Gravadora Mata Sul)
Original Soundtrack: Carlos Sá
Sound Design, Mixing: Nicolau Domingues
Colorist: Pablo Nóbrega
Translations, Subtitles: Stephen Rimmer
Supported by: Fundação Joaquim Nabuco (Fundaj), Instituto Moreira Salles (IMS), Portomídia, Dubcolor
Acknowledgments: Moacir Dos Anjos, Thyago Nogueira, Valentina Tong, Diego Medeiros, Djota Oliveira, Petrus Carvalho, Giovanna Simões, Dona Zuleide, Joyce Sá, Clara Arruda, Clara Vasconcelos, Gustavo Montenegro, Cícero Eraldo, Schumacher
Shot in Palmares, Pernambuco, Brazil
Produced in Brazil

Swinguerra, 2019

Two-channel video installation, 2K HD video, color, 5.1 sound; 21 min
Courtesy the artists and Fortes D'Aloia & Gabriel, São Paulo/Rio de Janeiro

Cast
Eduarda Lemos, Willam Vinícius, Stephane Melo, Daivson Lima, Clara Santos, Aline Linhares, Marcílio Gomes, Myllena Mello, Melissa Salazar, Hefrain Nunes, David Helder, Wallisson Vieira, Vinícius Lima, Renato Victor, Williams Ferreira, Diego Matarazzo, Edlys Rodrigues, Myllena Moura, Bethy Carvalho, Kally Albuquerque, Aline Marques, Julia Vitória, Higor Leandro, Ailton Silva, Deivesson Maksuel, Matheus Ferreira, Fábio Santos, Antonio Henrique da Sena Pinto (MC Fininho), Victor Adriano de Melo, Alex Martins da Silva, Wesley Victor da Silva, Clara Damaceno, Julian Letícia, Tamires Gonçalves, Vitória Caiury Gentil da Silva, Ângela Maria da Silva (Kinha do Tamburete)

Crew
Executive Producers: Dora Amorim, Thais Vidal
Cinematographer: Pedro Sotero
Art Director: André Antônio
Choreographers: Diego Matarazzo, Clara Santos, Edlys Rodrigues, Antonio Henrique da Sena Pinto (MC Fininho)
Editor: Eduardo Serrano
Colorist: Pablo Nóbrega (DubColor)
Sound Recordists: Lucas Caminha, Catharine Pimentel
Sound Design: Nicolau Domingues, Caio Domingues
Original Soundtrack: Carlos Sá
Production Manager: Julia Machado
Assistant Director: Gabriel Domingues
Second Assistant Director: David Moura
Set Producer: Jairo Dornelas
First Camera Assistant: Maíra Iabrudi
Second Camera Assistant, Logger: Lana Lo Bianco
Logger, Editing Assistant: Ivitch Barret
Gaffer: Marcinho Lima
Key Grip: Sandro dos Santos
Grip: Clóvis Albuquerque Lima
Costume Designer: Rita Azevedo
Styling: Zé Lucas
Graffiti: Carlos André
Sound Engineer: Bruno Lins (Carranca Estúdios)
Percussion: Renato Nogueira, Zé Paulo

Guitar: Caio Domingues
Vocals: Allison Marx
Finishing: Brunno Schiavon (Clandestino)
Translation: Pedro Neves
Commissioned by Fundação Bienal de São Paulo
Shot in Olinda and Jaboatão dos Guararapes, Pernambuco, Brazil
Produced in Brazil

Fala da Terra [Voice of the Land], 2022

2K HD video, color, 5.1 sound; 20 min
Courtesy the artists and Fortes D'Aloia & Gabriel, São Paulo/Rio de Janeiro

Cast
Mileny Alves Bezerra, Rodrigues Silva, Alan Leite, Aline Silva, Wildianei Celiniclis, Maria Luísa, Pablo Neri, Romário Rodrigues, Kananda Rocha, Luciana Melo, Agnes de Almeida Muniz Bezerra, Maria Raimunda César, Maria Zelzuita, Laurindo Costa, Luzenira Paula da Silva, Batista do Nascimento, Maria Olinda de Almeida, Eliene Silva, Maria Gouveia, Joari Procópio, Izabel Rodrigues, Maria Goreth, Suely Gomes, Deusa Sales, Giselda Coelho

Crew
Executive Producers: Dora Amorim, Júlia Machado (Ponte Produtoras)
Cinematographer: Pedro Sotero
Art Director: Benjamin de Burca
Assistant Art Director: Hemerson Souza
Editors: Daniela de Lamare, Benjamin de Burca
Edit Consultant: Eduardo Serrano
Colorist: Brunno Schiavon
Sound Recordists: Lucas Caminha, Daniel Moraes
Sound Design: Nicolau Domingues
Original Soundtrack: Carlos Sá
Production Manager: Henrique Lapa
Production Coordinator: João Lucas
Assistant Director: Gabriel Domingues
Second Assistant Director: Daniela de Lamare
Researcher: André Telles do Rosário
Assistant Researcher: Alan Leite
First Camera Assistant: Maíra Iabrudi
Second Camera Assistant: Tainá Bicalho
Logger: Liz Dórea
Production Assistant: Davi Fleury
Local Production Coordinator: Maria Raimunda César
Local Production Assistant: Trevo Ribeiro
Gaffer: Vitinho Espínola
Light Assistant: Almir Costa
Key Grip: Alex Índio
Grip: Aldo Cardoso
Costume Designer: Rita Azevedo
Assistant Costume Designer: Luciana Melo
Makeup Artists: Victória Tavares, Roptykwyi Kuxware Bebka
Supported by Fundo de Incentivo à Cultura do Estado de Pernambuco (Funcultura)
Acknowledgments: Movimento dos Trabalhadores Rurais Sem Terra (MST), Rafael Villas Boas, Douglas Estevam, Dan Baron Cohen, Haroldo de Souza, Vangela Pereira Silva, Benedito de Jesus Bastos, Luzinete Nunes Pinto, Etevaldo Arantes, Manuel Fábio Matos Barros, Ian Almeida Borella, Rosilda Bezerra Nogueira, Tito Moura, Cici Ferraz
Shot in Marabá, Serra Pelada and Parauapebas, Pará, Brazil
Produced in Brazil

About the Artists

Bárbara Wagner (b. 1980, Brasília) and Benjamin de Burca (b. 1975, Munich) live and work between Recife and Berlin. They have had recent solo exhibitions at the Institute of Contemporary Art, Boston (2022); Kunsthall Stavanger, Norway (2021); Maison Européenne de la Photographie, Paris (2021); Temple Bar Gallery and Studios, Dublin (2020); Brazilian Pavilion, 58th Venice Biennale (2019); Stedelijk Museum, Amsterdam (2019); Pérez Art Museum Miami (2019); Museo Jumex, Mexico City (2019); Wexner Center for the Arts, Columbus, OH (2018); and Museum of Contemporary Art Detroit (2017).

Their work has been featured in group shows including Manifesta 13, Marseille, France (2020); Institute of Contemporary Arts Singapore (2019); Solar dos Abacaxis, Rio de Janeiro (2019); Toronto Biennial of Art (2019); Instituto Moreira Salles, Rio de Janeiro (2018); Front International: Cleveland Triennial for Contemporary Art, OH (2018); Museu do Arte do Rio, Rio de Janeiro (2018; 2014); 35th Panorama da Arte Brasileira, Museu de Arte Moderna de São Paulo (2017; 2013); 5th Skulptur Projekte, Münster, Germany (2017); 20th Festival de Arte Contemporânea, SESC VideoBrasil, São Paulo (2017); Museu de Arte Contemporânea de Serralves, Porto, Portugal (2017); Museo de Arte Moderna de Bogotá, Colombia (2017); 32nd São Paulo Biennial, Pavilhão da Bienal de São Paulo (2016); Museu de Arte Moderna de São Paulo (2016); Latvian Museum of Contemporary Art, Riga (2014); Berlin Art Prize (2014); 36th EVA International, Limerick, Ireland (2014); Frestas, Art Triennial, SESC Sorocaba, São Paulo (2014); and 4th Contemporary Art Biennial, La Réunion, France (2013).

They have also been included in the Berlin International Film Festival (2019; 2018; 2017; 2021); Locarno International Film Festival (2019); and Tel Aviv International Documentary Film Festival (2017).

Board of Trustees

Photography Credits

All images courtesy the artists and Fortes D'Aloia & Gabriel, São Paulo/Rio de Janeiro, unless otherwise noted.

Courtesy TENT, Rotterdam. Photo: Aad Hoogendoorn: pp. 86–87

Courtesy Fundação Bienal de São Paulo. Photo: Leo Eloy/Estúdio Garagem: pp. 118–19

Courtesy Instituto Moreira Salles. Photo: Leonardo Wen: pp. 150–51

Courtesy Temple Bar Gallery + Studios. Photo: Kate-Bowe O'Brien: pp. 182–83

Published by
New Museum
235 Bowery
New York, NY 10002

On the occasion of the exhibition
"Bárbara Wagner and Benjamin de Burca: Five Times Brazil"
June 30–October 16, 2022

Curators: Margot Norton,
Allen and Lola Goldring Curator,
and Bernardo Mosqueira,
ISLAA Curatorial Fellow

Contributors:
Benjamin de Burca
Vivian A. Crockett
Bernardo Mosqueira
Margot Norton
Wendelien van Oldenborgh
Bárbara Wagner

Copy Editor: Sarah Stephenson
Design Template: An Art Service
Design Production: Nicholas Weltyk
Printing: SPC, Poland

Cover: *Fala da Terra* [Voice of the Land], 2022 (still). 2K HD video, color, 5.1 sound; 20 min

ISBN: 978-0-915557-98-1

Major support for this exhibition is provided by the International Leadership Council of the New Museum.

Support for this exhibition is provided by the Toby Devan Lewis Emerging Artists Exhibitions Fund.

Artist commissions are generously supported by the Neeson/Edlis Artist Commissions Fund.

Additional support provided by Marcelo Martins, Frances Reynolds / Instituto Inclusartiz, and Brenda Valansi.

Education and community programs are supported, in part, by the American Chai Trust.

Thanks to Camila Yunes Guarita.

Support for the publication has been provided by the J. McSweeney and G. Mills Publications Fund at the New Museum.

This exhibition is made possible, in part, by in-kind support from Kvadrat.

kvadrat

NEW
235 BOWERY
NEW YORK NY
10002 USA
MUSEUM